IMAGES
of America

STOUGHTON

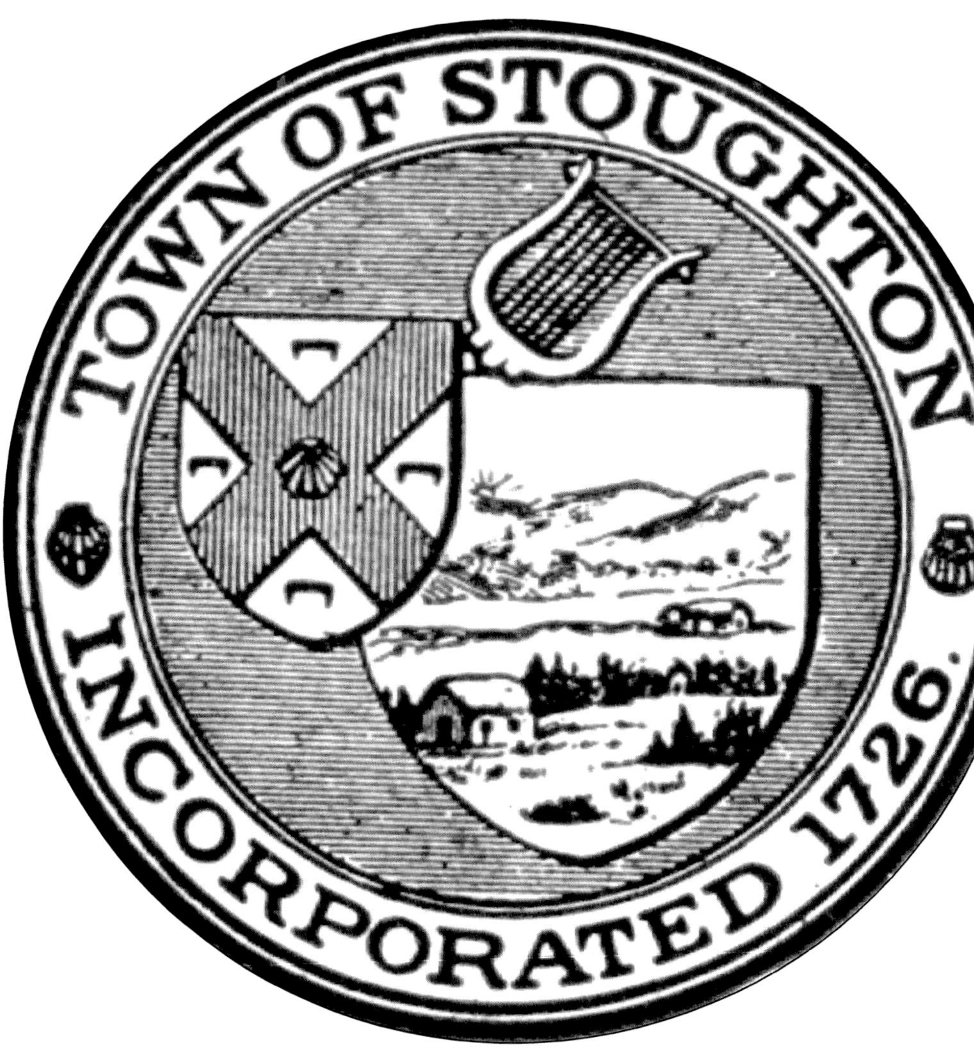

THE TOWN SEAL OF STOUGHTON, DESIGNED BY EDWIN A. JONES OF STOUGHTON IN 1892. The shield in the lower right represents a landscape showing the territory in the Colonial days. The overlapping shield shows the Stoughton family coat of arms. The harp represents the fact that Stoughton is the birthplace of the first musical society in the country. This seal is still used to adorn all official town documents.

IMAGES
of America

STOUGHTON

David Allen Lambert

ARCADIA
PUBLISHING

ISBN 978-0-7385-0941-9

Published by Arcadia Publishing
Charleston, South Carolina

Printed in the United States of America

Library of Congress Catalog Card Number: 2001092295

For all general information contact Arcadia Publishing at:
Telephone 843-853-2070
Fax 843-853-0044
E-mail sales@arcadiapublishing.com
For customer service and orders:
Toll-Free 1-888-313-2665

Visit us on the Internet at www.arcadiapublishing.com

This book is dedicated in memory of my parents,
George and Joan Lambert, who will forever remain in my heart.

CONTENTS

ACKNOWLEDGMENTS

I would like to thank the following individuals from the Stoughton Historical Society for their support and encouragement on this project: Denise Peterson, Hank Herbowy, Edward Meserve, Howard Hansen, Joan O'Hare, and Alice Petruzzo. Their assistance with obtaining photographs for this book was extremely important. All photographs, unless otherwise noted, came from the archives of the Stoughton Historical Society.

I would like to recognize the photographs taken by my late friend and Stoughton historian John Cyrns Stiles, who encouraged my early interest in the history of Stoughton.

Many thanks to my editor, Megan Dumm, for her wonderful assistance throughout this project.

I would also like to thank my wife, Anne-Marie, my daughter Brenda and my sister Carol for all their love and support during this project.

INTRODUCTION

The present town of Stoughton was once under the domain of the Massachuset Indians, who fished and hunted along the streams and woods in our town. At the time of the arrival of the Winthrop Fleet, the Massachuset sachem was the great Chicatabut. He died in 1633 from a case of smallpox. In the years following, his people would be forced to move from their lands along the Neponset River so settlers of the Massachusetts Bay Colony could establish permanent settlements of their own. Under the rule of the late Chicatabut's brother Kitchamakin, some of the Massachuset Indians heard the call of Rev. John Eliot, who actively sought to christianize them. Some 40,000 acres of land south of the Great Blue Hill were set off for the town of Dorchester as the New Grant. This land was divided into 12 divisions for 480 members called the Dorchester Proprietors. This desire for more land by the colonists concerned Eliot to seek a secure settlement for Kitchamakin's people from the town of Dorchester. In 1657, a 6,000-acre plantation was established around Punkapoag Pond from the 40,000-acre tract for this purpose. Punkapoag Plantation would consist of a simple wooden chapel, a cemetery, and a community living in bark wigwams in the shadow of the Great Blue Hill. Many of the Punkapoags and other Christian Native Americans from Massachusetts were held by the Massachusetts Bay Colony at Deer Island for their own protection from King Philip in 1675.

By the end of King Philip's War, many of the Punkapoag had died from disease and exposure at Deer Island. Their numbers having depleted greatly had caused them to lease to colonists some land they could not maintain. By this time, their English neighbors were acquiring land and settling in great numbers in the New Grant. On May 12, 1707, a vote from the town of Dorchester allowed petitioners from the New Grant to settle a minister and raise taxes to construct a meetinghouse. Rev. Joseph Morse (1671–1732) became the first minister in the town of Stoughton, serving until 1727. The Massachusetts General Court allowed an area of Dorchester to be set aside as the South Precinct on December 19, 1715. Many of the leases established by the Punkapoags in the South Precinct were slated to exist for over 100 and 200 years. These original leases to their English tenants were later deemed illegal by the Commonwealth of Massachusetts. The leases of land in the years previous to 1726–1727 would now have to be conveyed by deed from the Punkapoags to these tenants.

The town of Stoughton was incorporated by an act of the Massachusetts General Court on December 22, 1726. The town chose its name in honor of William Stoughton (1631–1701), who had served as lieutenant governor of Massachusetts and also as chief justice over the Salem witchcraft trials of 1692. Both William and his father, Israel Stoughton, had been substantial landowners in the New Grant. The town of Stoughton developed as an agricultural community under the watchful guidance of one church and one minister. By August 3, 1727, a new minister, Rev. Samuel Dunbar, had been called to the parish church. The first survey of the town (1727) found 2 gristmills, 7 sawmills, 4 ironworks, 121 houses, and 275 individuals who were taxable. Land was annexed to Dedham from Stoughton in 1733 and 1737. Due to the size of the original town, the concept of one parish caused many to seek their own parishes and ministers in a closer proximity. The first major division occurred when the Second Precinct was incorporated on July 2, 1740. The Second Precinct became the town of Stoughtonham on June 21, 1765. The name was changed to Sharon on February 25, 1783. Part of the town of Foxboro, incorporated on June 10, 1778, was from the Second Precinct land.

On November 9, 1743, the Third Precinct of Stoughton was established by petition from those who resided south of the First Parish house, which was located on land in present-day Canton. On August 10, 1744, the Church of Christ meetinghouse was constructed on the green in Stoughton Center. From the area around this meetinghouse, the present town of Stoughton was comprised. The old First Parish separated from present-day Stoughton and, on February 23, 1797, incorporated as the town of Canton. A final separation from the original town occurred when East Stoughton petitioned to separate and, on February 21, 1888, formed the new town of Avon.

The men of Stoughton, leaving their farms bravely, answered the call of the guns of Lexington and Concord. Their descendants would set aside their factory jobs to answer President Lincoln's, President Wilson's, and President Roosevelt's calls for volunteers. This agricultural community was transformed into a hub for Massachusetts during the Industrial Revolution. From home shoe shops on family farms and water-powered mills to emerging smokestacks of shoe and boot factories, Stoughton would see an increase in population and wealth. Besides boots and shoes, Stoughton would be a manufacturer of a variety of products ranging from blocks from her granite quarries, the invention of packaged popcorn, rubber fabrics, textile and metal products, and, eventually, electronics and computer technology. At the close of the 19th century, both the old Yankee families along with recent European immigrants in search of new opportunity would call Stoughton home. Both their generation and descendants would work side by side on the farms, at the stores, and in the factories to help create the success of present-day Stoughton.

—David Allen Lambert

One

EARLY IMAGES OF STOUGHTON

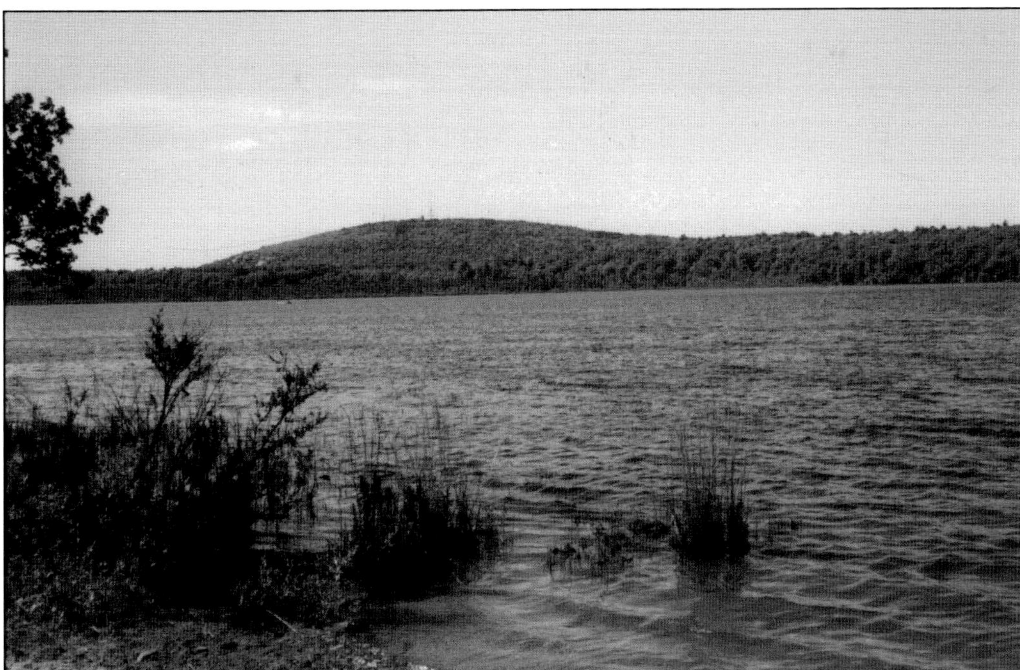

A VIEW FROM THE SHORE OF PUNKAPOAG POND AND GREAT BLUE HILL. This view has remained unchanged for centuries. In 1657, Rev. John Eliot helped establish a 6,000-acre plantation for the Massachuset Indians surrounding Punkapoag Pond. This community was the second successful Native American praying village in the Massachusetts Bay Colony. Many descendants of the Punkapoag Indians still live in the nearby area, and the Massachuset Punkapoag Tribal Council still holds an annual celebration and ceremony near their ancient homeland. (Author's collection.)

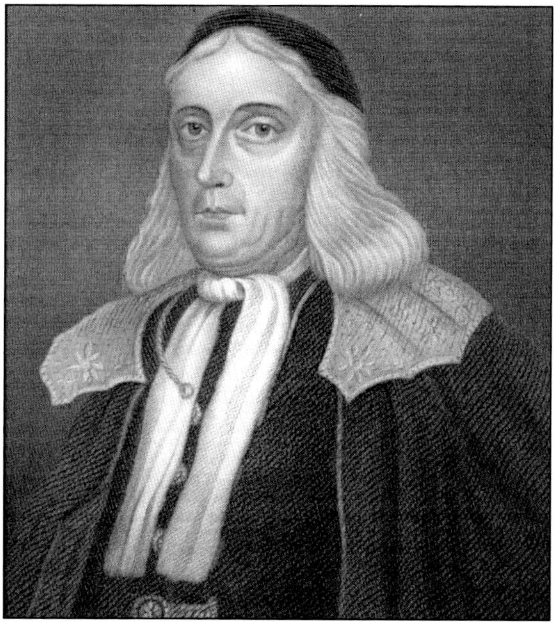

THE SECOND PRECINCT OF DORCHESTER, INCORPORATED DECEMBER 22, 1726, AS THE TOWN OF STOUGHTON. The town was named for Lt. Gov. William Stoughton (1631–1701). Stoughton had served as lieutenant governor, acting governor, and chief justice over the infamous Salem witchcraft trials in 1692. While Stoughton was serving as chief justice, many individuals accused of witchcraft were jailed and hung. Until the day he died, Stoughton never believed his judgment was in error during the Salem hysteria of 1692. (Author's collection.)

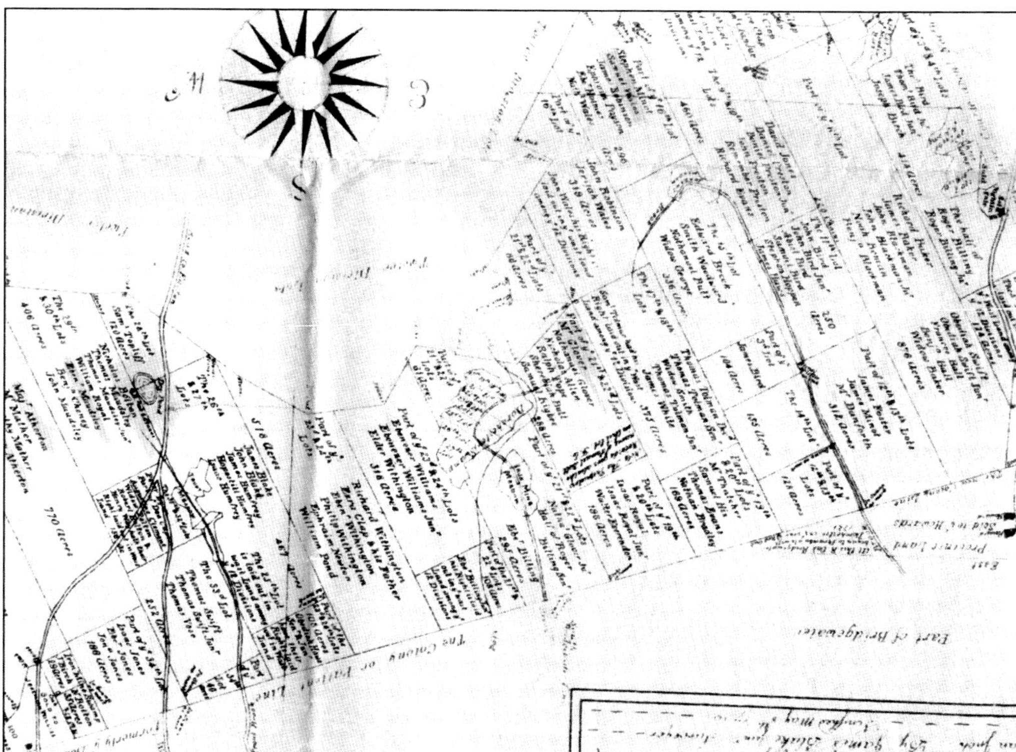

A 1730 MAP SHOWING THE NEW GRANT LAND. This version of a 1730 map showing the New Grant land was created from two maps by historian Frederic Endicott in 1895. This portion of the map clearly shows the snake-shaped curve of Bay Road on the Sharon and Stoughton border. Trout Meadow also illustrated would later be flooded to become what is now Ames Pond off West and Highland Streets. (Author's collection.)

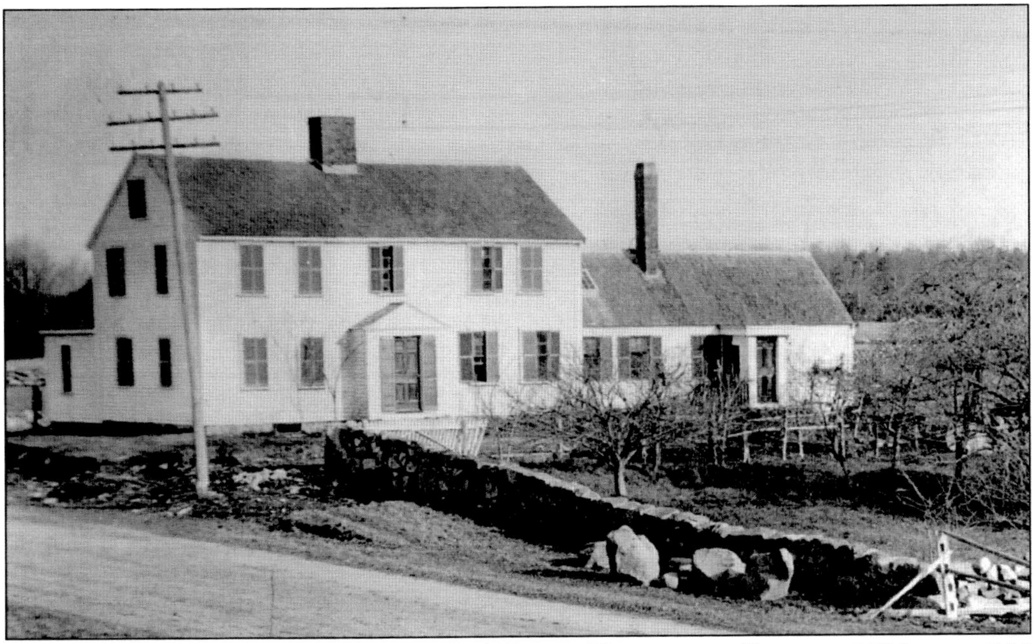

THE CAPT. GEORGE TALBOT (1688–1760) FAMILY HOMESTEAD, BUILT C. 1720 NEAR 564 WASHINGTON STREET. This house was located on the easterly side of Washington Street until it was demolished after a heavy wind caused structural damage in 1929. The first Stoughton Third Parish town meeting was held in this building on December 12, 1743. Talbot and his wife, Mary (Turrell), were dismissed from the First Parish Church to help form the Third Parish Church on July 29, 1744.

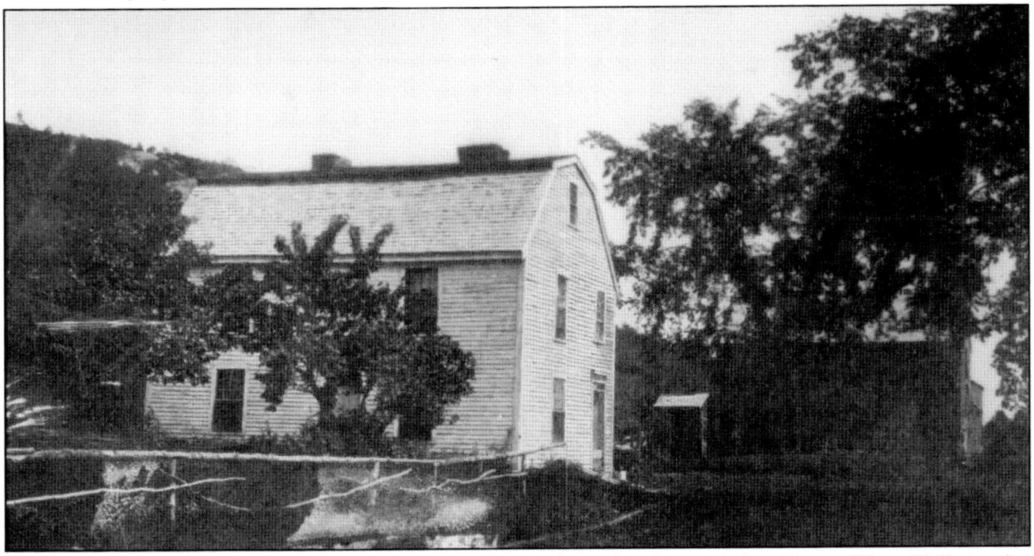

DOTY'S TAVERN. Doty's Tavern was once located at the foot of the Great Blue Hill in the original boundary of Stoughton. This structure was built as a tavern for Maj. John Shephard in 1726 and was later occupied by Col. Thomas Doty. Within this building, Samuel Adams, John Hancock, and Gen. Joseph Warren met on August 16, 1774, to formulate the beginning work toward the Suffolk Resolves. On December 19, 1888, the old tavern was burned to the ground, where the cradle of American liberty began. (Author's collection.)

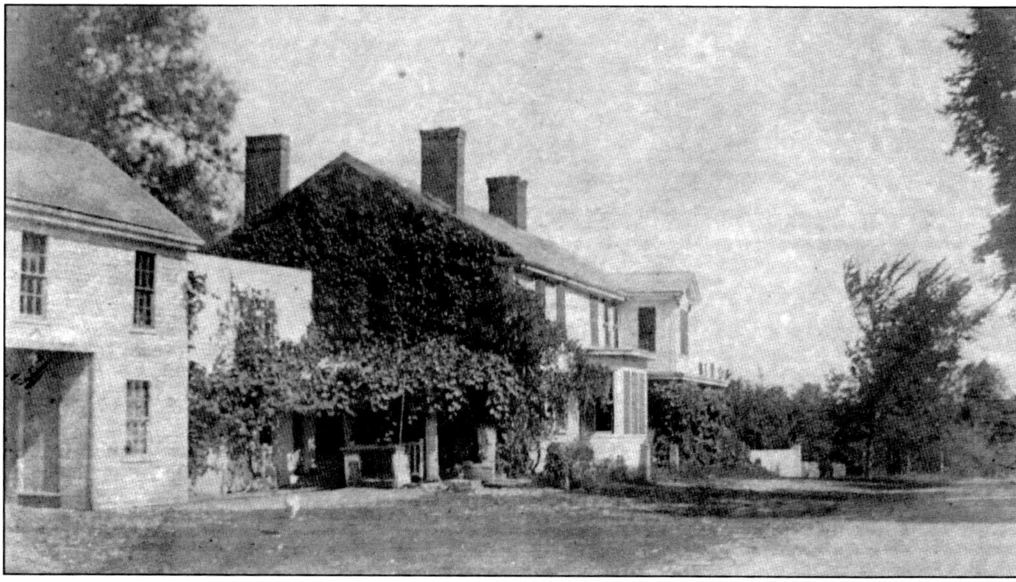

COBB'S TAVERN AND ELIJAH FISHER'S OLD FARM ON BAY ROAD. In 1797, Jonathan Cobb (1770–1845) purchased the land of Elijah Fisher of Sharon. The oldest section of the tavern is believed to have been built *c.* 1740 and moved from across Bay Road. Cobb enlarged the tavern after purchasing it. The Old Stoughton Musical Society met at the tavern from November 12, 1804, until June 6, 1808. The tavern was also the home to the Rising Star Lodge of Stoughton from September 14, 1815, until December 18, 1817. The original tavern tap room, post office, and Masonic Lodge room are still preserved in the building today.

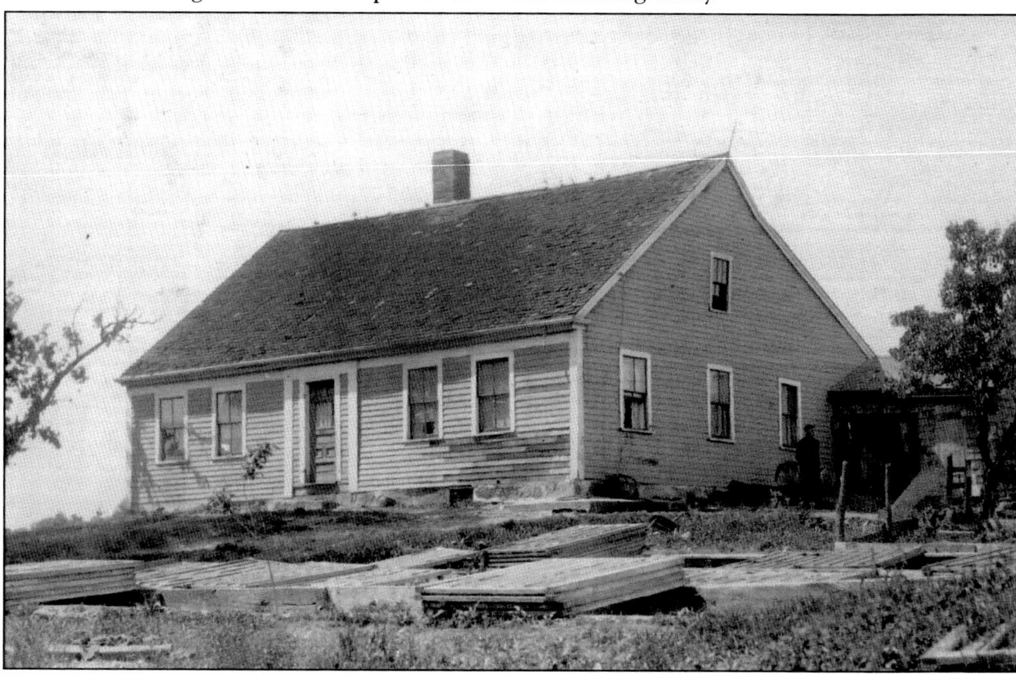

THE HOUSE OF HEZEKIAH GAY (1700–1774), BUILT IN 1734 AT 2125 CENTRAL STREET. Gay was born in Dedham and, in 1727, moved to Stoughton. This house was owned by Frank Polillio in 1929, when it was photographed.

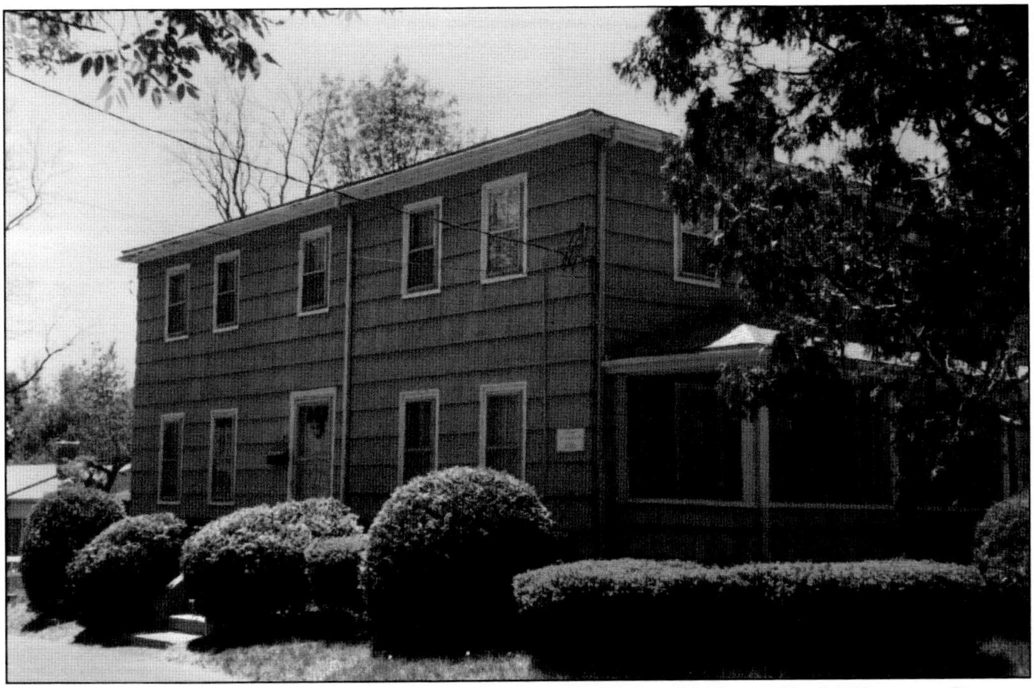

The Homestead of Capt. Consider Atherton (1716–1812) at 33–35 Pratts Court. This house was built in 1740. Captain Atherton married in Stoughton on July 2, 1744, to Mary Bailey (1724–1782). This is believed to be the oldest house standing in Stoughton. The date of 1740 appears in the files of Stoughton historian William H. Capen (1871–1939).

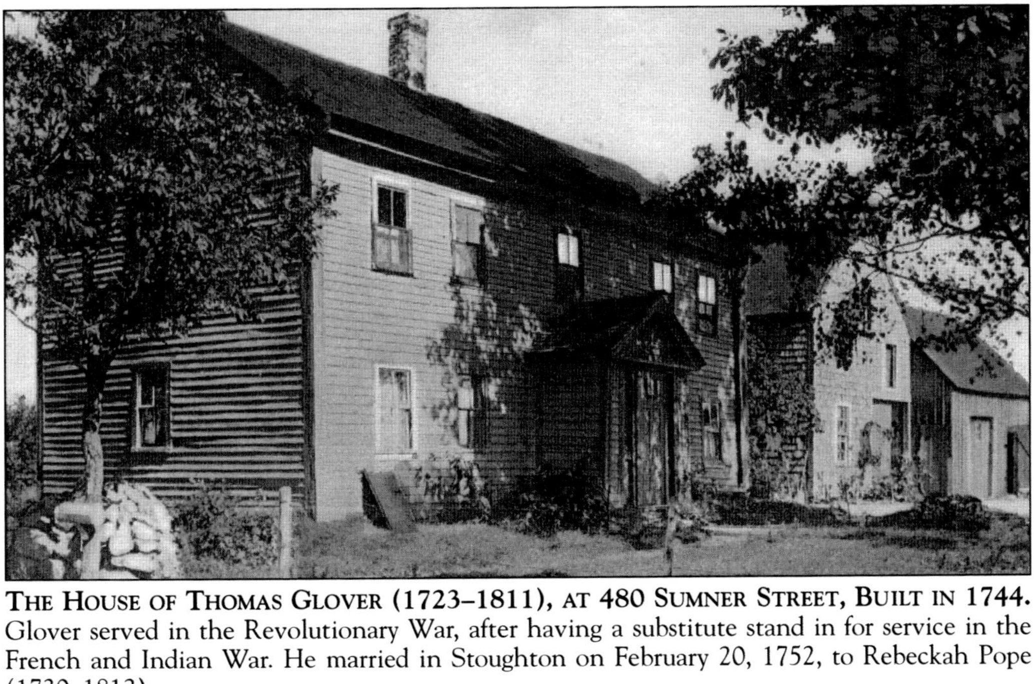

The House of Thomas Glover (1723–1811), at 480 Sumner Street, Built in 1744. Glover served in the Revolutionary War, after having a substitute stand in for service in the French and Indian War. He married in Stoughton on February 20, 1752, to Rebeckah Pope (1730–1812).

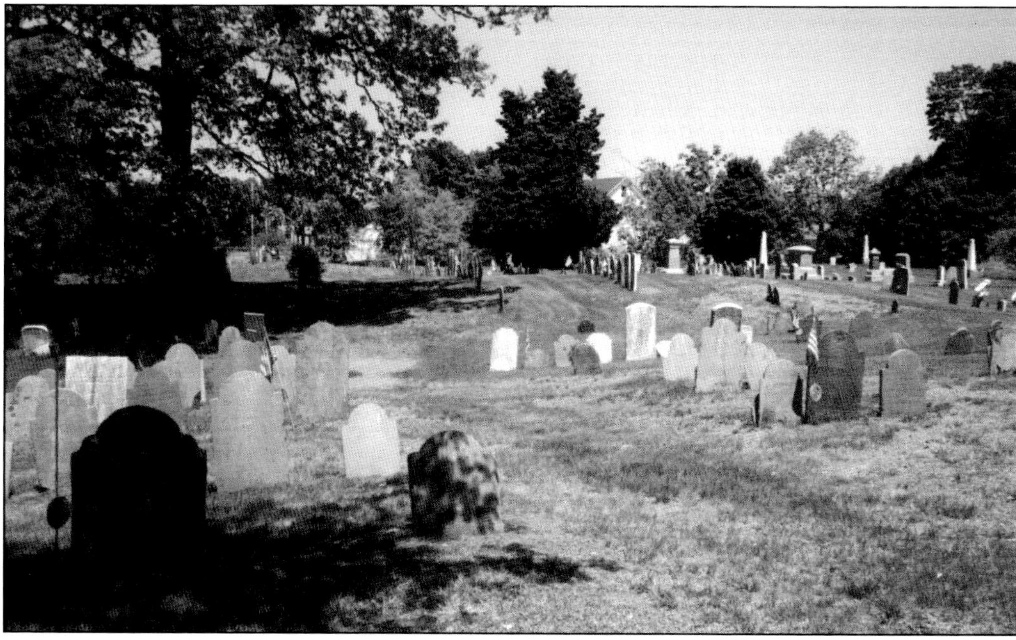

The Pearl Street Cemetery across from 102 Pearl Street. This cemetery was laid out on land given to Stoughton by George Talbot in 1748. This cemetery is the oldest cemetery in present-day Stoughton. Buried in this cemetery are some of the earliest residents of Stoughton, including the Talbot, Wenthworth, Gay, Holmes, and Estey families. (Author's collection.)

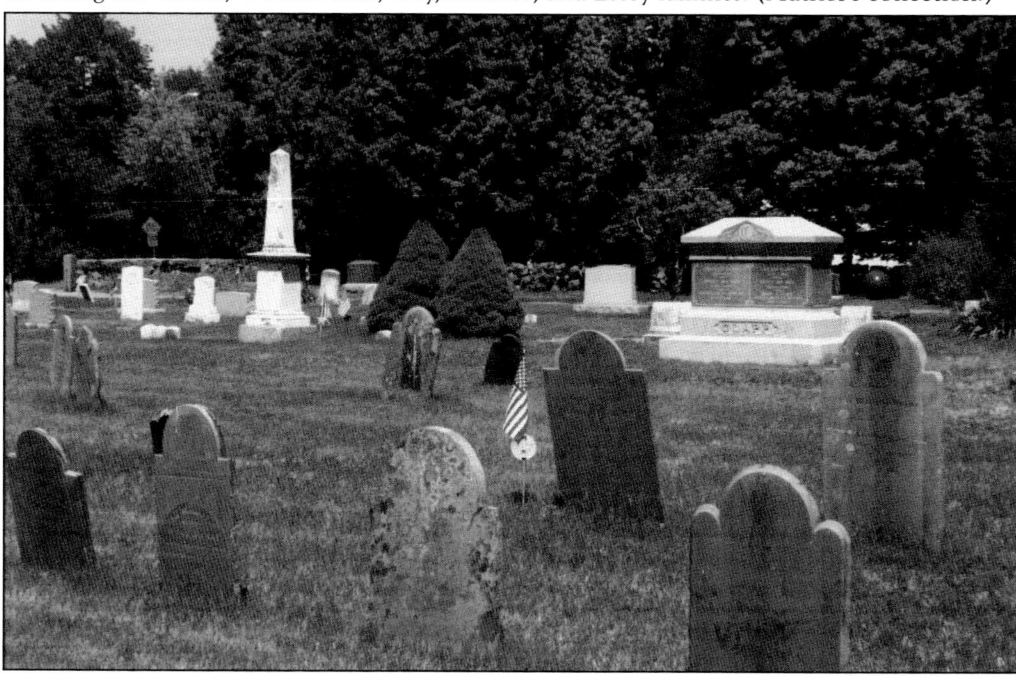

The Dry Pond Cemetery at the Corner of Bay Road and Plain Street. The oldest gravestone in this cemetery is that of Zachariah Lyon, who died in 1749. Buried in this cemetery are families from the Dry Pond area, including the Smith, Gay, Drake, Waters, and Clapp families. (Author's collection.)

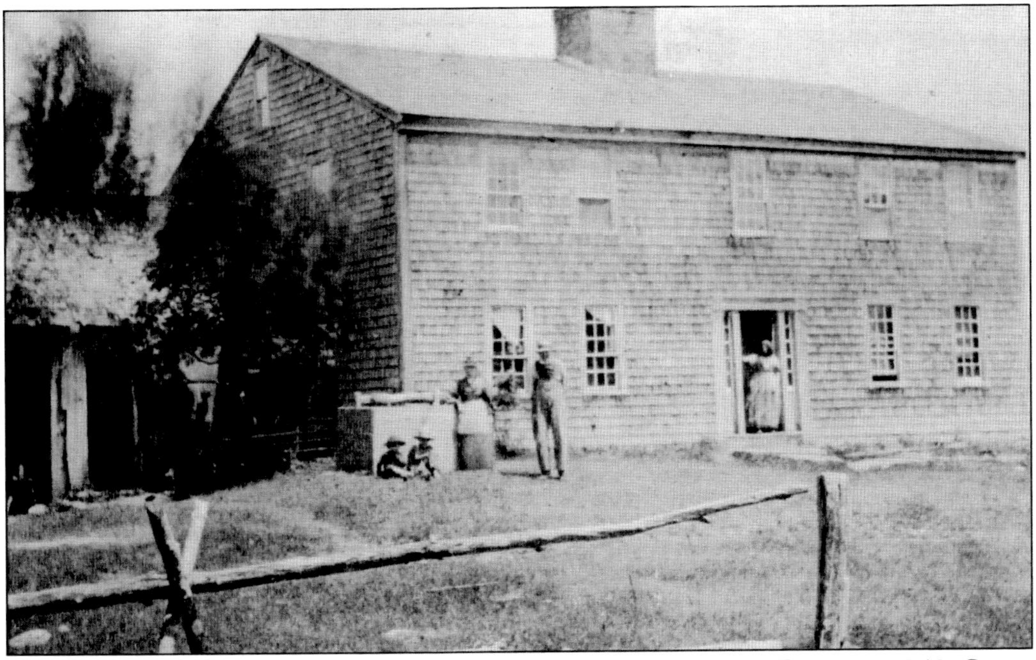

The House of Jonathan Capen (1724–1813), off Pine Street, Built in 1749. Capen served as a guardian to the Punkapoag Indians of Stoughton in the 18th century. He married in Stoughton on November 20, 1746, to Jerusha Talbot (1721–1817), the daughter of Capt. George Talbot of Stoughton.

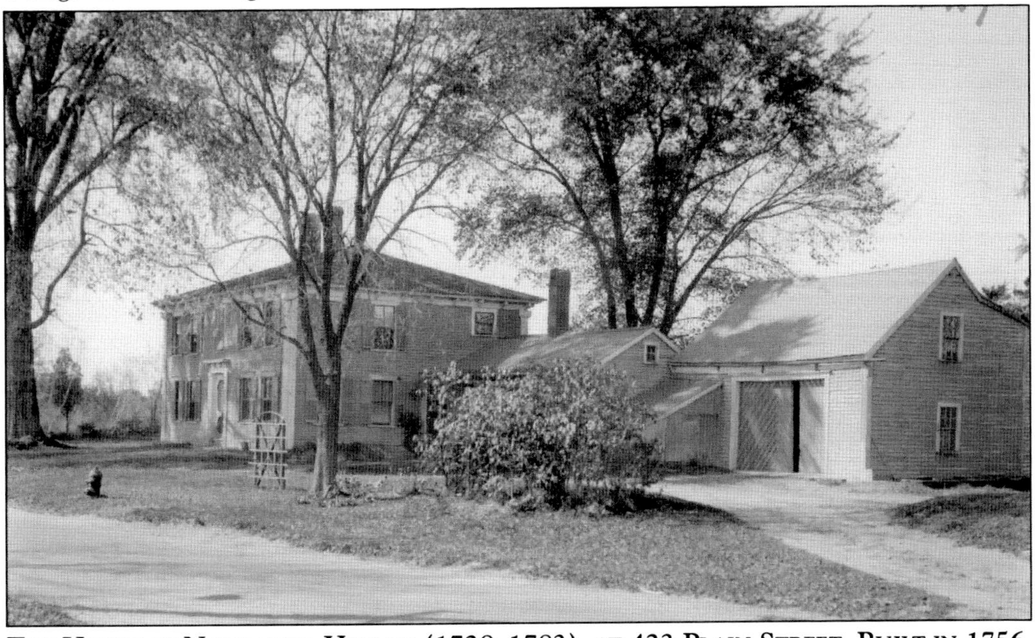

The House of Nathaniel Holmes (1728–1783), at 423 Plain Street, Built in 1756. The house received its first addition in 1806. Holmes was a tax collector in Stoughton and was a member of the William Billings singing school. This home would serve as home of the First Congregational Church and Society on July 14, 1822, after the its initial split from the First Parish Church of Christ.

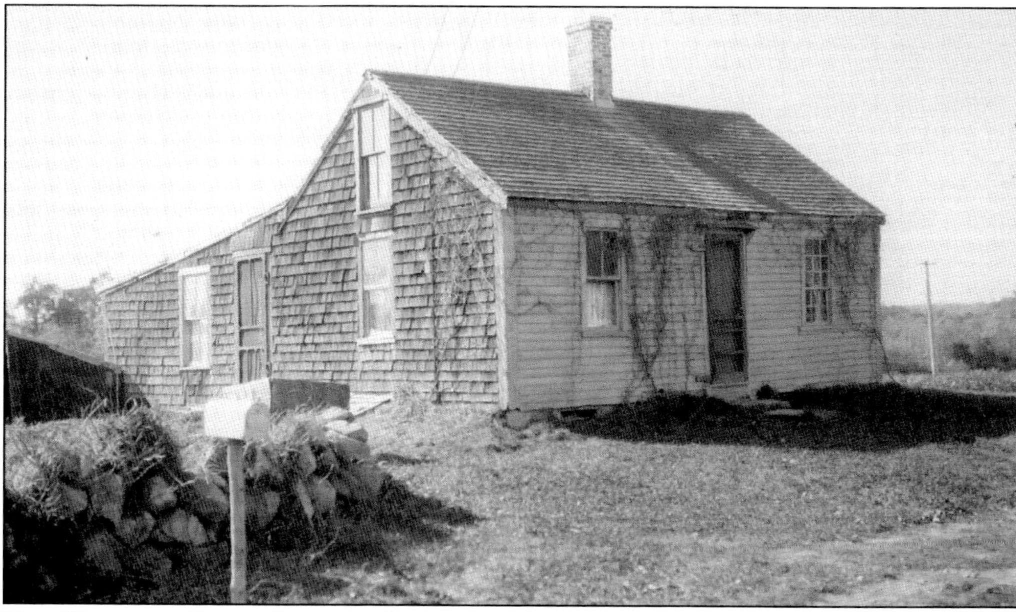

THE HOUSE OF SIMON STEARNS (1733–1816), AT 1127 WEST STREET, BUILT IN 1764. Stearns was the grandson of Dea. Isaac Stearns (1665–1741), who built the first house within the boundaries of present-day Stoughton on West Street in 1716. In 1899, the Stoughton Historical Society placed a marker by the cellar hole of his grandfather's homestead located next to 363 West Street. This house would later be the farm of Stephen Monk and his son Frank Monk. The house was razed by the McNamara family in the 1960s.

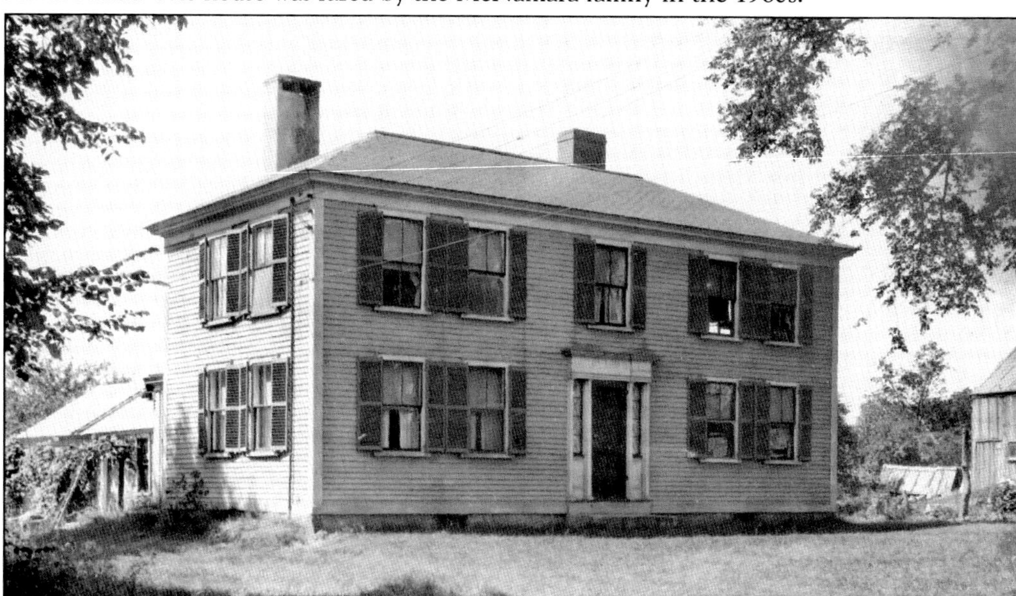

THE HOUSE OF JOHN ATHERTON JR. (1747–1835), AT 470 CENTRAL STREET, BUILT IN 1769. Atherton married in Stoughton on June 27, 1769, to Mary Adams the daughter of Rev. Jedediah Adams of Stoughton. Atherton served in the Revolutionary War and was a church deacon. This house had an addition built in 1829. It is believed the portion in the back of the house is the older structure.

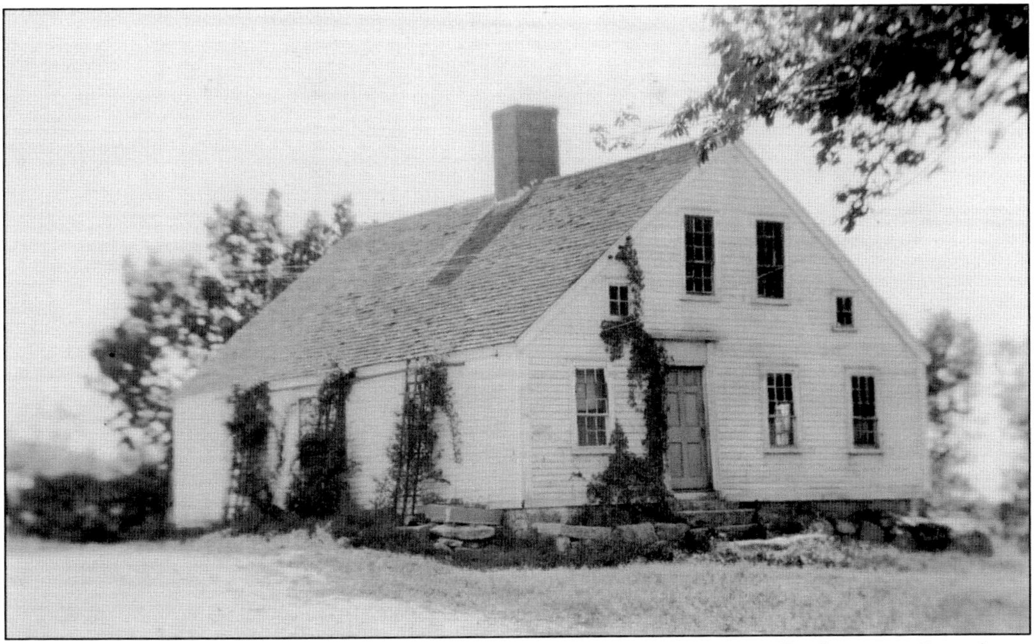

THE LEMUEL BIRD HOUSE, OFF BIRD STREET, BUILT C. 1775. Bird was a Stoughton minuteman marching on the alarm of April 19, 1775, with Capt. Peter Talbot's company in Col. Lemuel Robinson's regiment. This house burned down after 1929, and the foundation and front steps can be seen at the Bird Street Conservation area in Stoughton.

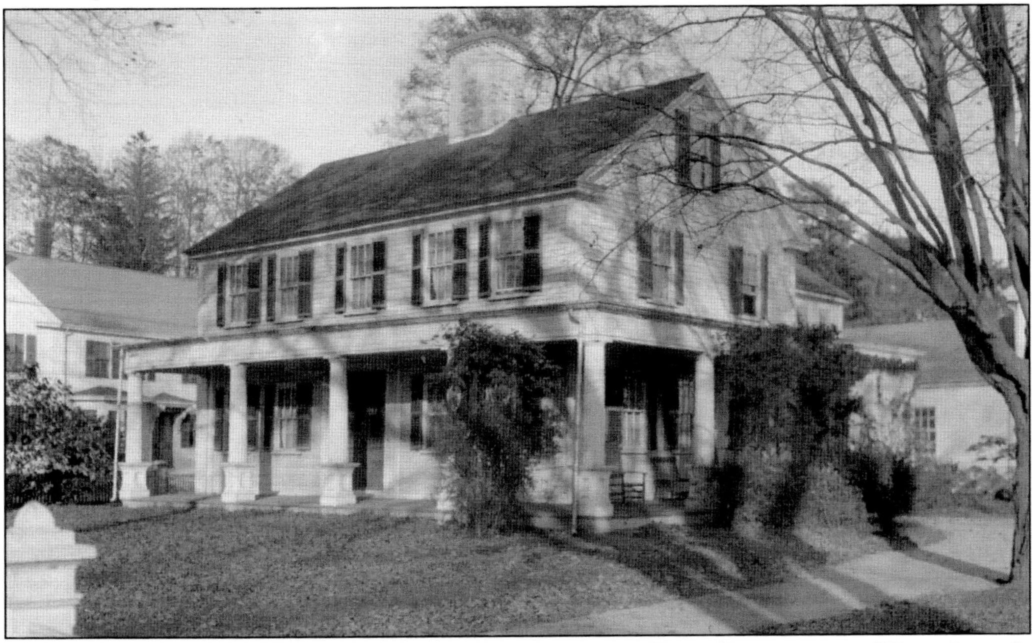

BLANCHARD'S TAVERN, AT 98 NORTH MAIN STREET IN EAST STOUGHTON (NOW AVON). This structure was built in 1748 by Samuel Blanchard and was operated by William Blanchard as a tavern in 1780. William Blanchard had served in the Revolutionary War and had been at Valley Forge. The old tavern would be home to Avon's town hall from 1938 to 1975. The structure has resumed its previous use as a tavern in recent years.

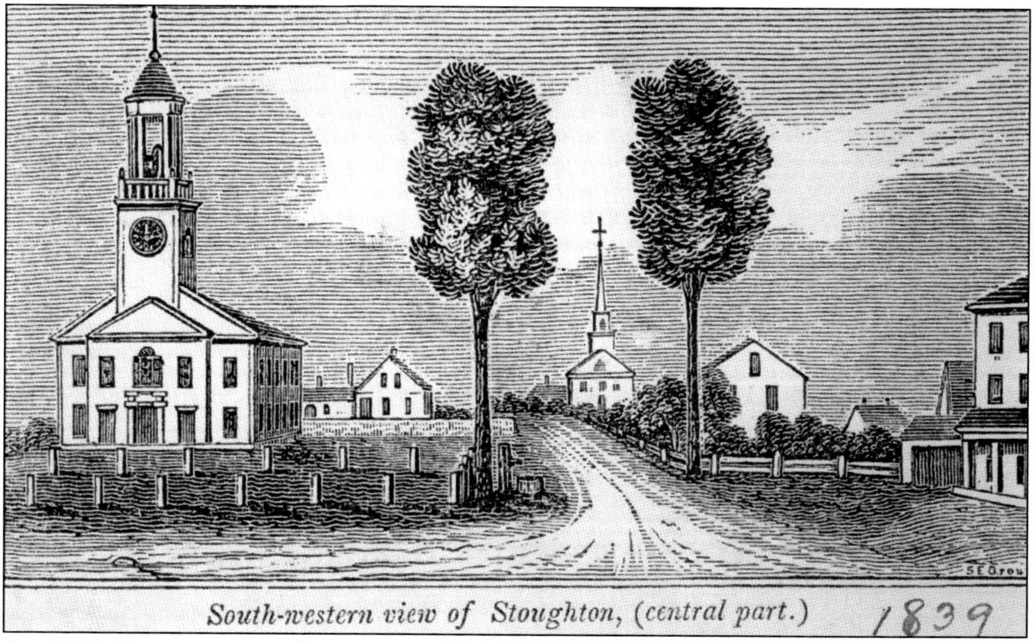

AN 1839 ENGRAVING OF STOUGHTON CENTER, LOOKING EAST DOWN PLEASANT STREET. On the left is the Universalist church and, in the background, the old Methodist Episcopal church on Pleasant Street. The structure on the right-hand side is Abraham Capen's Tavern, built in 1799. (Author's collection.)

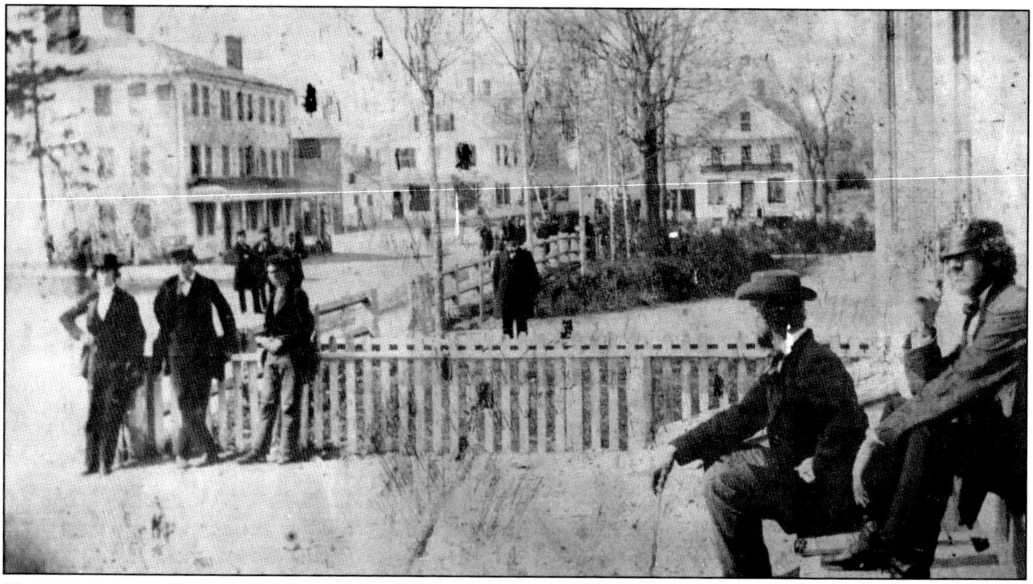

THE EARLIEST-KNOWN OUTDOOR PHOTOGRAPHIC IMAGE OF STOUGHTON, C. 1860. This daguerreotype image was taken from the steps of a building behind the First Parish Church on Pleasant Street. The camera was faced westerly down Pleasant Street and toward the town center. The Federal-era structure on the immediate left is the old Abraham Capen Tavern, built in 1799 on the corner of Pleasant and Park Streets. The Leonard Drake Hotel, in the center, and the Northrup Building, on the right, were destroyed in the great fire of February 27, 1880.

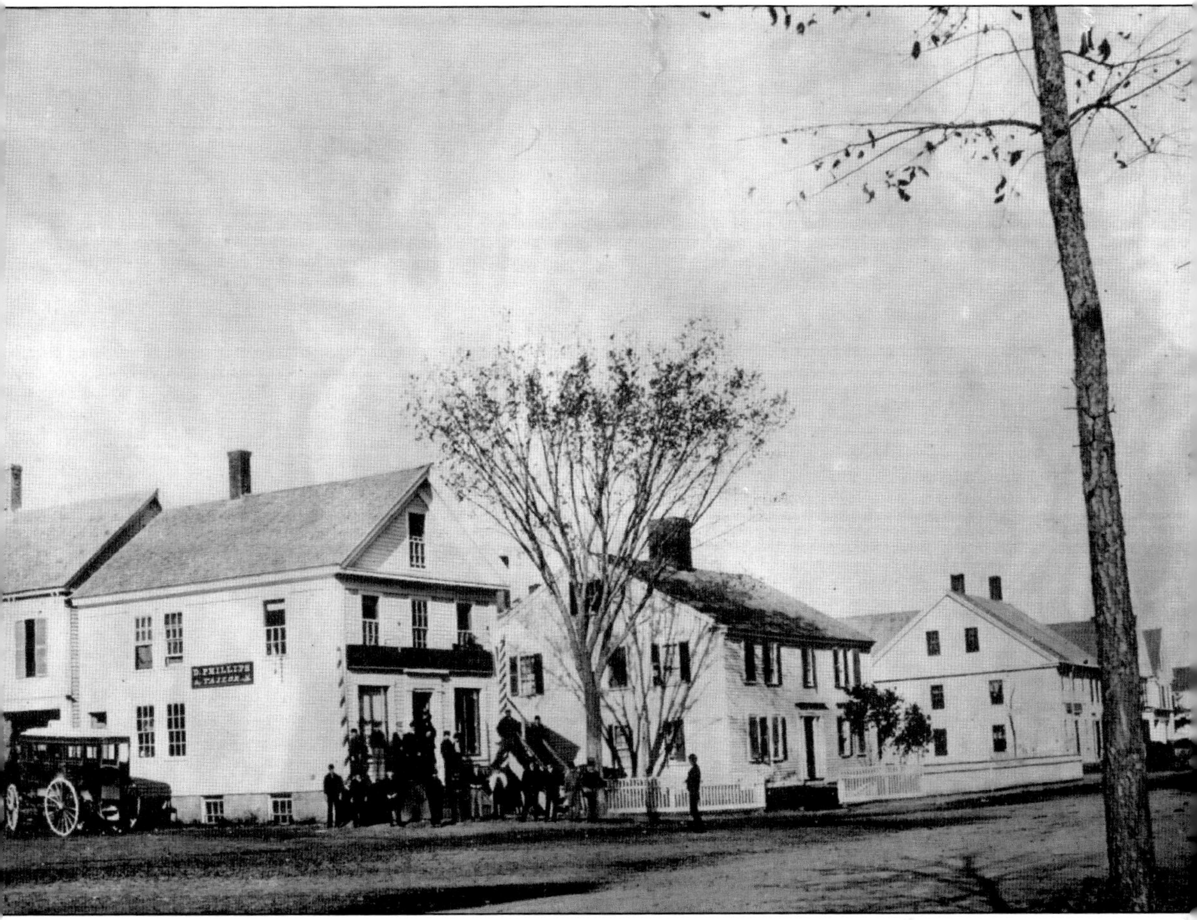

THE NORTHRUP BUILDING AND ROBERT SWAN'S HOUSE ON WASHINGTON STREET, C. 1870. The Northrup Building was north of Atwood's stable; this building has a sign advertising D. Phillips-Tailor. One of the coaches of Nathan Warren can be seen next to this building. To the right of the Northrup Building is the homestead of Joseph Withington, who sold this house and land to Lewis Johnson, December 24, 1764. This house was later the home of Robert and Luther Swan. In 1821, part of this building was used to house Isaac Beal's shoe shop. This entire block was destroyed by the fire of February 27, 1880. The next building is Joseph Swan's store and residence, which survived the fire.

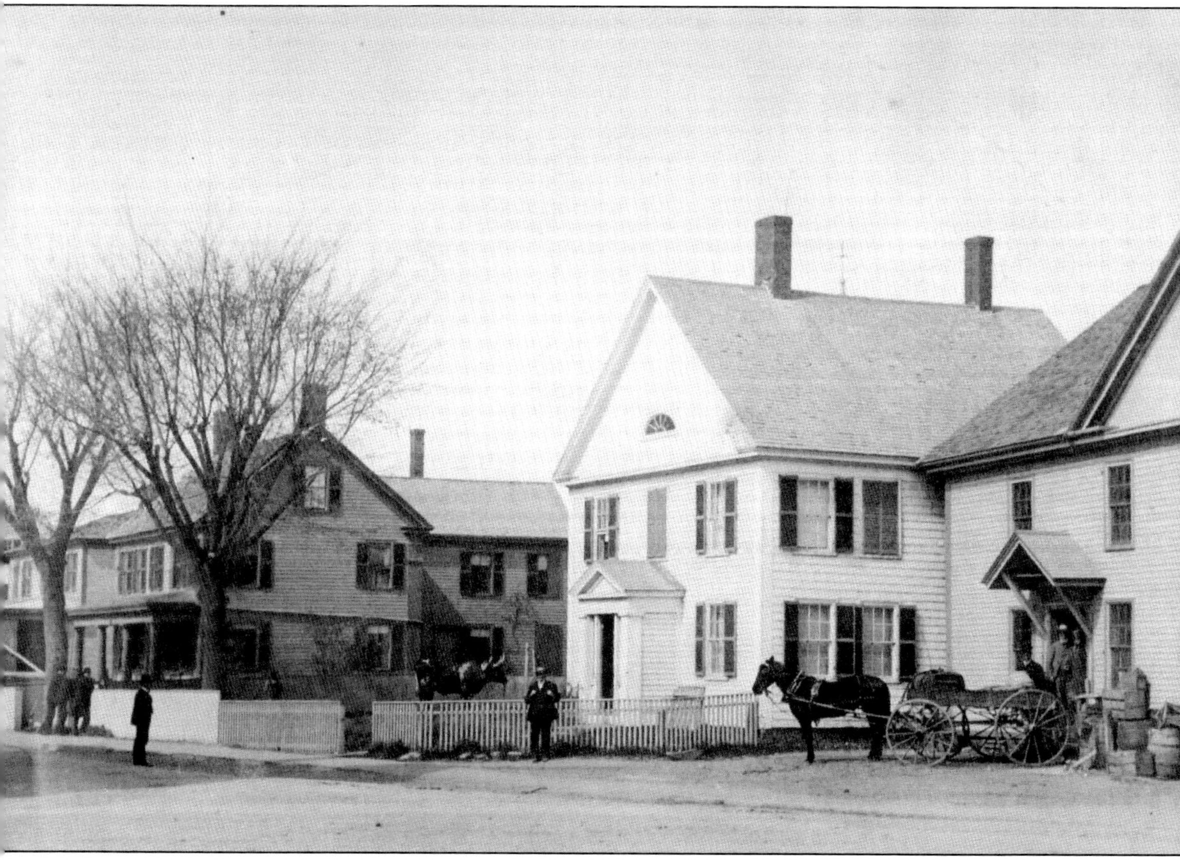

JOSEPH SWAN'S STORE AND RESIDENCE, ON WYMAN AND WASHINGTON STREETS. Brothers Robert and Joseph Swan purchased this corner lot *c.* 1830. One of the buildings was moved from North Easton by oxen. These building were razed to build Swan's Building on the same corner in 1892.

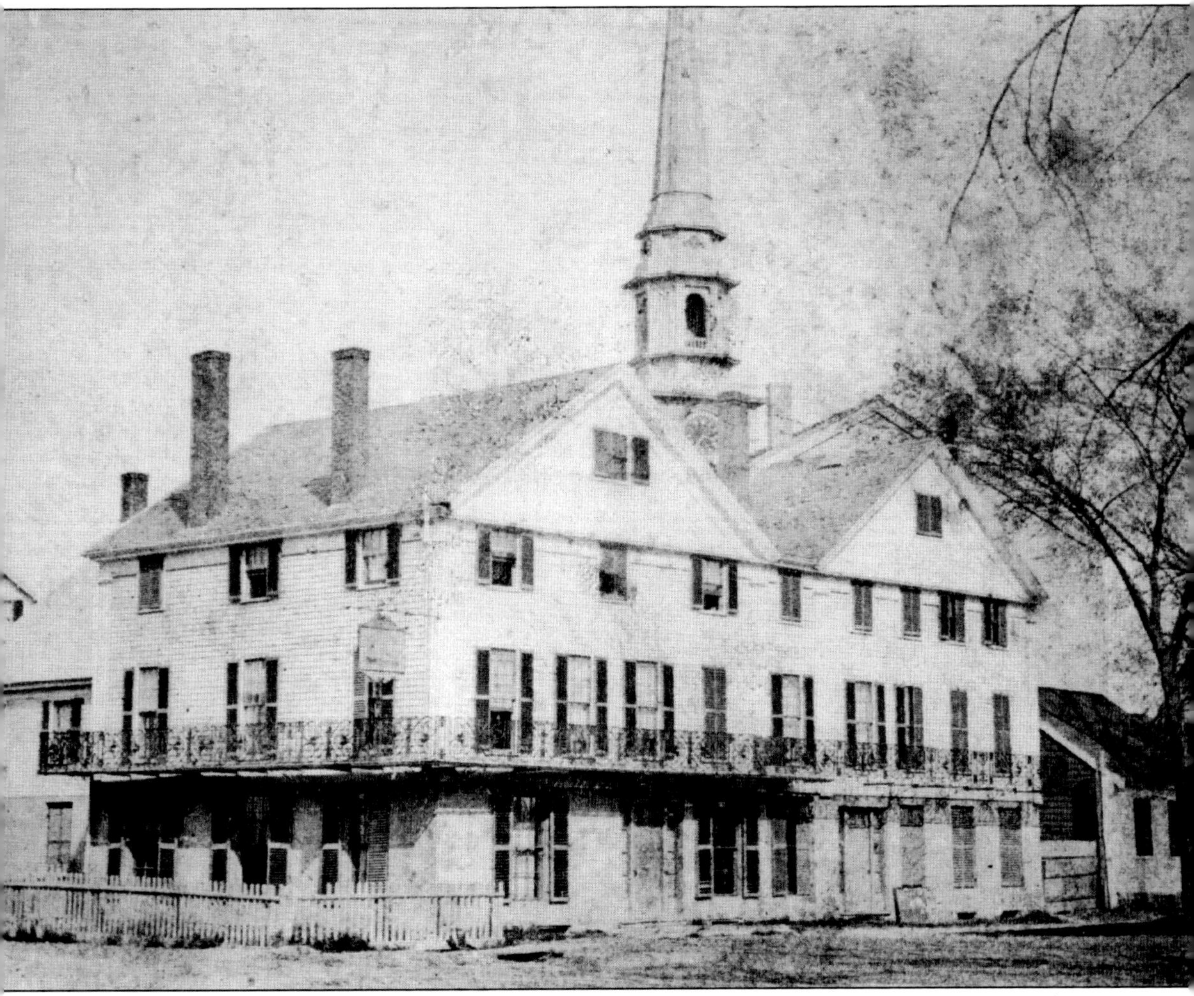

THE TISDALE HOUSE ON RAILROAD AVENUE, BUILT BETWEEN 1845 AND 1850. This structure was built to accommodate boarders and travelers from the nearby railroad depot. It was later known as the Stoughton House and was run by William Keith. It burned on January 12, 1903.

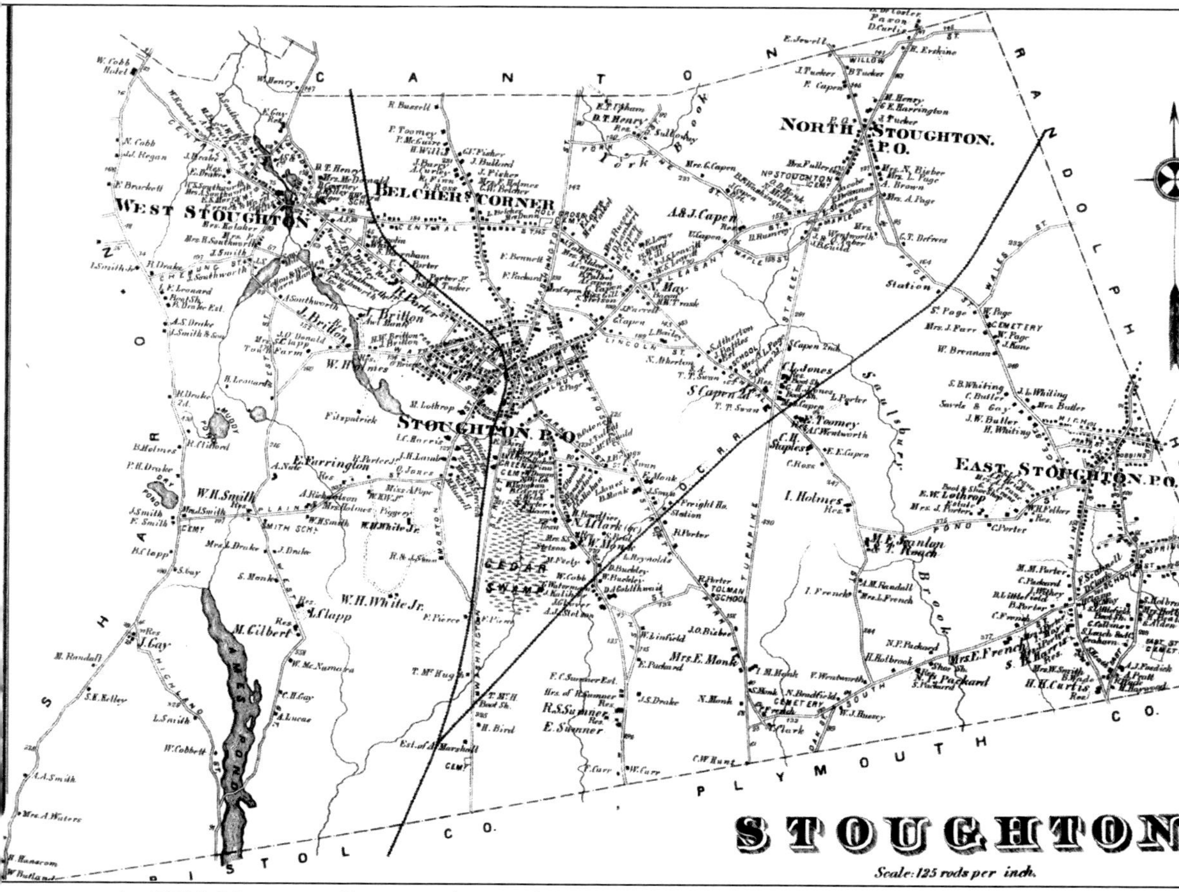

A 1876 NORFOLK COUNTY ATLAS MAP OF STOUGHTON. This detailed map shows the locations of all residences in the town of Stoughton at that time. (Author's collection.)

Two

PLACES OF WORSHIP

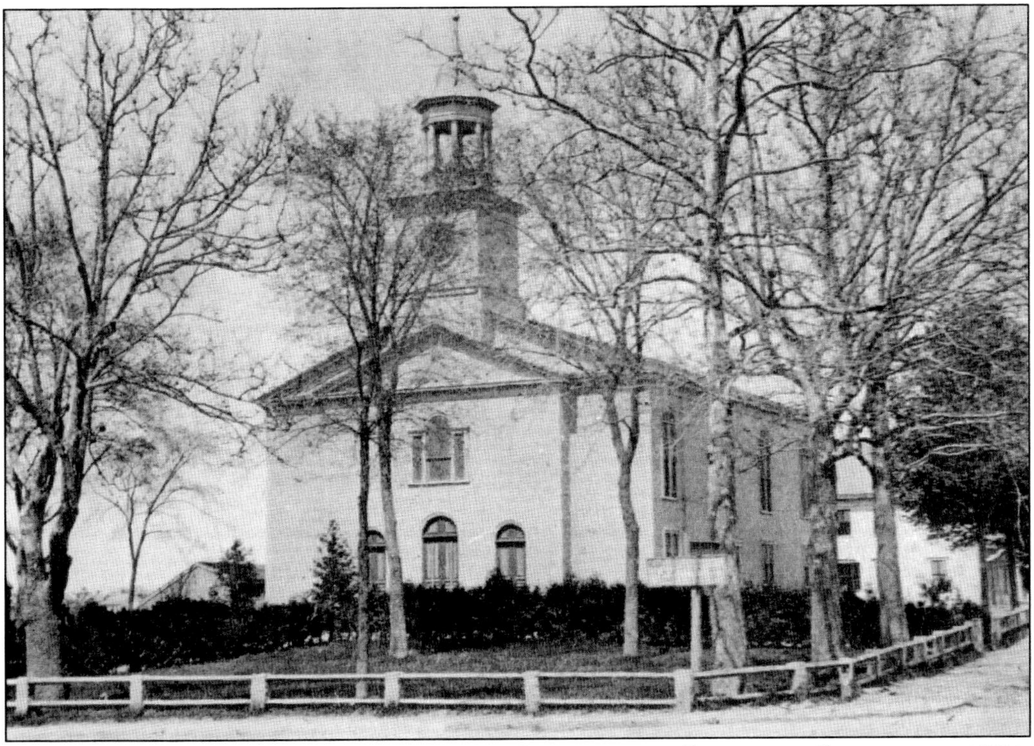

FIRST PARISH CHURCH, AT STOUGHTON CENTER AND PLEASANT STREET, IN 1874. Construction of this meetinghouse began in July 1806 and was completed in 1808. The meetinghouse was dedicated on June 2, 1808. This church is where the split occurred on July 10, 1822, dividing the Church of Christ into the Congregationalists and the Unitarians. The structure became formally known as a Universalist church in 1838. It was altered in 1848 and remodeled and enlarged in 1870. For many years, the Stoughton town offices were located at Chemung Hall in this structure. This building was destroyed by fire on June 29, 1966.

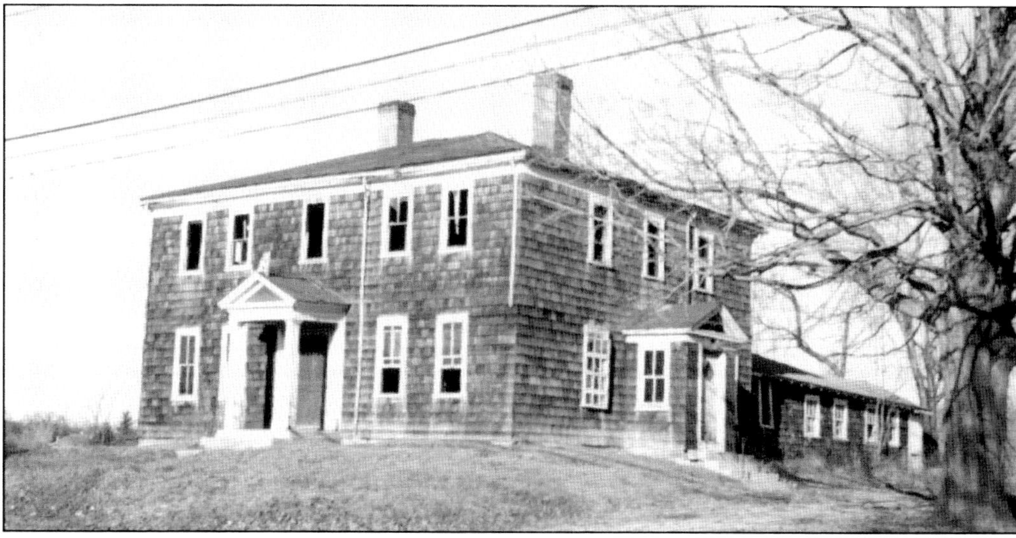

The House of Rev. Jedediah Adams (1710–1799), on Pearl Street, across from the New Stoughton High School. Rev. Jedediah Adams graduated from Harvard University in 1733. This building was built shortly after his call to Stoughton's Third Parish as minister of the Church of Christ, January 5, 1746. He turned his pulpit to Rev. Edward Richmond in 1792; however, he remained an associate minister until his death. Adams raised his family in this house. One of his sons, Dr. Peter Adams (1756–1832), served as the Stoughton town clerk in 1795–1796. Dr. Adams was an early Stoughton physician and became the first worshipful master of Stoughton's Rising Star Lodge, chartered in 1799. The Adams homestead was burned down in 1970.

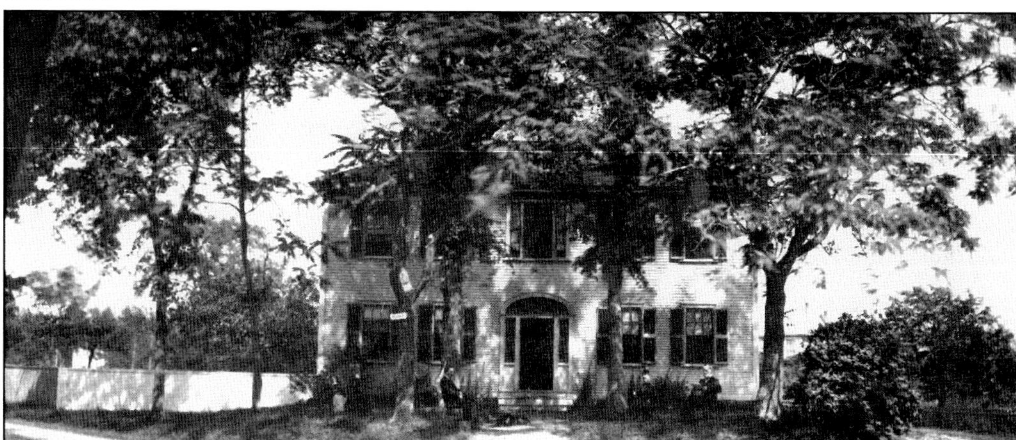

Robert Capen's Tavern and House, at the Corner of Seaver and Park Streets. The tavern was where an early meeting of a singing school met on January 13, 1762. This early meeting was the root of the current Old Stoughton Musical Society. This building was purchased as a parsonage for the Church of Christ in 1793 by Rev. Edward Richmond (1767–1842). Richmond was ordained a colleague of Rev. Jedediah Adams on December 5, 1792, and continued his preaching at Stoughton's First Parish Christ Church until his resignation in 1817. In 1826, the parsonage was purchased by Rev. Calvin Park of the First Congregational Church as a parsonage. In 1888, this structure was moved to 15 Seaver Street to make room for a two-family house erected by Newell S. Atwood.

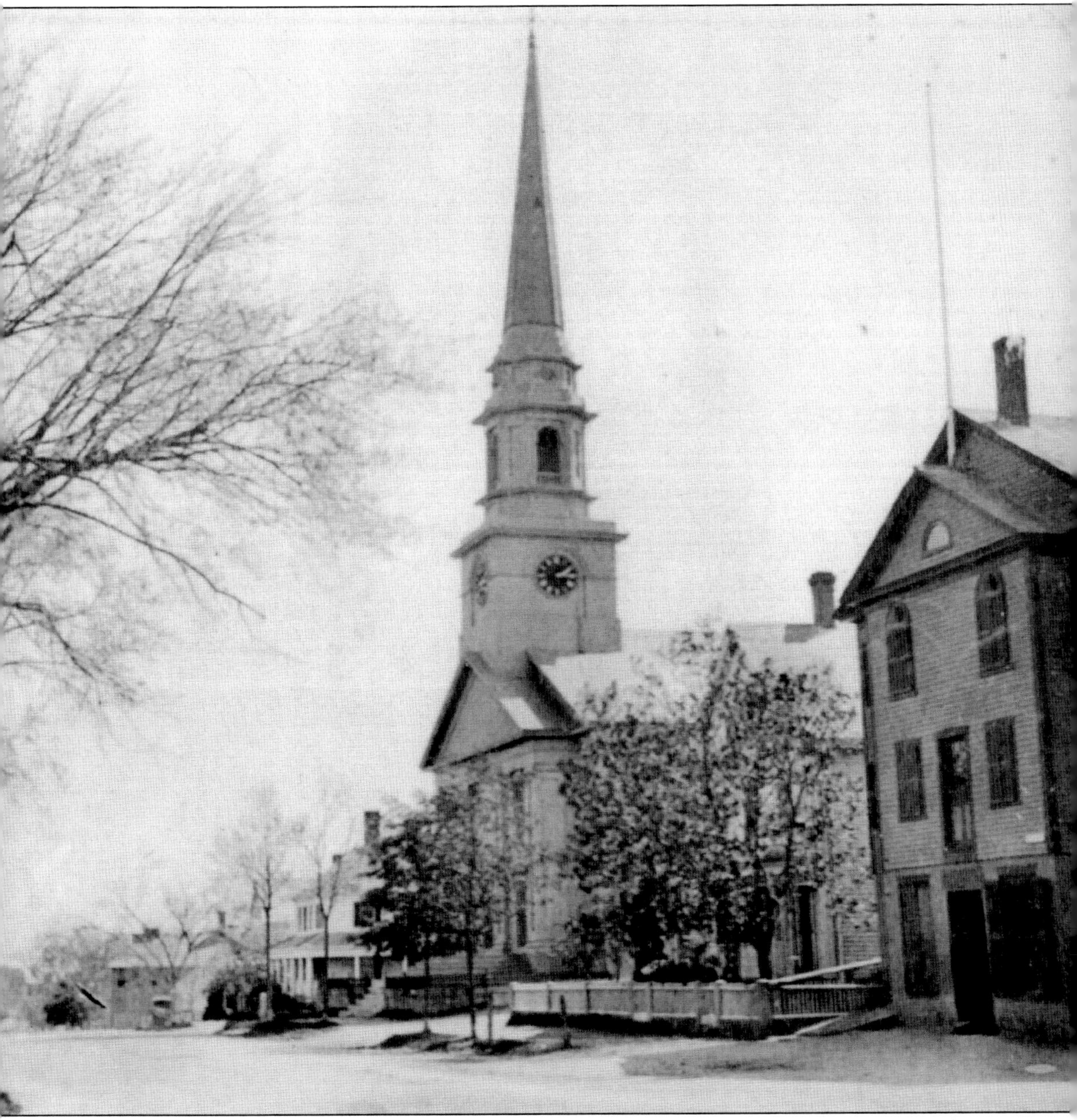

Two Structures of the Congregational Church on Washington Street. The structure on the right is the edifice where construction was begun by Benjamin Clapp in 1824. The building was dedicated on June 1, 1825, and was altered in 1842. This building proved to be too small for the congregation and was later sold to Willard White for $450. White had the building moved slightly north of its location and hoisted to the second floor of his White's Market. The building was used as a skating rink and club rooms. The old structure would be destroyed by fire on October 5, 1897. Seen on the left is the 1852 edifice of the church. Construction on this building began in 1851. The church was dedicated on January 28, 1852, at a cost of $12,000. It was destroyed by fire on March 9, 1942.

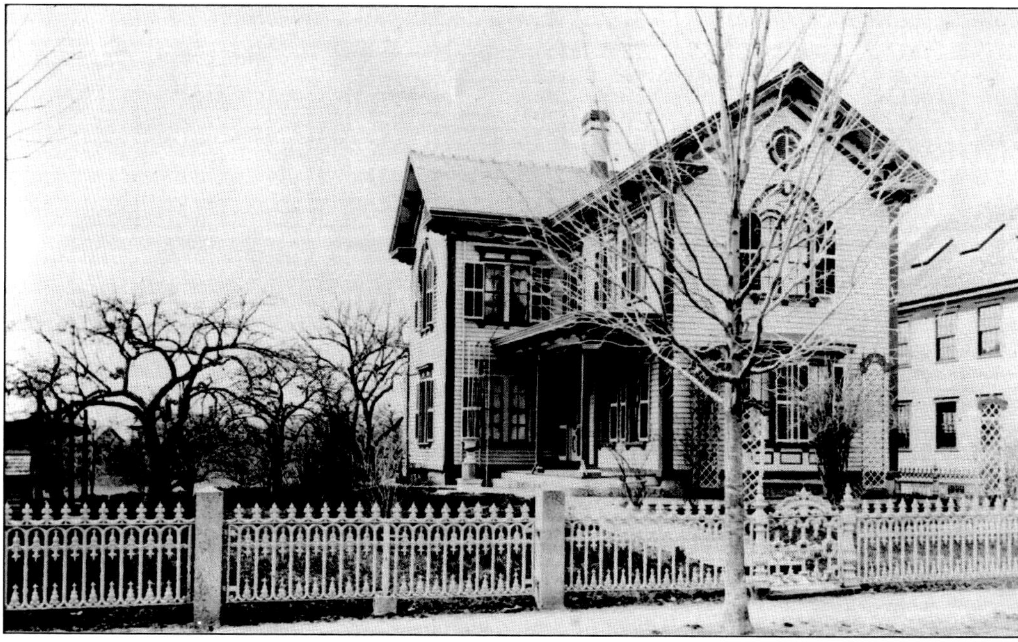

THE FIRST CONGREGATIONAL CHURCH BUILDING (1949–1958), AT 30 PEARL STREET. This building was purchased from the estate of the widow of Dr. Charles L. Swan Sr. on December 27, 1948. After major renovation, the church dedicated this structure on November 20, 1949. The First Congregational Church sold this structure to Ahavath Torah Synagogue in 1958.

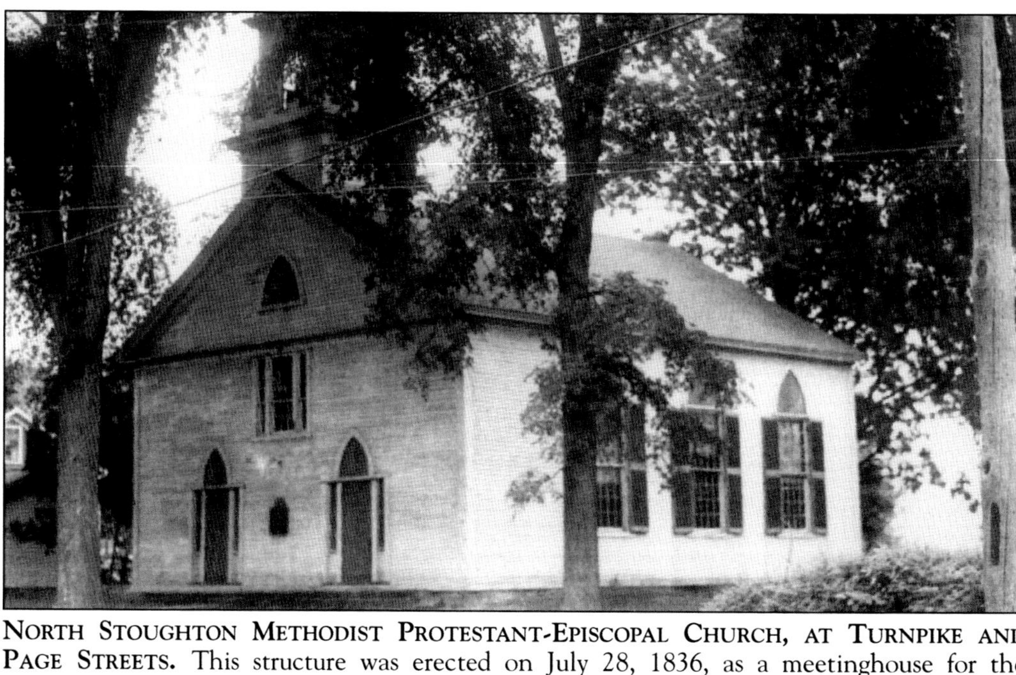

NORTH STOUGHTON METHODIST PROTESTANT-EPISCOPAL CHURCH, AT TURNPIKE AND PAGE STREETS. This structure was erected on July 28, 1836, as a meetinghouse for the Methodist Protestant Church. The denomination was changed to Methodist Episcopal on February 23, 1873. The church closed its doors for the last time in 1943 and was soon after torn down. (Author's collection.)

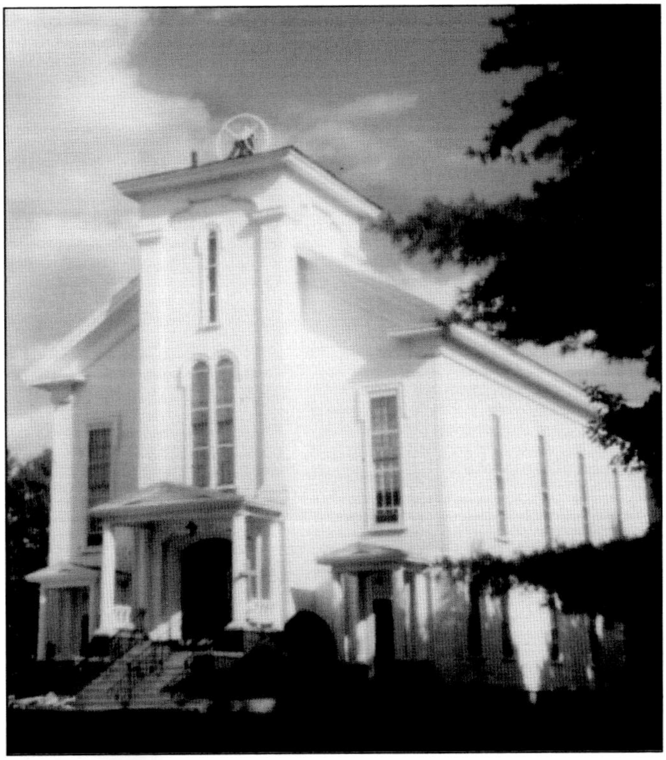

The First United Methodist Church, at 100 Pleasant Street. Construction began in 1865 and was completed upon dedication, on December 5, 1866, as a Methodist Episcopal church. This building occupies the site of an earlier edifice (built in 1835) that faced westerly toward Stoughton Center. This earlier structure was removed *c.* 1865 to make room for the current structure. (Author's collection.)

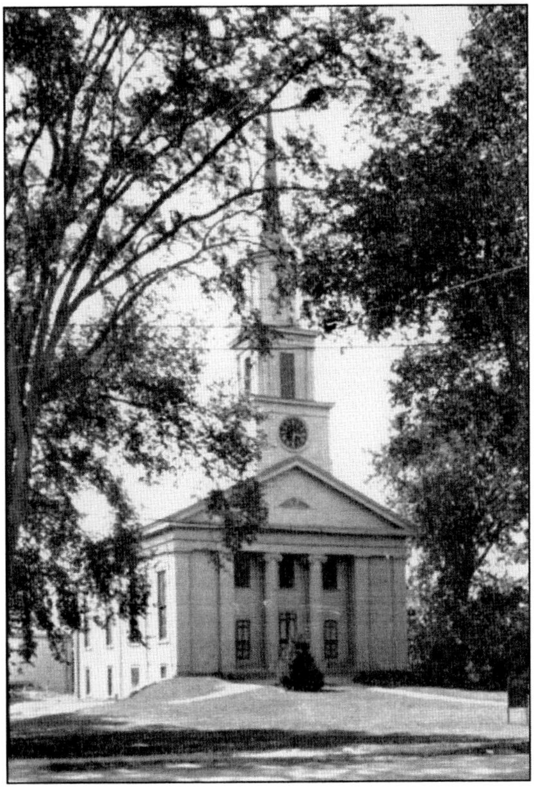

The Old East Stoughton Baptist Church, on North Main Street in Avon. This structure was dedicated as the third Baptist meetinghouse in East Stoughton on March 30, 1848. After 1888, this church served as a parish for Avon citizens.

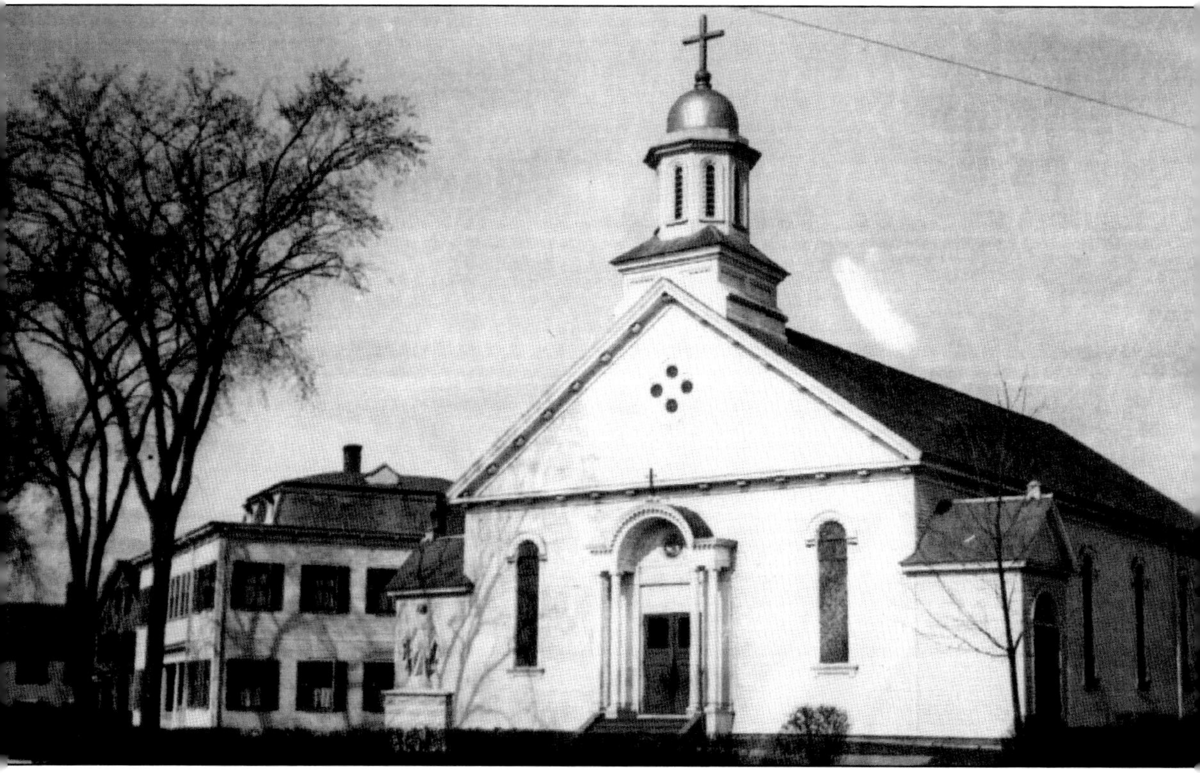

The Immaculate Conception Church, on the Corner of Canton and School Streets. The original half-acre plot for this structure was purchased by Fr. John Flatley. This edifice was dedicated on November 10, 1859, by Bishop John B. Fitzpatrick. It was removed in the early 1970s to make room for a newer building.

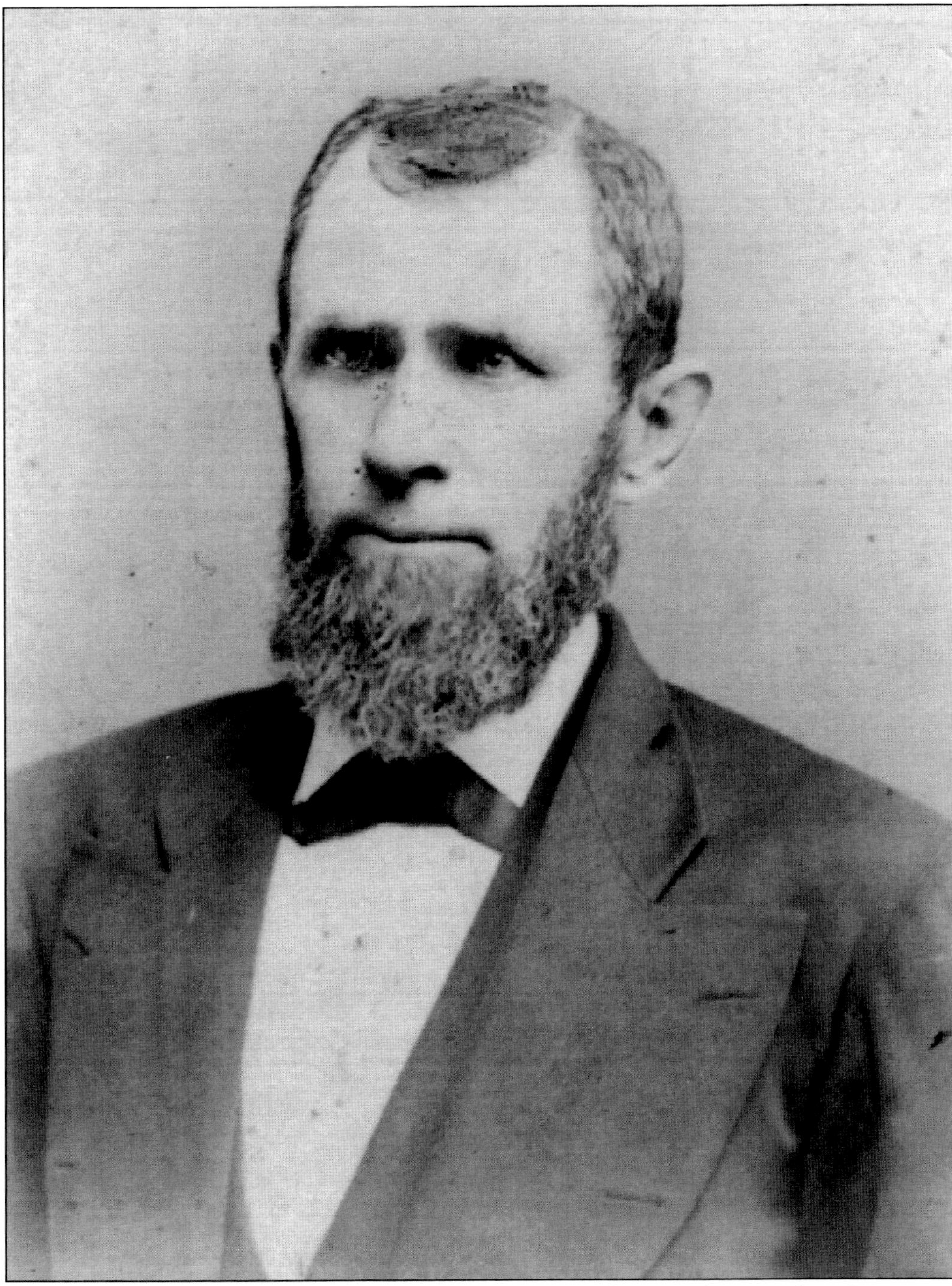

JOSEPH ROWAN (1835–1884). Joseph Rowan was a parishioner of Immaculate Conception Church. He was born in County Clare, Ireland, and immigrated to New York on January 10, 1853. He moved to Stoughton soon after and lived out the rest of his life there at his home across from the convent he helped purchase. He became a naturalized U.S. citizen on October 26, 1858. His descendants still reside at his same house at 49 Winter Street. (Courtesy of Denise [Theriault] Peterson.)

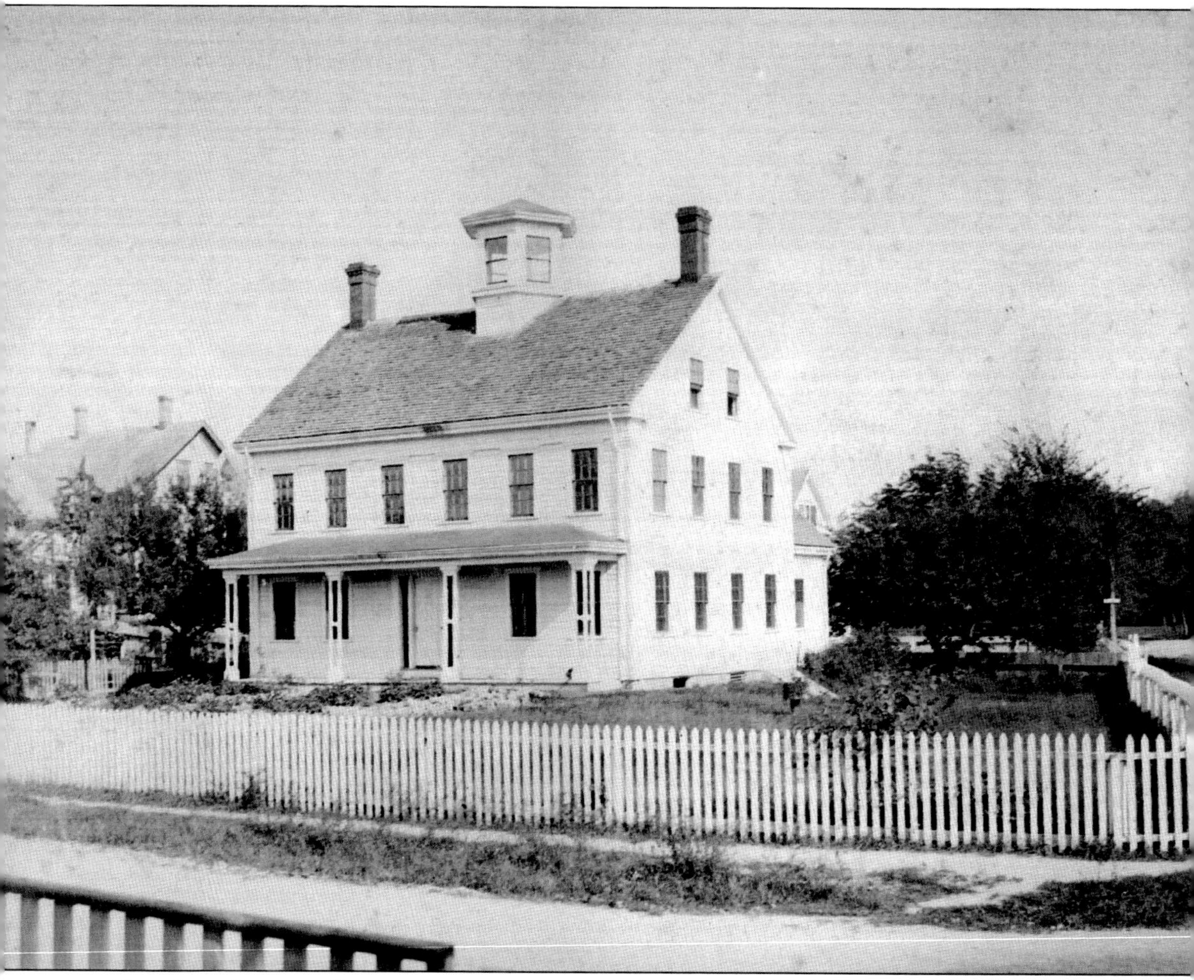

The Old Sacred Heart Convent for the Sisters of St. Joseph, on the Corner of Summer and Winter Streets. This building and land was purchased by Joseph Rowan for $2,500 from factory owner John Greenleaf Phinney on October 17, 1882. Rowan then turned the property over to the Sisters of St. Joseph, who would teach at the newly formed St. Mary's School.

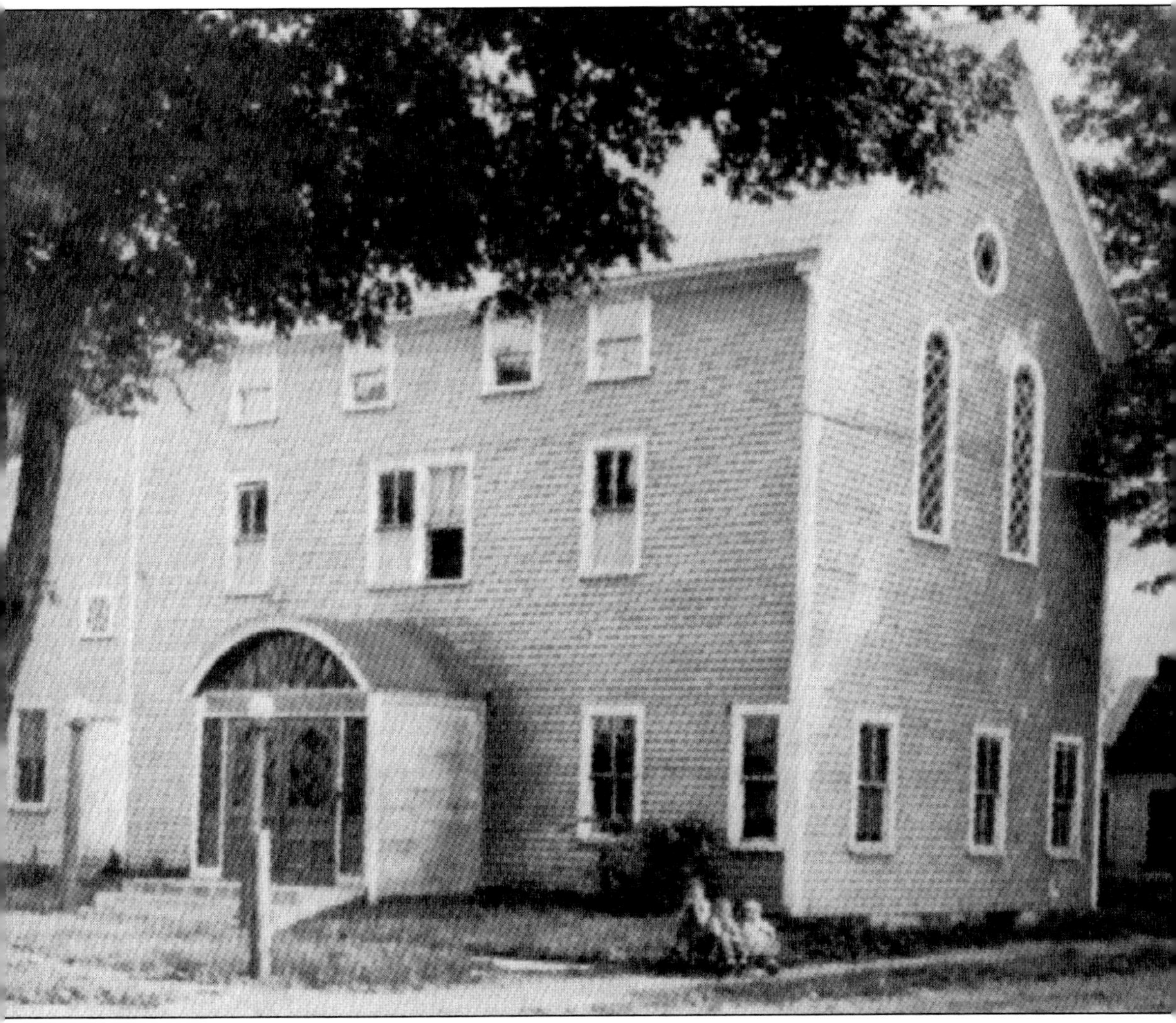

THE AHAVATH TORAH SYNAGOGUE ON PORTER STREET, BUILT IN 1918. The first meeting of Ahavath Achim Congregation occurred in 1893. By 1895, Congregation Talmud Torah organized at the home of Benjamin Lipsky in Stoughton. In 1918, the two congregations combined to form the Ahavath Torah Congregation. They would later move to the old Dr. Swan house at 30 Pearl Street, after the First Congregational Church sold the remodeled structure they used from 1949 to 1958. The old synagogue would become home to the Knights of Columbus. The structure was later sold and torn down to make room for a new meeting place for the Club Luiz de Camoes.

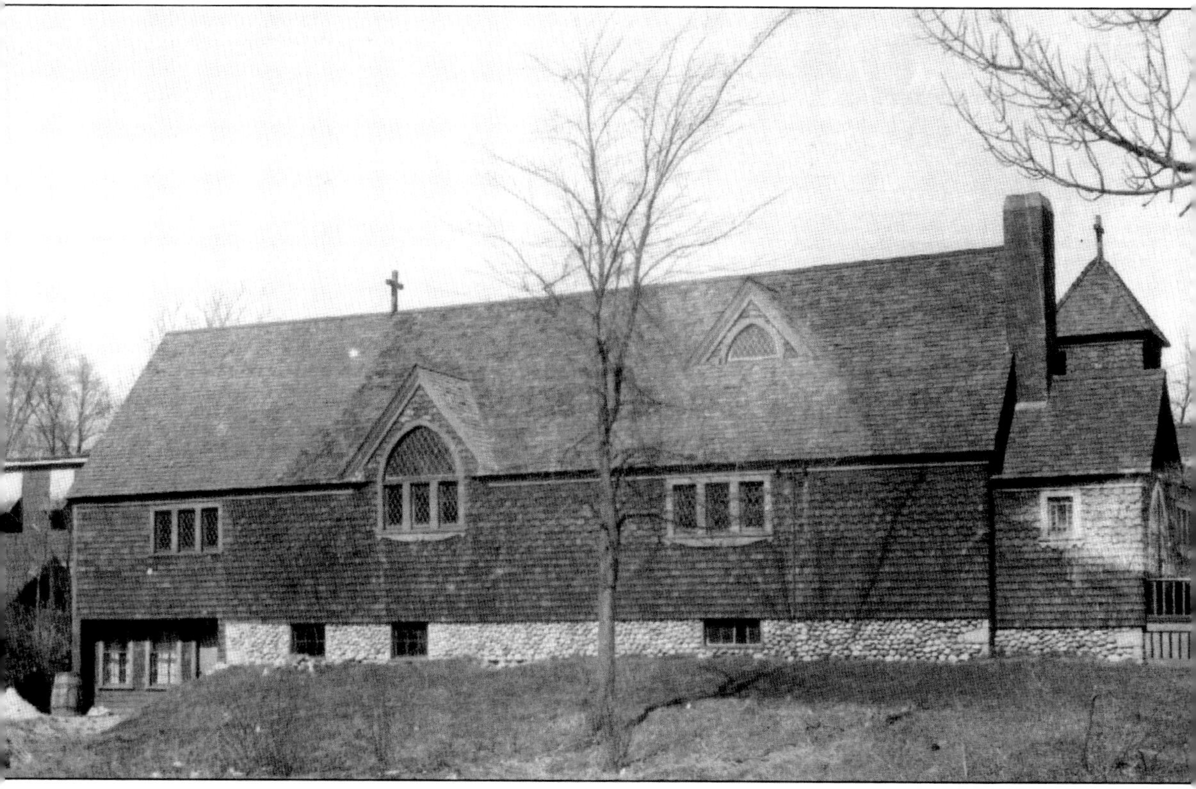

THE TRINITY EPISCOPAL CHURCH, AT 34 FREEMAN STREET, BUILT IN 1898. The Trinity Episcopal Church formed in Stoughton on October 1, 1893, and met at the Masonic Block on Wyman Street until its structure was completed. The church later sold the structure to the Christadelphian Ecclesia and, in 1969, moved to 414 Sumner Street.

Three

SCHOOLS

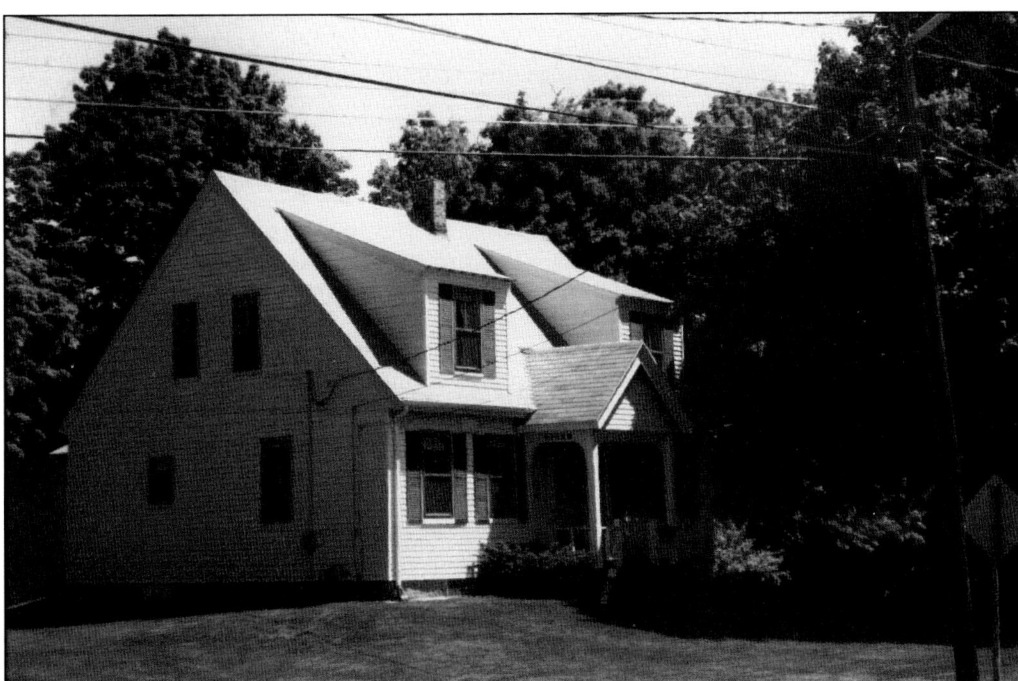

THE WEST STOUGHTON SCHOOLHOUSE, BUILT ON CENTRAL STREET IN 1818. This structure was constructed as a schoolhouse. It was later moved to Chestnut Street and then to Seaver Street. The building was finally moved to its current location, 27 Leach Street, *c.* 1906. (Author's collection.)

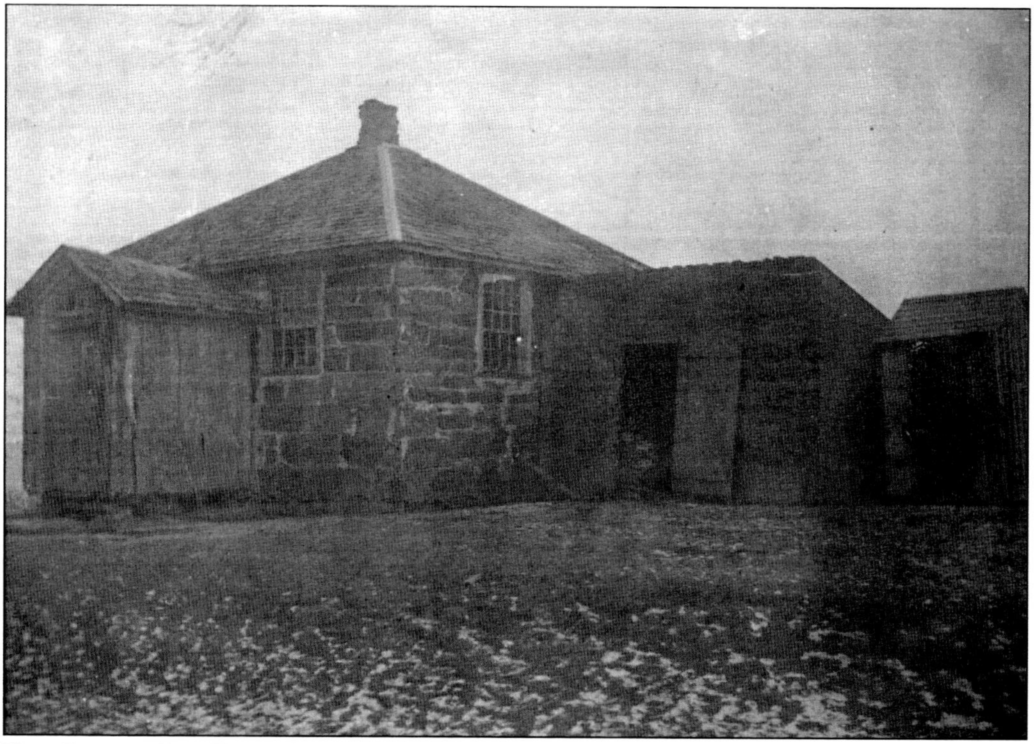

THE SECOND DRY POND SCHOOLHOUSE, C. 1880. This square schoolhouse was made out of granite blocks *c.* 1827 and was referred by the pupils as the "jail." Lucius Clapp (1817–1909) was a teacher at this building for several winters before 1837. This building stood on the site of the original wooden Dry Pond Schoolhouse, built in 1798 at the southeast corner of West and Plain Streets.

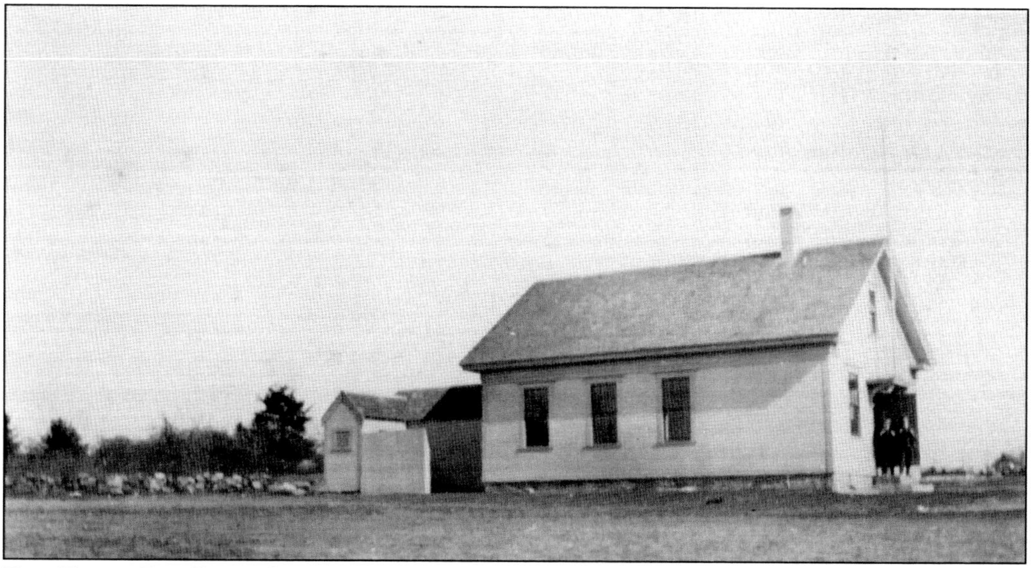

THE THIRD DRY POND-SMITH SCHOOLHOUSE IN 1915. In 1871, a new schoolhouse was built on the same plot of land as the previous two structures at West and Plain Streets. This school was closed in 1933 and was converted into a single-family house by the Dykeman family.

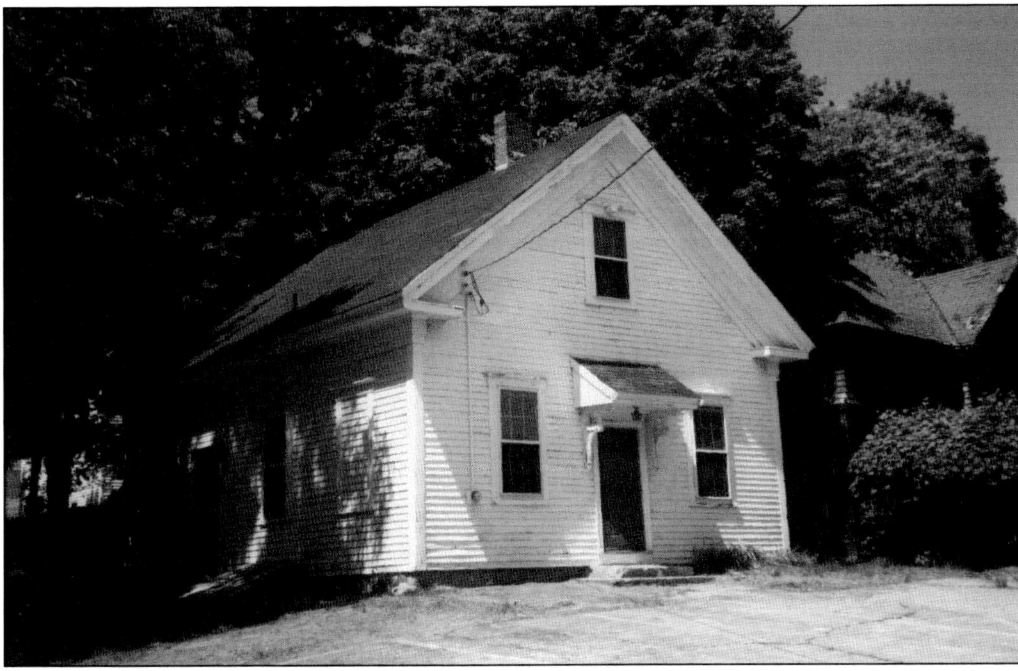

THE PARK SCHOOL ON SEAVER STREET, BEHIND THE METHODIST CHURCH. This two-room schoolhouse was built in 1859 and named for Rev. Calvin Park (1774–1847), a longstanding member of the school committee and minister of the First Congregational Church of Stoughton from 1826 to 1840. This building was last used as a school in 1917. In the 1980s, Richard A. Venanzi of Stoughton restored this structure for a Scout project while in Stoughton's Troop 57.

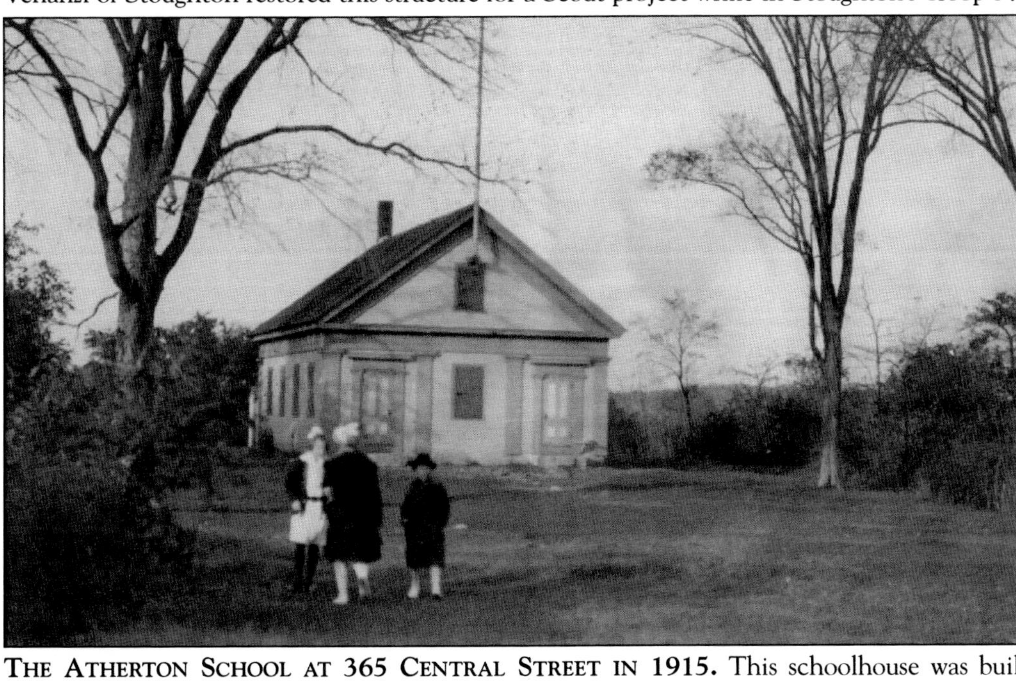

THE ATHERTON SCHOOL AT 365 CENTRAL STREET IN 1915. This schoolhouse was built c. 1895 and closed in 1933. The original structure is now incorporated into a modern structure at the same location on Central Street.

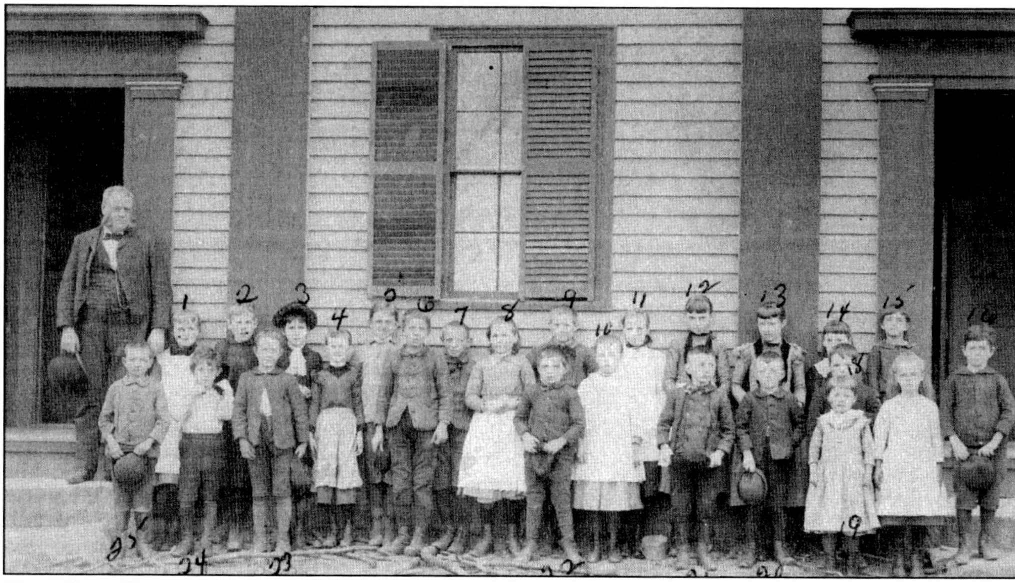

THE OLD TOLMAN SCHOOL, ON PARK STREET, C. 1880–1885. The school was taught by Francis Capen (d. 1892) from 1879 to 1890. From left to right are the following: (front row) unidentified, Billie Walters, unidentified, Lester Raymond, Sam Savory, two unidentified, Arthur Porter, Sade Corbett, and Charles Blanchard; (back row) Francis Capen (teacher), unidentified, Billie Corbett, Feenie McCarron, Nelle Corbett, George Faunce, Lester Randall, Fred Lawrence, unidentified, Ed Lawrence, Sadie Watts, Bertha Skinner, Eddie Monk, Helen Monk, Maude Savory, and Sadie Randall. This school was burned on November 27, 1924.

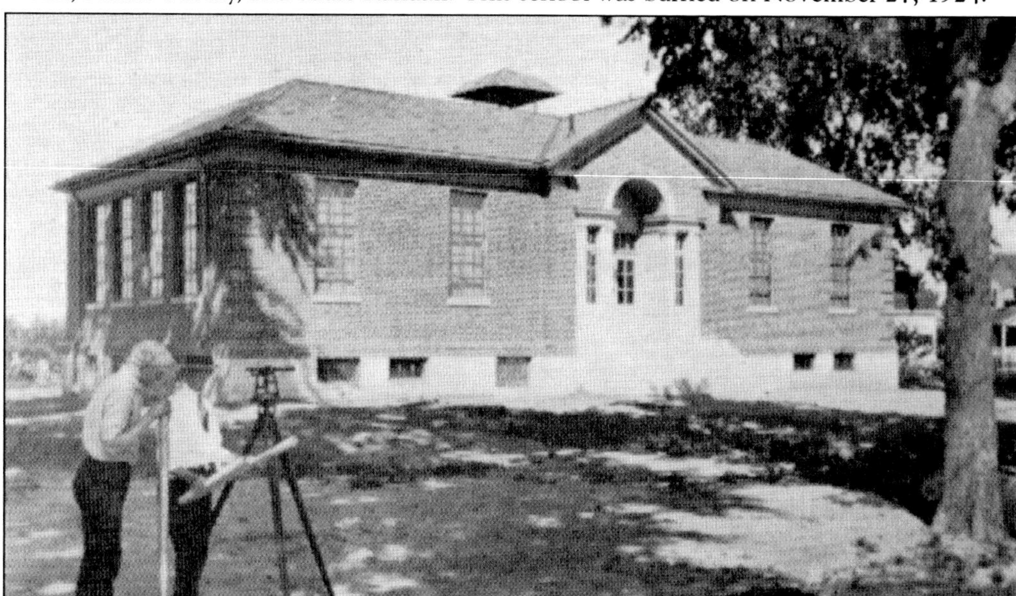

THE NEW TOLMAN SCHOOL, ON PARK STREET, BUILT IN 1925. This new building was constructed for a cost of $16,400. The town of Stoughton discontinued use of the Tolman School in 1970. Shortly after the close, the building was used for the school of nursing for the Southeastern Regional Vocational Technical High School. The building is currently a private home on the corner of Park and Ninth Streets.

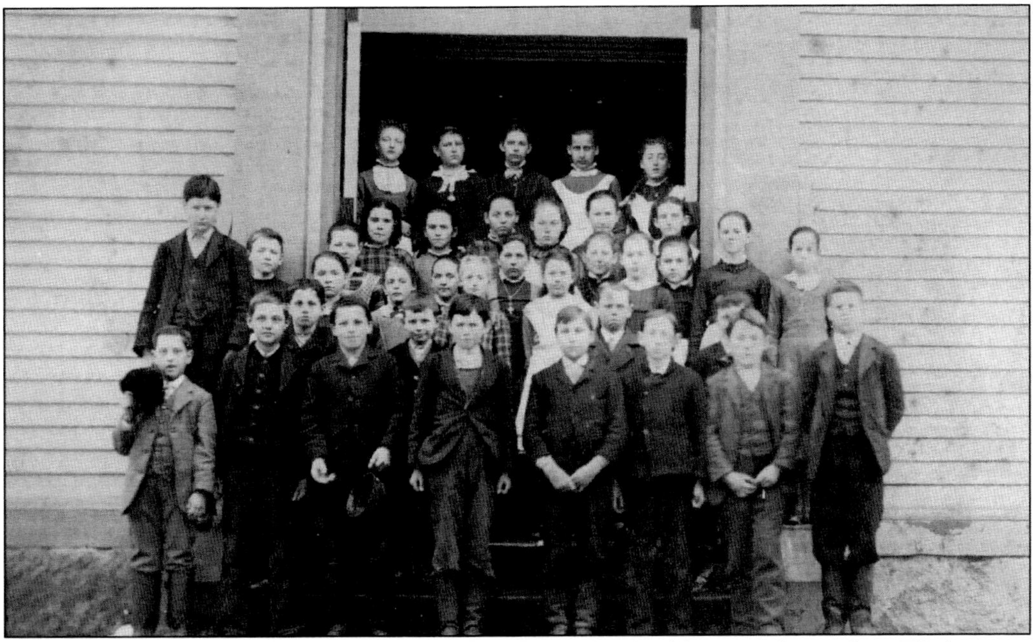

STUDENTS AT THE OLD DRAKE SCHOOL IN 1880. This building was located on Washington Street, across from the entrance to School Street. It housed the first Stoughton High School in room 4 in May 1865. By 1873, the Stoughton High School had been moved into a new structure on Walnut Street. This schoolhouse was razed in 1890 to make room for a new building.

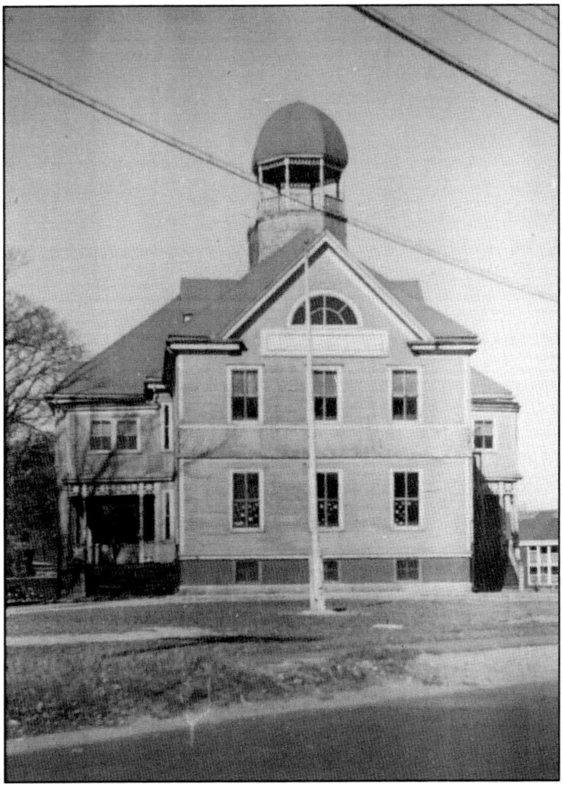

THE NEW DRAKE SCHOOL, AT THE CORNER OF WASHINGTON AND MONK STREETS IN 1950. This was the second school on this site, replacing an earlier structure that was home to Stoughton High School in 1865. This structure was built in 1892 and designed by architect Fergus H. McKain. The Drake School eventually closed and, in 1952, was torn down.

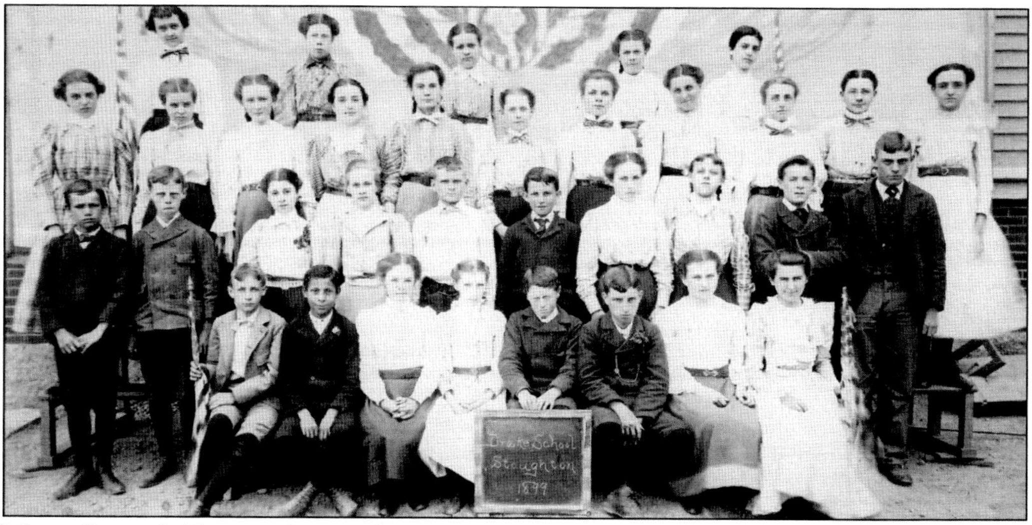

MYRA COFFIN'S EIGHTH-GRADE CLASS AT THE DRAKE SCHOOL IN 1899. From left to right are the following: (first row) Hobart Tower, Abraham Presse, Grace Carpenter, Viola Humem, Albert Whiting, Roy Russell, Mabel Fisher, and Effie Griffin; (second row) Eugene Toomey, Annie Stickney, Edith Perkins, Henry Cutting, William Hallowell, Elizabeth Blye, Annie Knosky, Charles Curtis, and Abner Corbett; (third row) Celia Clapp, Jennie Connel, Annie Cassidy, Mabel Kingham, Bella Porter, Retta Murphy, Jennie Hooper, Annie Walker, Nellie Webb, Lucia Clifford, and Ethel Smith; (fourth row) Bessie Curtis, Frances Mosman, Ethel Austin, Ruth Mosman, and Ruey Burnham. It is interesting to note in the photograph records that the back-row girls all had the mumps at the time of the photograph.

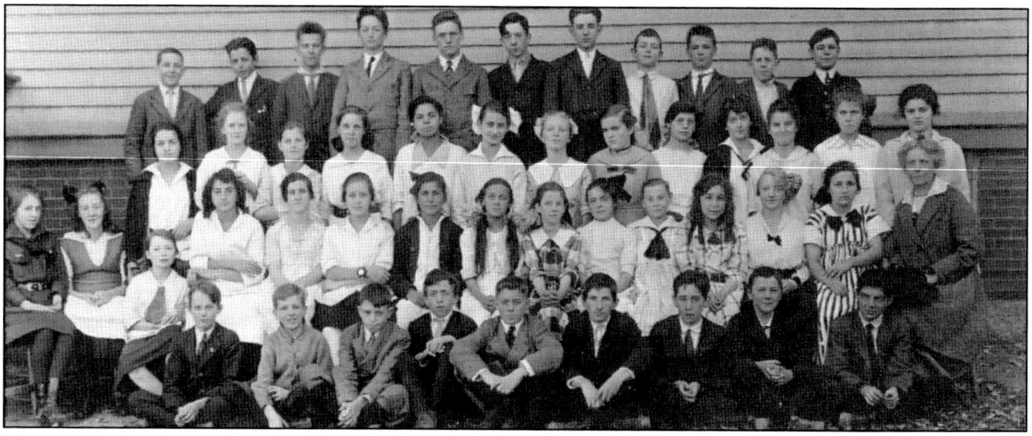

MYRA COFFIN'S EIGHTH-GRADE GRADUATING CLASS AT THE DRAKE SCHOOL IN 1918. From left to right are the following: (first row) Frederick Fobes, George Rockwood, Eugene Russell, Willard Emery, Charles H. Clapp, Benjamin Cohan, unidentified, Melvin MacGavin, and Charles Dillon; (second row) Agnes MacCalmont, Frances Kovolosey, Helen ?, Alice Cornell, Lena Pollilio, Hazel Dykeman, Emily Goward, Catherine Shay, Sally Esty, Elsie Russell, Anna Allen, Ethel Bumpus, and Myra Coffin (teacher); (third row) Gladys Wood, Edwina Vanston, Ruth Connors, Irma Beal, Margaret Sweetman, Bessie Yarrish, Bella Mitchell, Mildred Botsch, Florence Buker, Ruth Hyde, Annie Andrews, Clara Barker, Helen Farrell, Grace Mosman, and ? Daniels (assistant teacher); (fourth row) John Strumitus, Edgar Barker, Felix Laport, Raymond Bete, Edward Moon, Andrew Mason, Forest Pratt, Leonard Berguson, Joe Greenwald, Ernest Murphy, and George Smith.

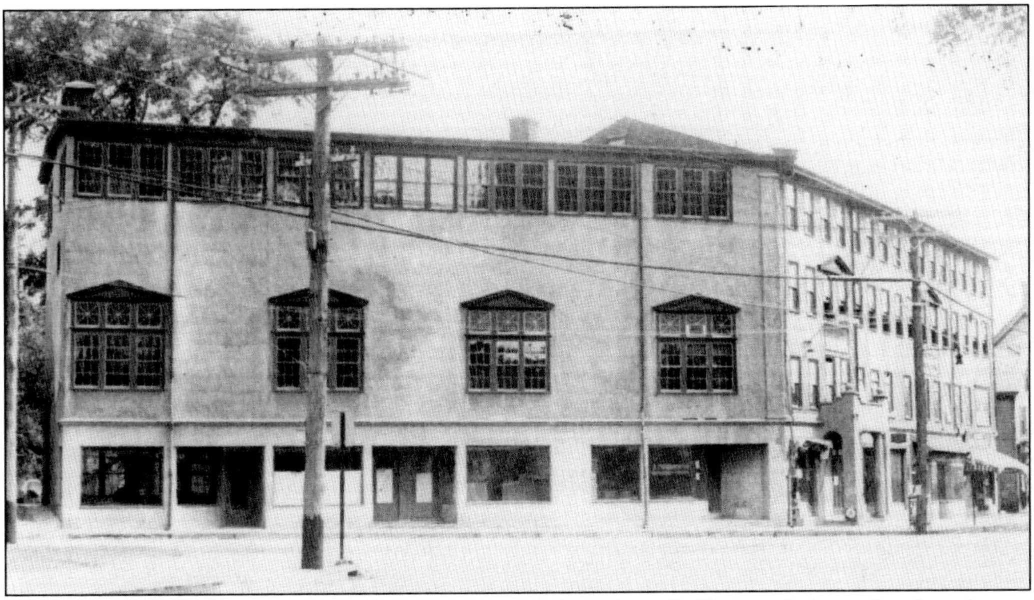

THE NOYES BLOCK. The Noyes Block was used for Myra Coffin's eighth-grade class due to overcrowding in the Drake School. The new Orpheum Theatre was opened by Anson Favor at the Noyes Block on April 4, 1914, for movies and vaudeville shows. The old Fitzpatrick Shoe Factory and later Stoughton Boot & Shoe Company were in the building next to the Noyes Block.

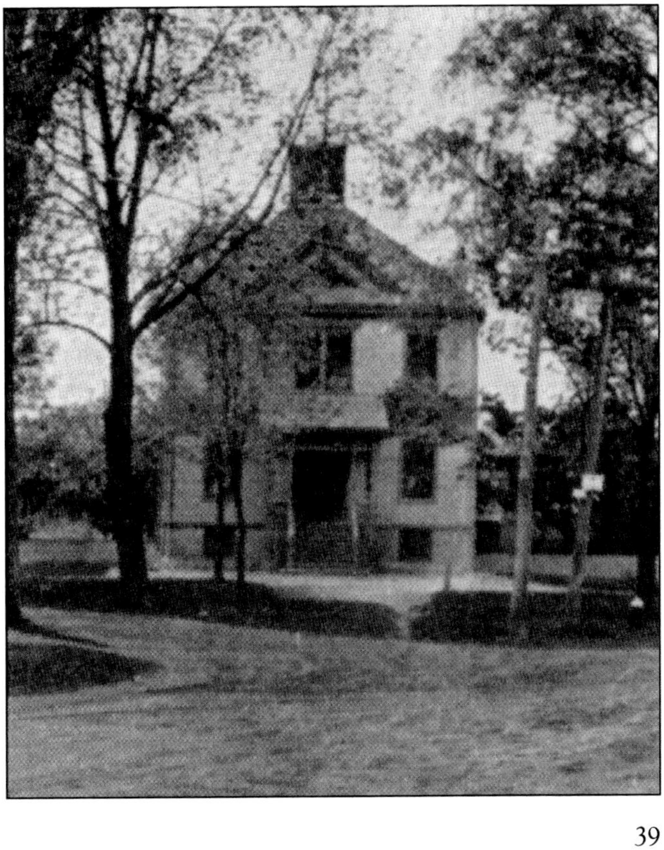

THE CAPEN SCHOOL. The Capen School was erected in North Stoughton at the intersection of Page and Turnpike Streets in 1892. The cost to purchase the land and erect this two-room schoolhouse by contractor Elisha S. Hawes was $5,921.34. In 1924, a failed attempt was made to make a branch public library for North Stoughton in this building after school. This schoolhouse served North Stoughton until it was closed in 1969 and torn down.

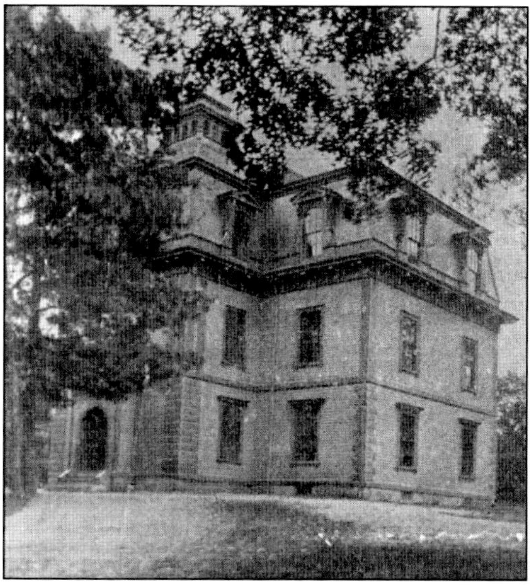

THE OLD STOUGHTON HIGH SCHOOL BUILDING, ON WALNUT STREET. This structure was built as a combination grammar and high school in 1873. In 1880, the building would be named for local benefactor Lucius Clapp (1817–1909). This building was destroyed by fire January 7, 1896.

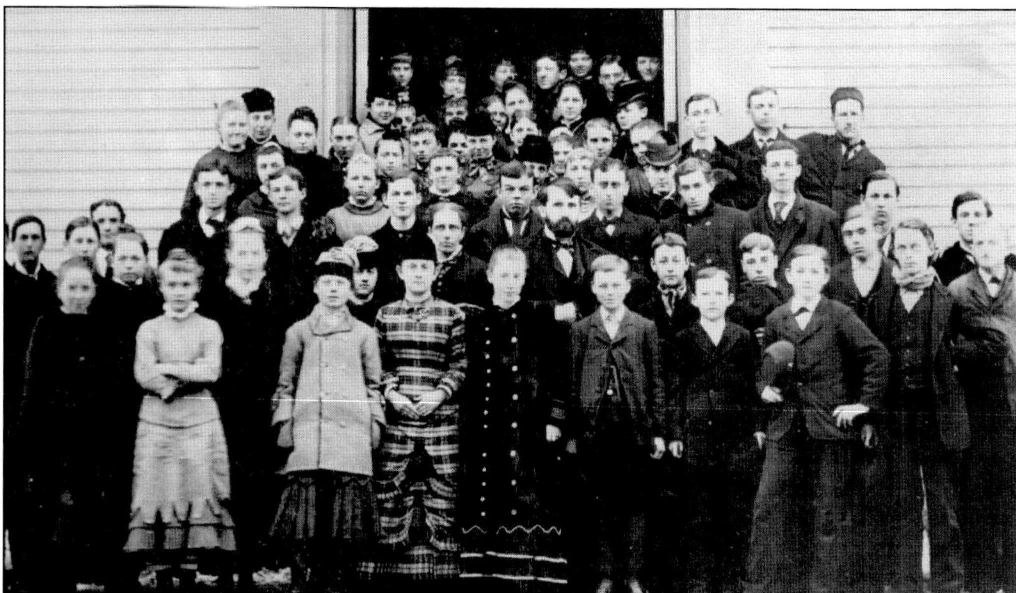

STUDENTS OF LUCIUS CLAPP HIGH SCHOOL IN 1880. Those who are identified in this photograph are, in no particular order, as follows: Maggie Kennedy, Nellie Cowgill, Martha Wall, Nellie Marron, Mattie Pierce, Evie Drake, Grace Waugh, Frank Crane, Clyde Clark, Willie Dolan, Wallace Hill, Charles Brownell, Lester Johnson, Clinton Holbrook, Cornelius Sullivan, Harry Drake, Joseph Marriott, George Drake, Willett Clark, John Mulligan, Amelia Clifton (assistant principal), Henry Burns, William E. Pulsifer (principal), Archie Thompson, Dan Young, Charles Upham, Wallace Capen, Charlie Gardner, Jacob Gray, Lena Underwood, Kate Fleming, Ethel Lamb, Georgie Capen, Mattie B. Capen, Carrie Freeman, M. Lellias Bryden, Alice Burnham, Lucy Johnson, Edith Farrington, Bert Dickerman, Henry Reynolds, Frank Hussey, Cora Brock, Agnes Waugh, Hattie Clapp, Mary Perkins, Hattie (Shute) Ripley, Harriet Curtis, Nellie M. Capen, Catherine Smith, Emma Pye, Fannie Bird, Clemmie Tucker, Helen Curtis, Jennie Guild, Jessie Folsom, Minnie Stone, Minot Linfield, Anna Crane, Will Marriott, Annie White, Dedie Tower, and William Clifford.

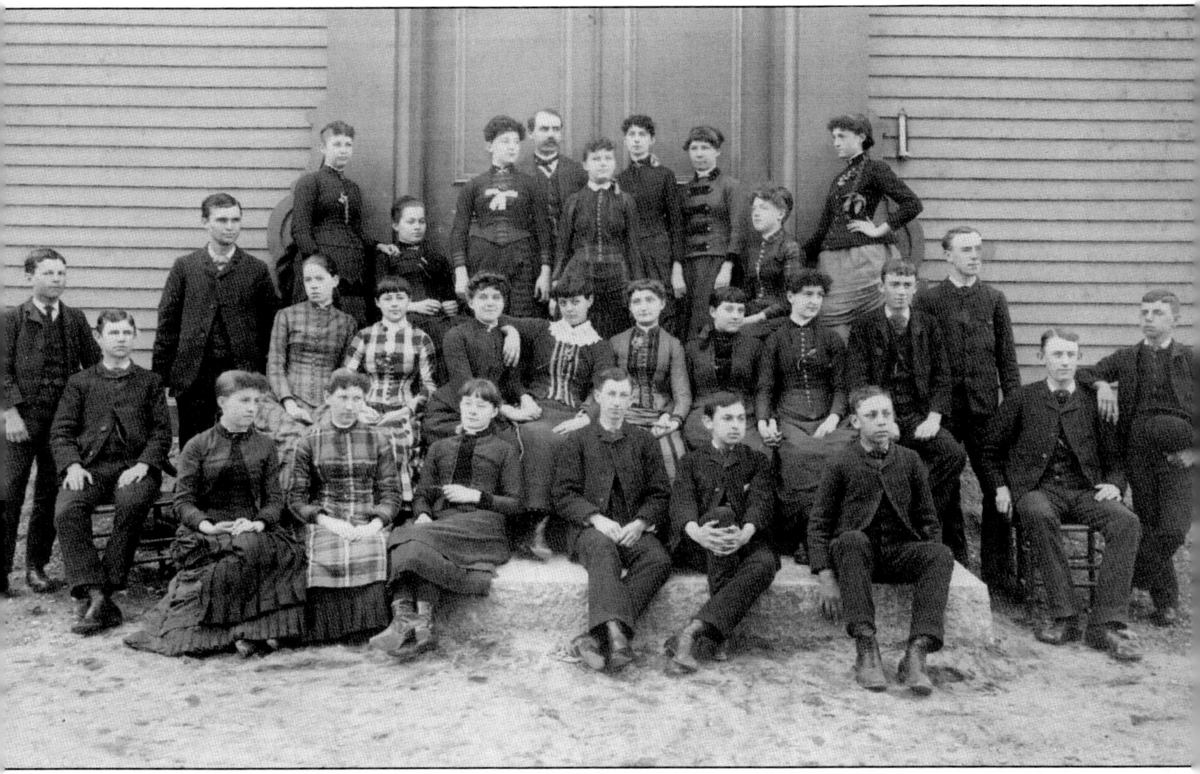

STOUGHTON HIGH SCHOOL STUDENTS, C. 1886. This photograph was taken in front of the original Clapp High School building on Walnut Street. From left to right are the following: (first row) Alma Bisbee, Bessie Porter, Mattie Sawyer, Charles Tuttle, Fred Staples, and Harry Cornish; (second row) Eugene Clark, Ernest Goward, Charles Tucker, Gertrude Cooper, May Bird, Hattie Tucker, Pauline Blanchard, Mabelle Hamilton, Nellie Reynolds, Blanch Bright, ? Parker, Martin Southworth, ? Porter, and Willie Capen; (third row) Florence Walker and Edith Southworth; (fourth row) Alice Belcher, Mamie Atwood, ? Gifford, Claire Rogers, Raychel Upham, Minnie Hussey, and Nellie Hall.

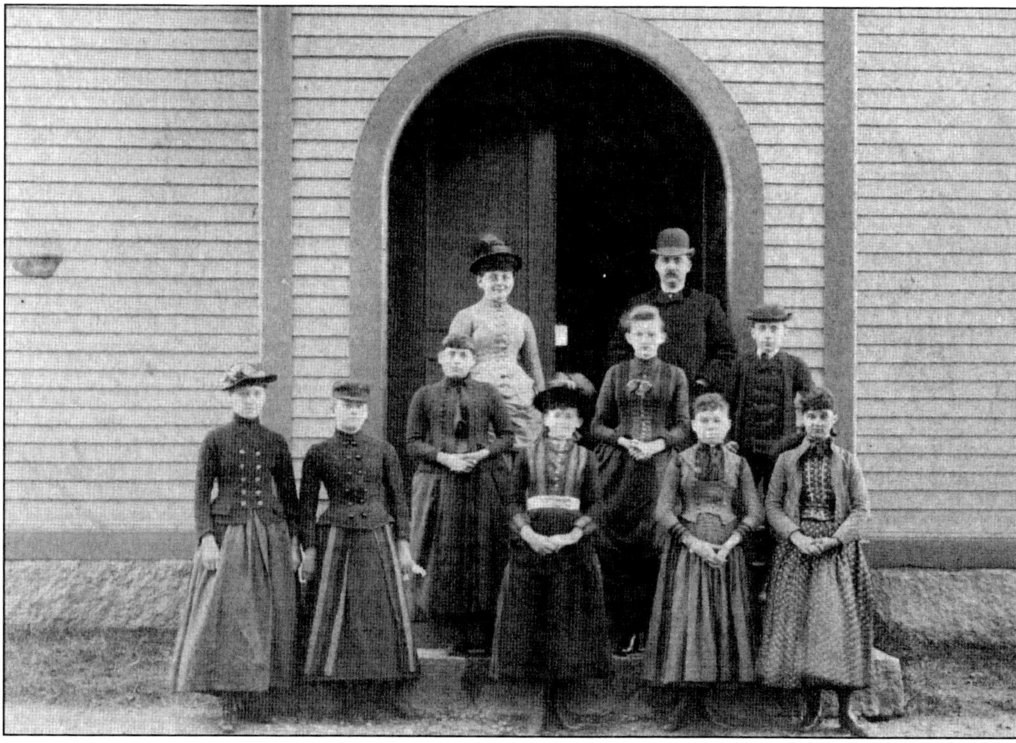

THE STOUGHTON HIGH SCHOOL CLASS OF 1892 AT THE CLAPP SCHOOL. From left to right are the following: (front row) Harriet Hussey, Elizabeth Farrell, Anne Clapp, Ruth Shephard, and Ada Hewett; (middle row) Grace Ward, Elizabeth ?, and Elwyn Capen; (back row) Jimmy Allen, and Benjamin Hill (teacher).

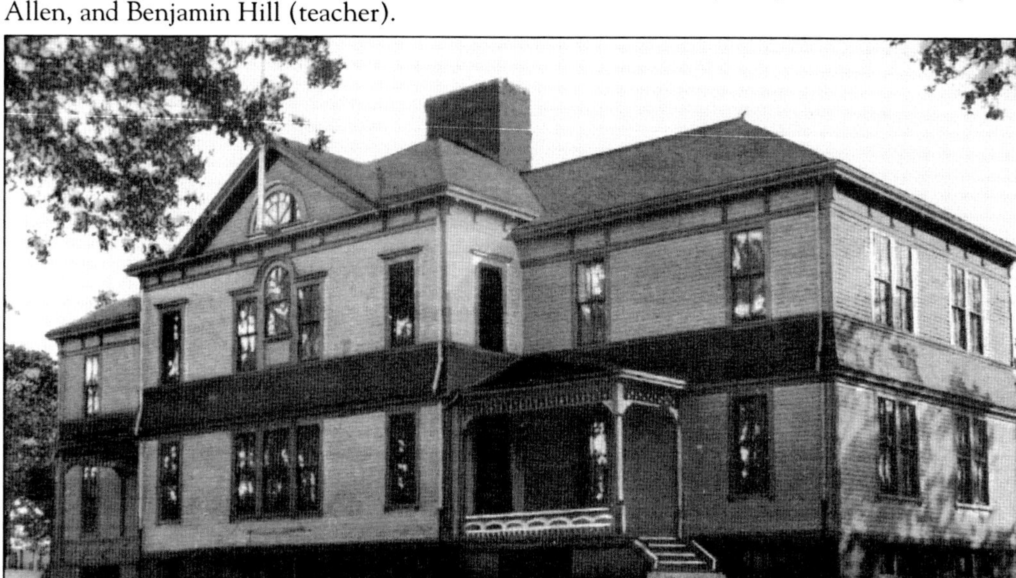

THE NEW CLAPP SCHOOL, LOCATED ON THE SITE OF THE EARLIER SCHOOL ON WALNUT STREET. This school building was designed by architect C.L. Mitchell and opened on November 30, 1896, at a cost of $14,521.01. This building was torn down in 1984 to make additional parking for the Jones School. (Author's collection.)

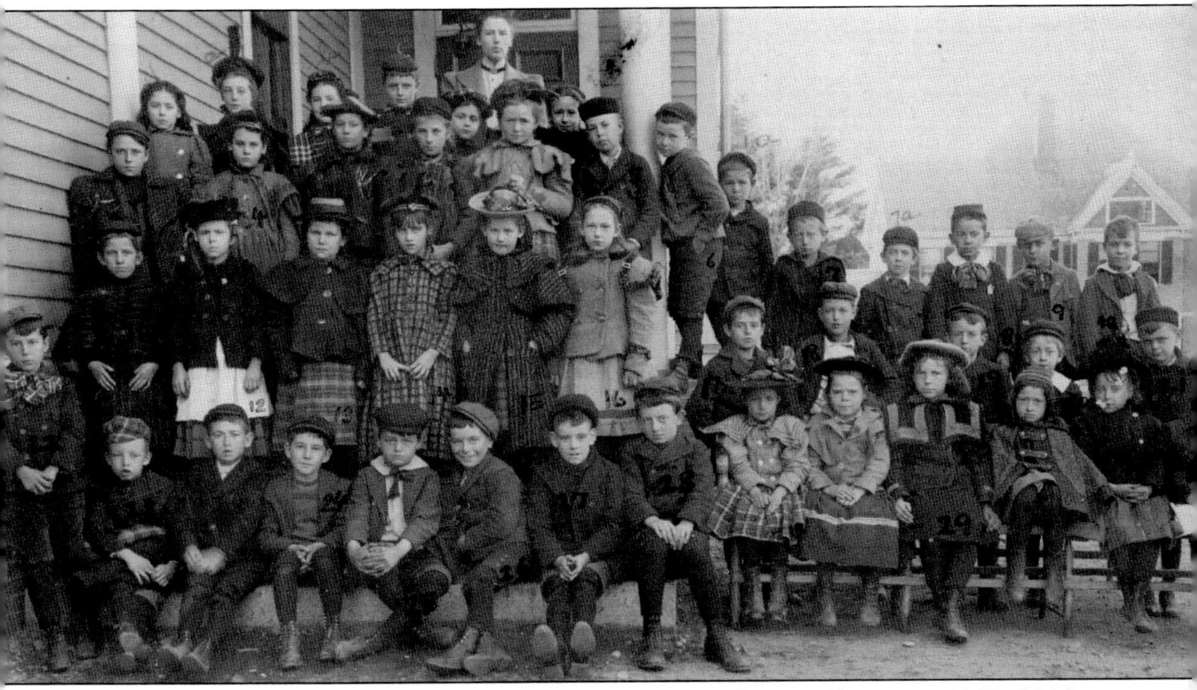

STUDENTS OF SUSAN L. PRATT'S THIRD- AND FOURTH-GRADE CLASSES, 1899–1900. Seen here outside of the new Clapp School are, from left to right, the following: (first row) Everett Winship, Harry Cheney, Robert McNamara, Joe Kelley, Billy Robbins, Bob Murphy, unidentified, Tom McCarty, Miss Goodnow, unidentified, Pearl Gay, Winifred Taylor, Miss Atwood, and Beatrice Clark; (second row) Eleanor Wells, Marion Clapp, Lulu Dykeman, Fannie Powers, Amy Leonard, Doris Holmes, Harry Conway, Brad Dykeman, William McCarty, E. Winslow Capen, and Clarence Taylor; (third row) unidentified, Katie Powers, Hazel Holmes, Miss Bunn, Louisa Lathrop, Earle Whitten, S.F. Blake, John Frank Pye, Harry Brovick, unidentified, William Curtis, George Wentworth, and Reuben Willis; (fourth row) Doris Burnham, Mamie Russell, Charlotte Cram, Nellie White, Susan L. Pratt (teacher), and Katie Steele.

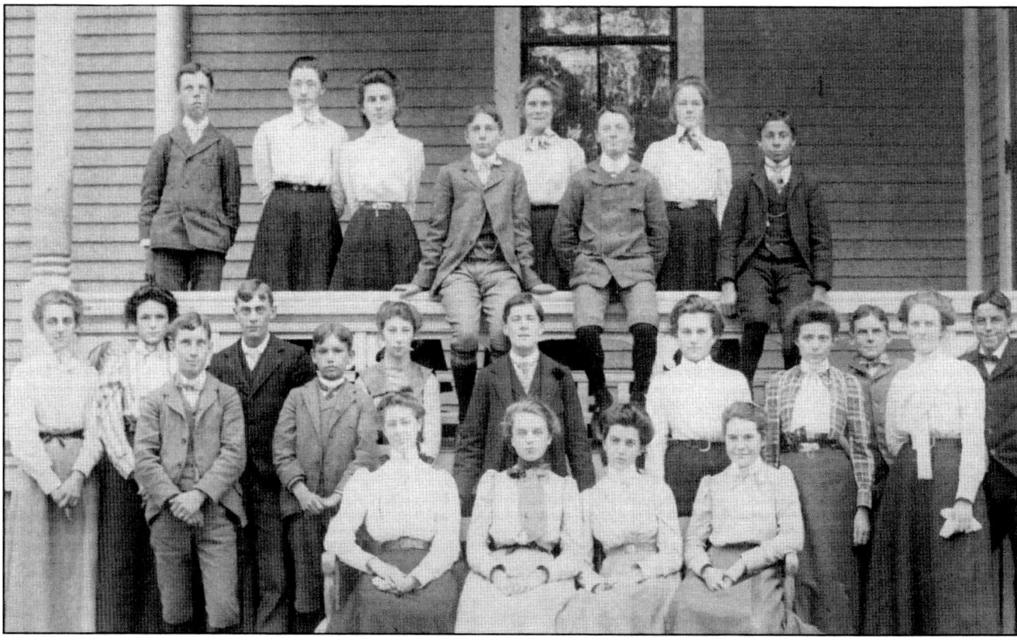

THE STOUGHTON HIGH SCHOOL CLASS OF 1903 IN FRONT OF THE CLAPP SCHOOL IN 1902. From left to right are the following: (front row) Mabel Morris, Celia Clapp, Ruey Burnham, and Bella Porter (class secretary); (middle row) Nellie Webb, Roy Russell, Abner Corbett, Alan Beausang, Viola Hume, Charlie Curtis, Mabel Fisher, Ethel Austin, Henry Cutting, Maud Guild, and Billy Healy; (back row) Eugene Toomey (class president), Lucia Clifford, Effie Griffin, Hobart Tower, Edith Perkins, Albert Whiting, Grace Carpenter, and Abram Press.

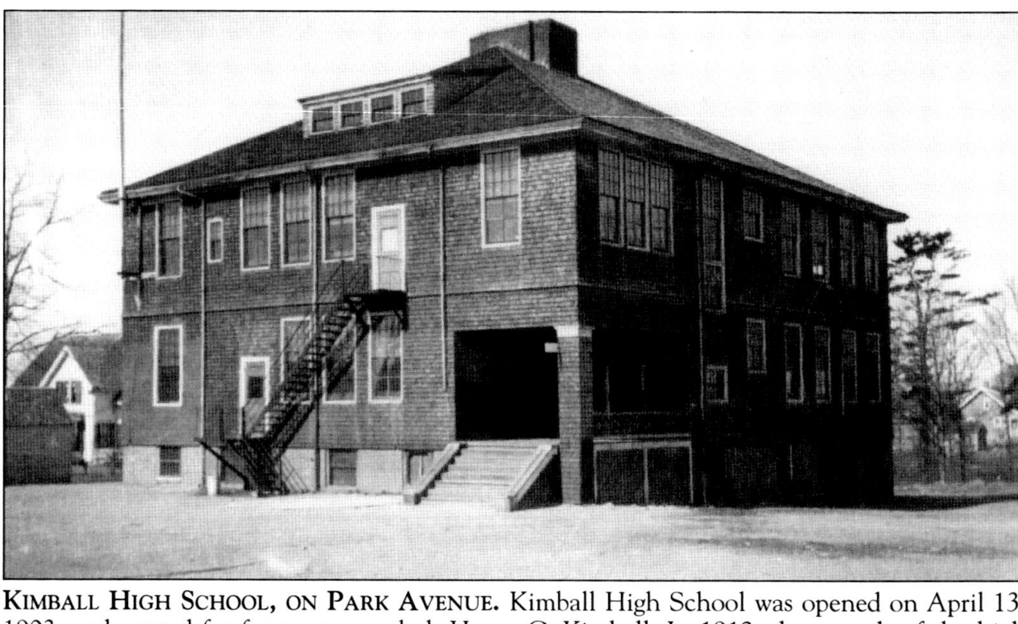

KIMBALL HIGH SCHOOL, ON PARK AVENUE. Kimball High School was opened on April 13, 1903, and named for former town clerk Henry C. Kimball. In 1912, the growth of the high school required the use of the entire building. This building would serve as a junior high school and, later, as an elementary school, after the new building on Pearl Street was finished.

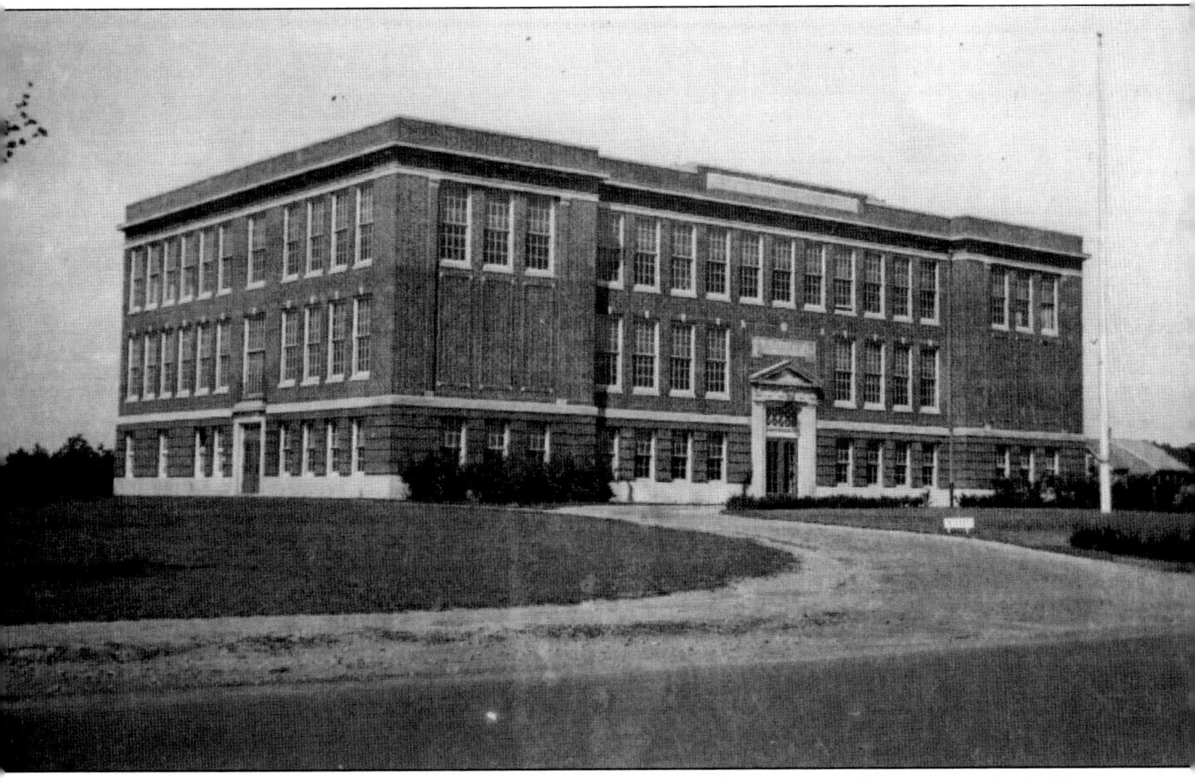

THE NEW STOUGHTON HIGH SCHOOL ON PEARL STREET, DEDICATED SEPTEMBER 8, 1923. Stoughton High School was built on 21 acres of land at a cost of $150,000. This section of the original building was enlarged in 1951 and had additions added in 1955 and 1965.

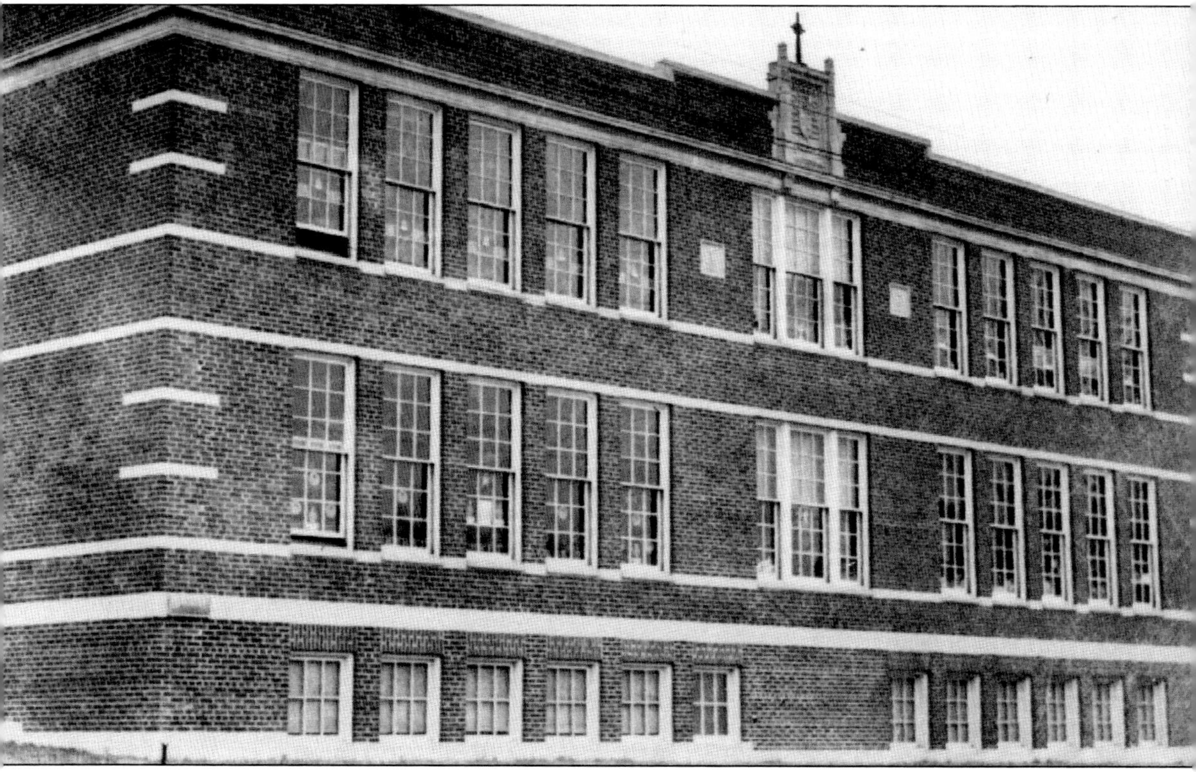

ST. MARY'S SCHOOL, BUILT IN 1931 ON ATHERTON STREET. This newer structure was completed for $160,000, replacing the earlier structure on Canton Street, which opened in September 1883. The sisters of St. Joseph were the teachers at St. Mary's from the day it opened. The school was closed in 1972 by the Catholic archdiocese.

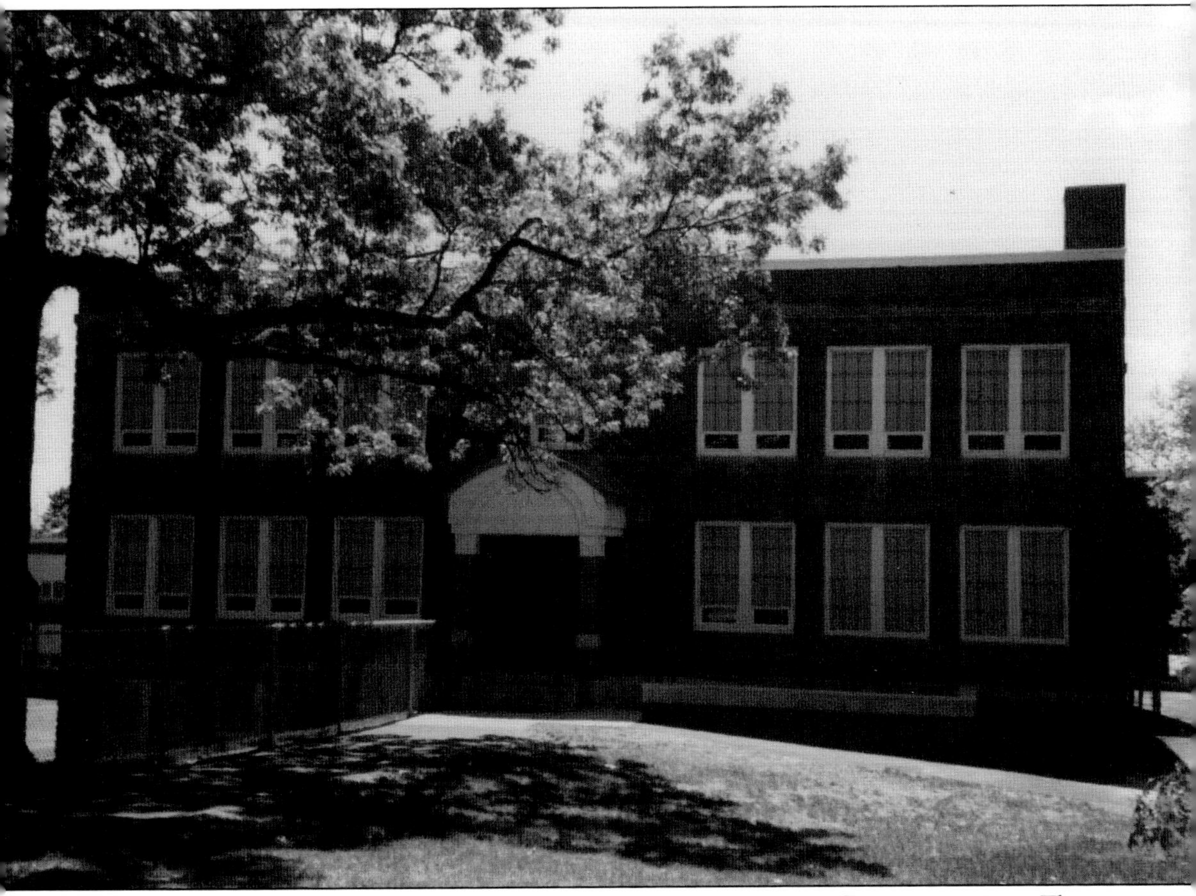

THE EDWIN A. JONES JUNIOR HIGH SCHOOL ON PIERCE STREET, BUILT IN 1930. The construction of this building cost $118,000. The building was named in honor of former school committee member Edwin Arthur Jones, who died in 1911. In 1954, an addition was added on the westerly end of the building. The Jones School still serves the community as an elementary school. (Author's collection.)

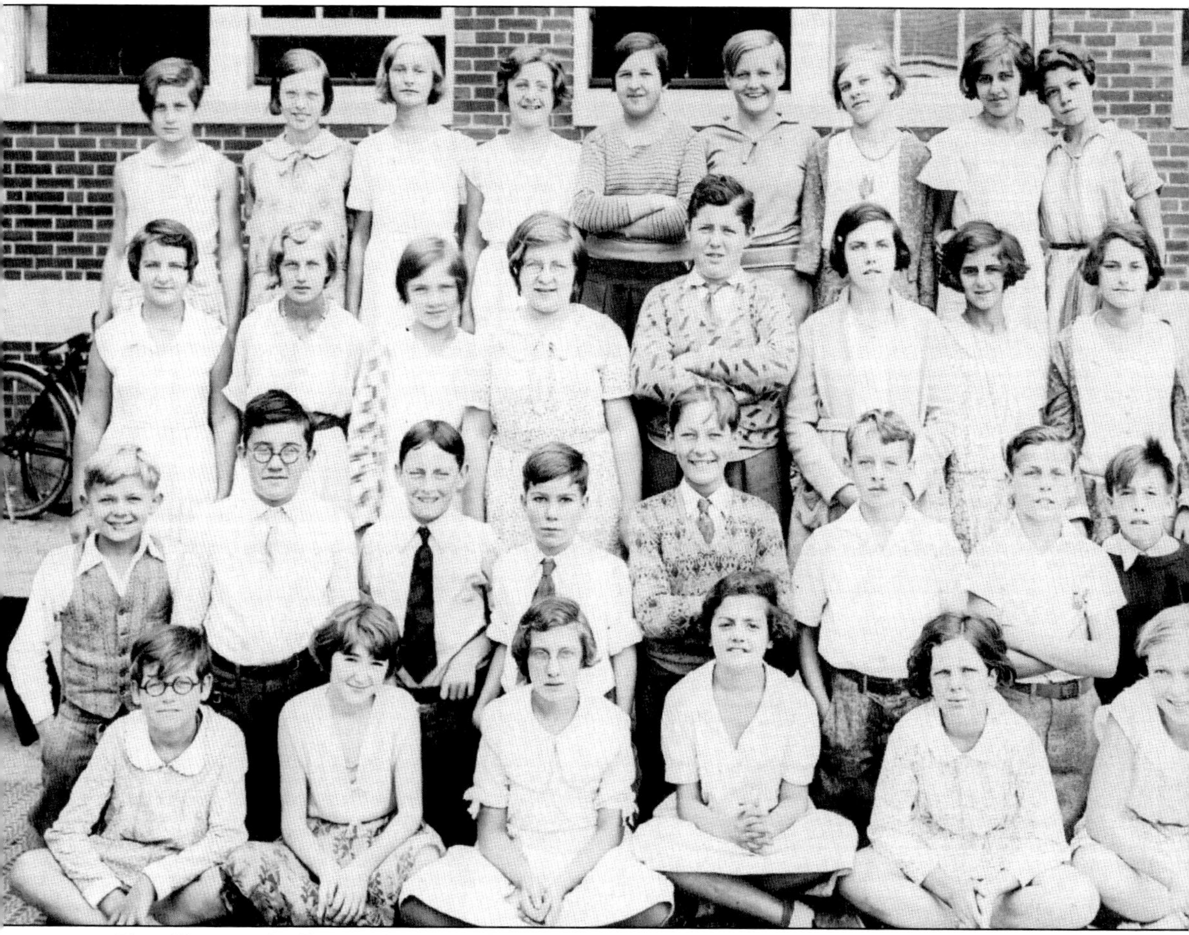

The Edwin A. Jones Junior High School Class of 1933. From left to right are the following: (first row) Vincy Zurblis, Eileen Crean, Virginia Creuti, Josephine DeLuca, Kathleen Kell, and Pauline Stockus; (second row) Michael Elkovitch, Robert Smith, Donald Hill, Robert Evans, Serge Wisotsky, Alfred Welton, Robert Beaton, and George Rist; (third row) Helen Lanigan, Bronia Blaizes, Marjorie Mosman, Nellie Kucinskies, James Heckart, Louise Thornell, Celia Drunker, and Anna DePaul; (fourth row) Aina Packard, Elsa-Jo Beatty, Angelyn Zienko, Mary Rivello, Helen Rakowsky, Ruth Bishop, Lena Grigas, Lillian Vitkauskis, and Florence Ponce.

Four

RAILROAD AND TRANSPORTATION

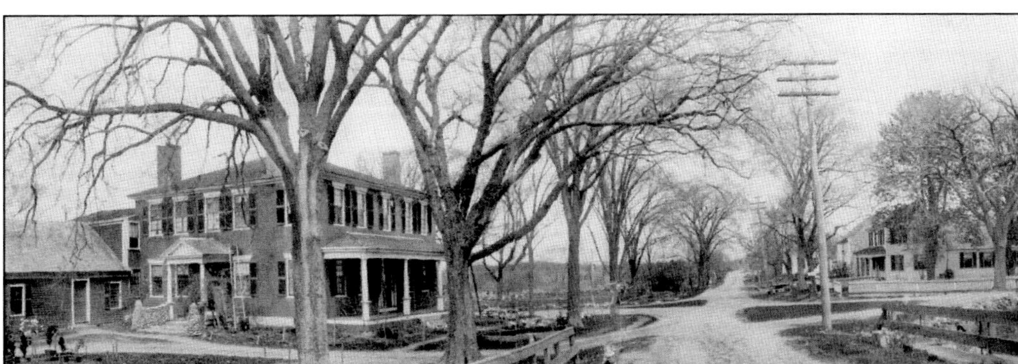

SWAN'S TAVERN AND THE INTERSECTION OF CENTRAL AND TURNPIKE STREETS. On June 24, 1806, the Taunton and South Boston Turnpike Corporation was formed and a stage line ran past this tavern. The tavern was constructed by the Turnpike Corporation in 1807 per William H. Capen or in 1810 per Howard Hansen and was originally called the Washington Hotel. The corporation sold the Washington Hotel to Capt. Elisha Swan in 1817. Swan operated it as a hotel and tavern under his own name. In 1824, Gen. Marquis de Lafayette visited this building on a visit to Boston. In 1959, the building was remodeled.

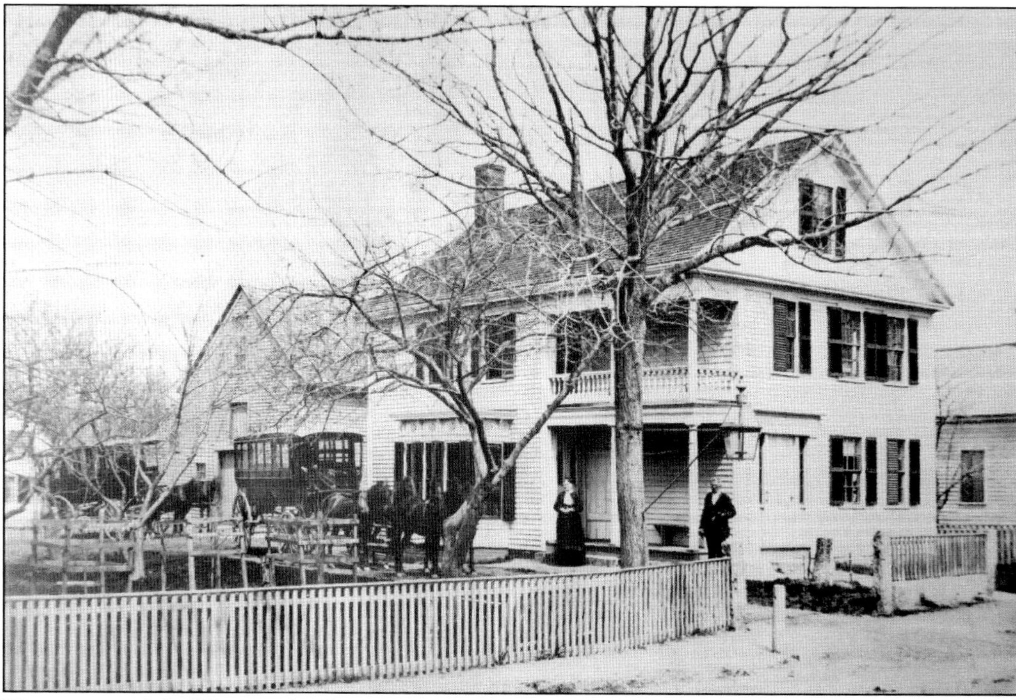

NATHANIEL M. WARREN'S COACHES AT PLEASANT STREET. This was the only means of transportation between Stoughton and Brockton prior to the railroad in 1888. This structure remains very unchanged and is near Capen Street.

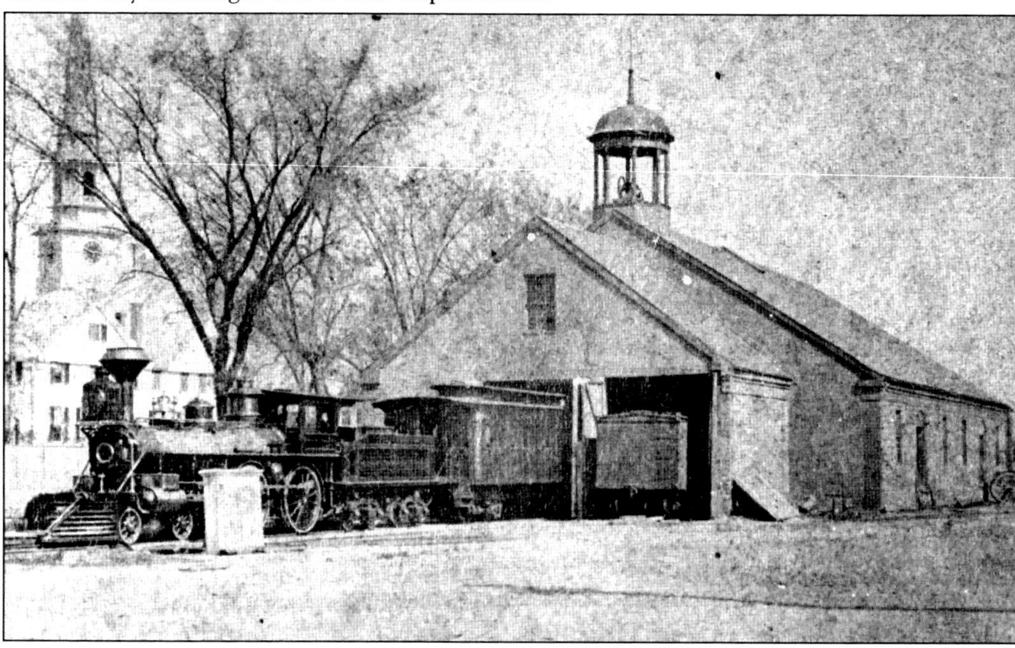

THE THIRD STOUGHTON DEPOT, BUILT IN 1845 AND LOCATED OFF RAILROAD AVENUE. This building served as an engine house, freight house, and passenger terminal until it was torn down in 1888. The previous structure, also constructed in 1845, burned to the ground the same year, and the second structure blew down in a heavy gale.

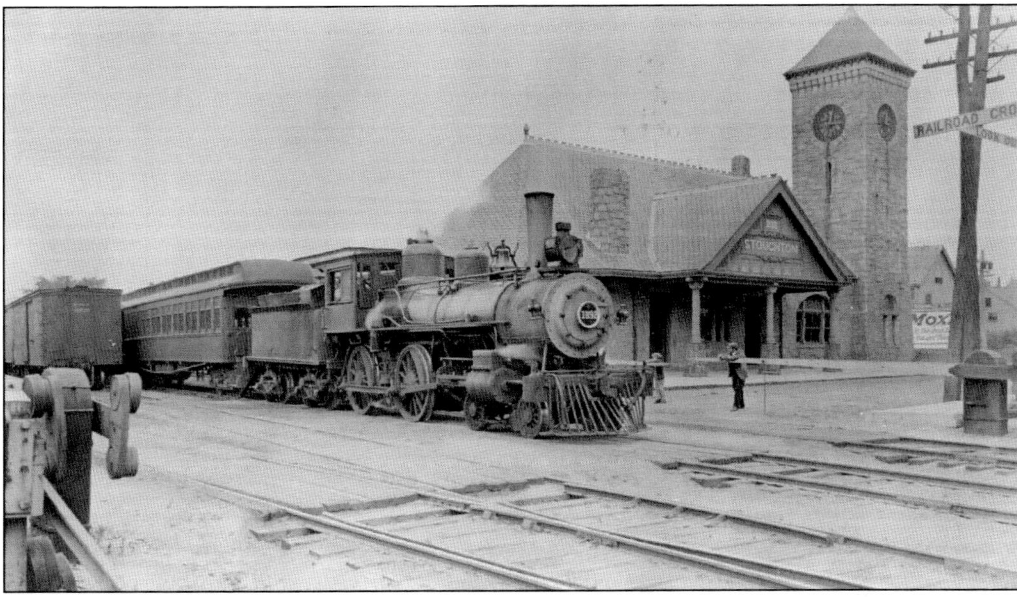

The Stoughton Railroad Station and Boston Outbound Steam Engine at Wyman Street in 1910. Construction of this station was financed by the Boston & Providence Railroad in 1887. This building, listed on the National Register of Historic Places, was built from 850 tons of stone from Myron Gilbert's granite quarry off West Street. Ground was broken on the former site of the house of Dr. Daniel C. Rose (1838–1914) on Wyman Street on May 28, 1887. The station was completed and opened to the public in March 1888. The 62-foot clock tower at the station is one of the last remaining in the northeast. In 1958, rail service to North Easton was discontinued and the Stoughton depot became the end of the line for passengers. The station continues to serve passengers to Boston.

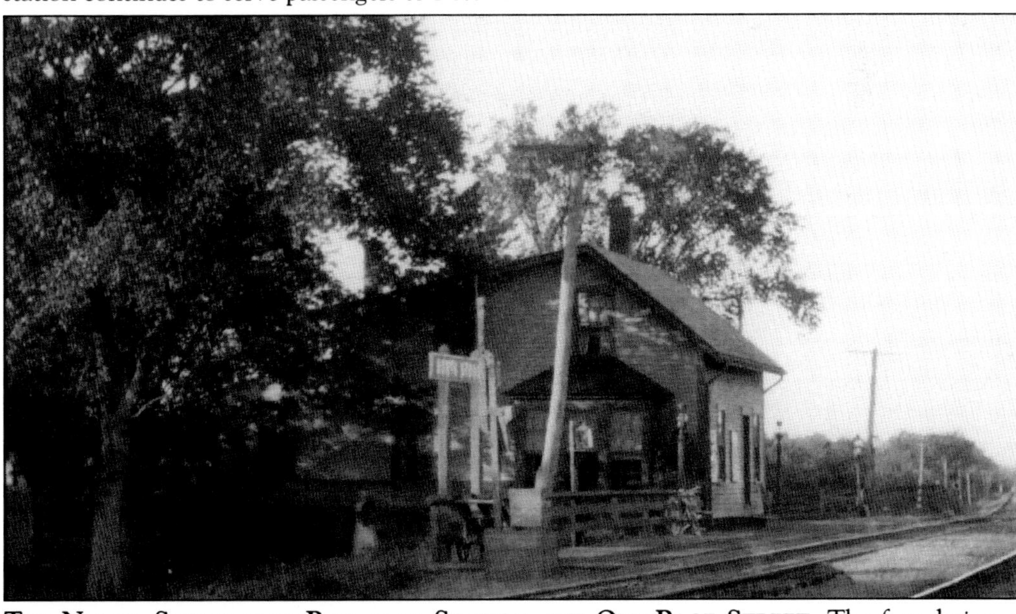

The North Stoughton Railroad Station, off Old Page Street. The foundation of this station can still be seen near the abandoned railroad bed off Page Street. This station was on the route of the original Old Colony Railroad.

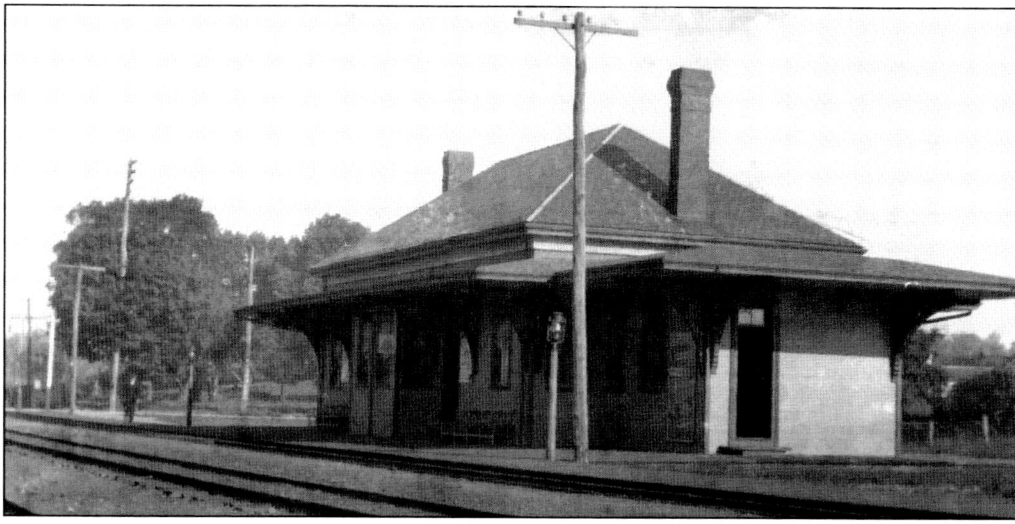

The West Stoughton Railroad Station, Located off Central Street. Nothing remains of this station, which was still standing in the 1950s. The station served as a stop along the New York, New Haven, & Hartford Railroad.

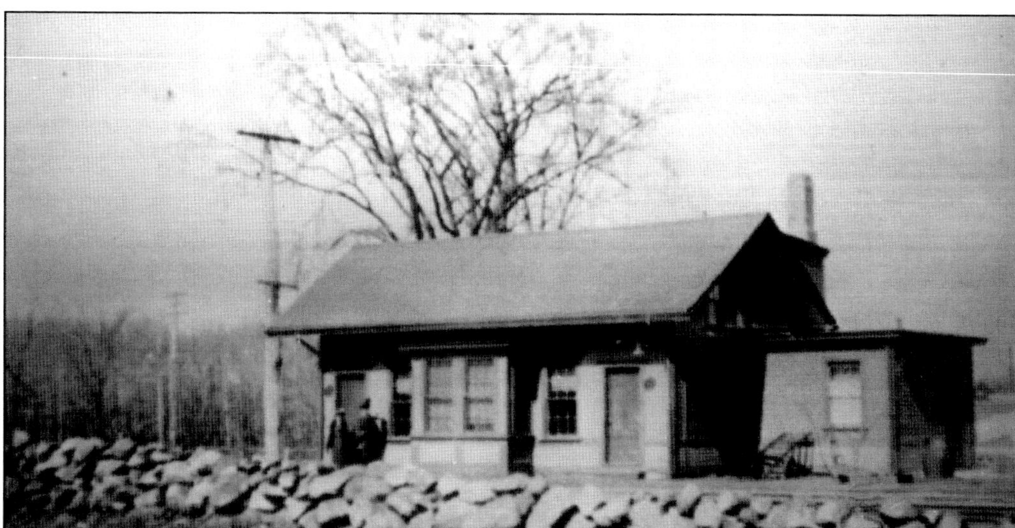

The South Stoughton Railroad Station on Park Street. This branch opened c. 1866 and was closed to passenger service in April 1925. The depot was demolished in 1944. The station served the Old Colony Railroad.

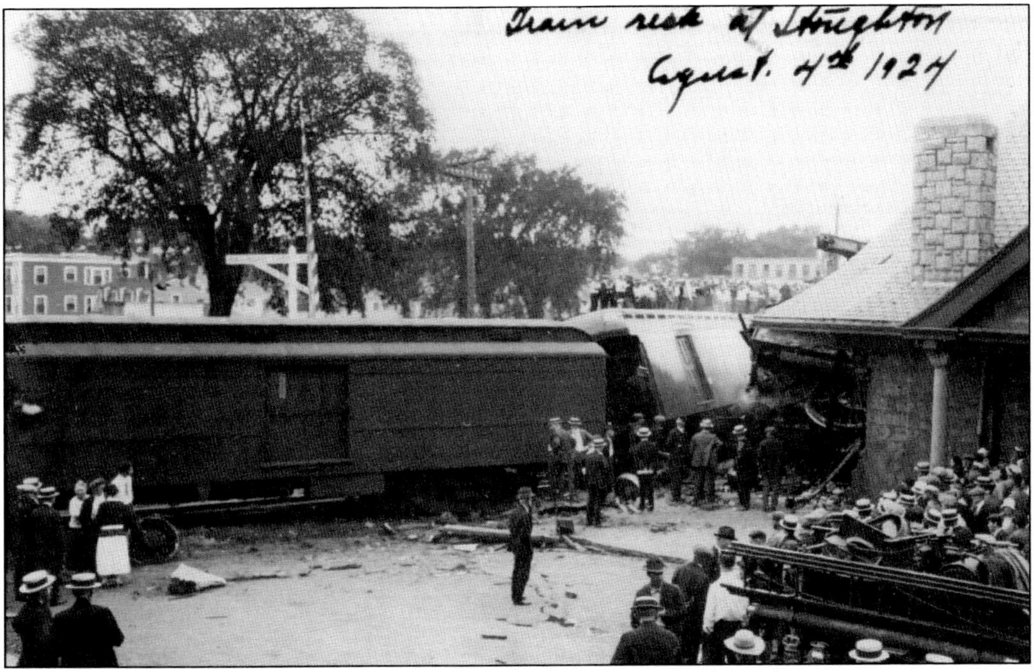

A STOUGHTON TRAIN WRECK. On August 4, 1924, the Boston-bound Newport train running an express service to Boston from Taunton derailed in front of the Stoughton depot and sent its locomotive crashing into the women's waiting room of the depot. This image shows the engine shortly after it crashed through the station walls.

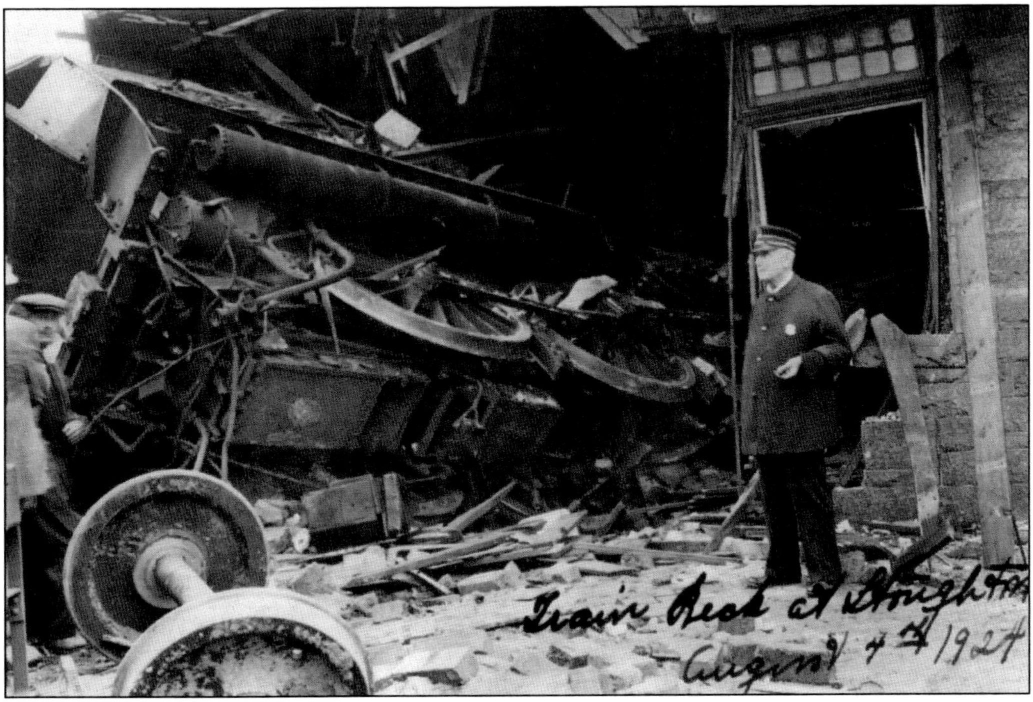

STOUGHTON TRAIN WRECK DAMAGE BEING INSPECTED BY POLICE CHIEF RICHARD J. VANSTON. This is the last known photograph of Vanston, who died in 1925.

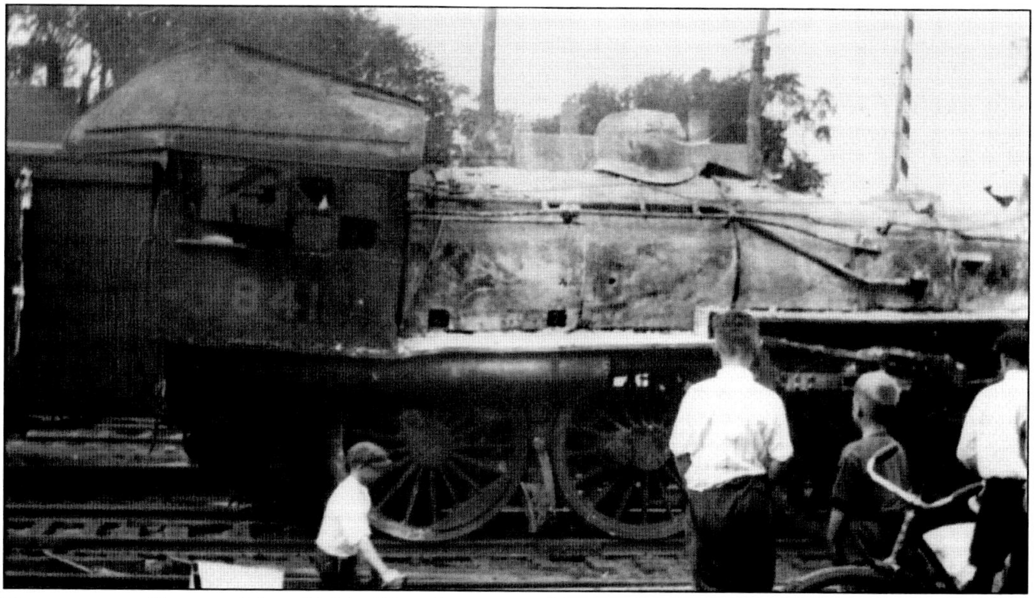

DAMAGE TO ENGINE NO. 1841. The damage to Engine No. 1841 is shown in detail after it was removed from the crash site. The engineer of this train died shortly afterward as the result of injuries sustained in the crash.

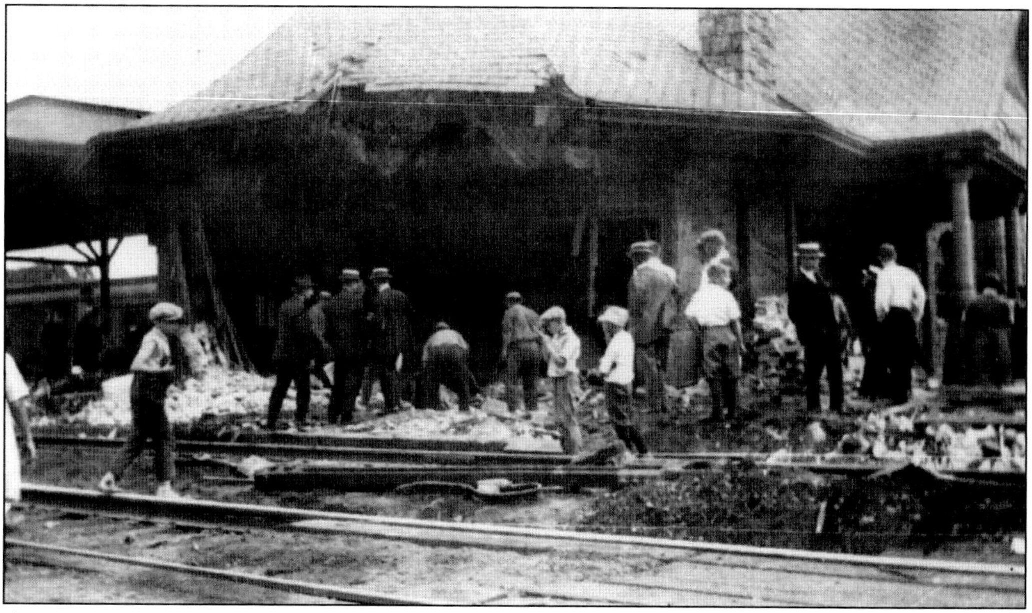

ANOTHER VIEW OF THE STOUGHTON TRAIN WRECK, AUGUST 4, 1924. After the train was removed, this gaping hole in the station remained. Granite from the closed Myron Gilbert's quarry was used once again for the station.

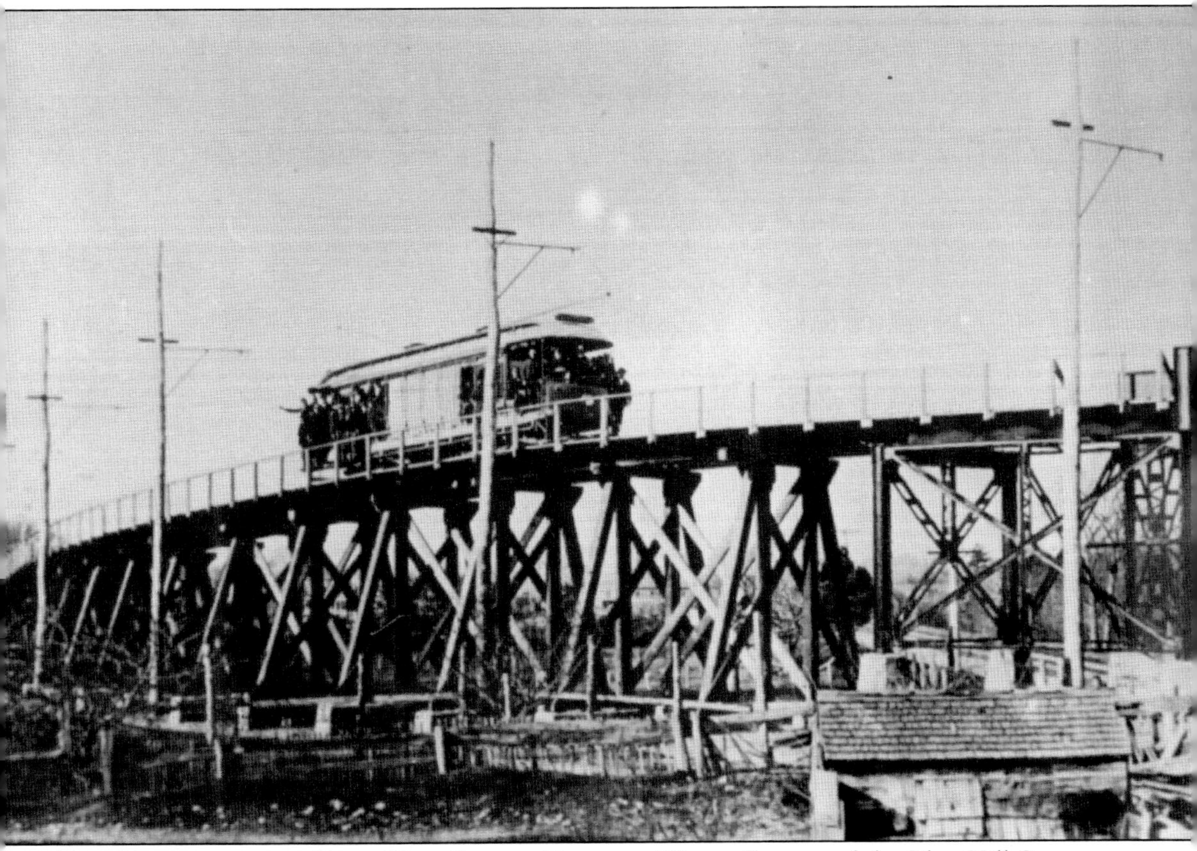

The Trolley of the Blue Hill Street Railway. The trolley car of the Blue Hill Street Railway is shown crossing the trolley trestle built in 1902 over the railroad tracks from Cushing to Canton Streets. This allowed trolleys to travel safely over the tracks of the New York, New Haven, & Hartford Railroad. The Blue Hill Street Railway operated from November 4, 1899, until February 5, 1920, after a terrible snow storm. The Brockton & Stoughton Street Railway Company operated through Stoughton from August 21, 1895, to August 25, 1933, when bus service replaced the trolley.

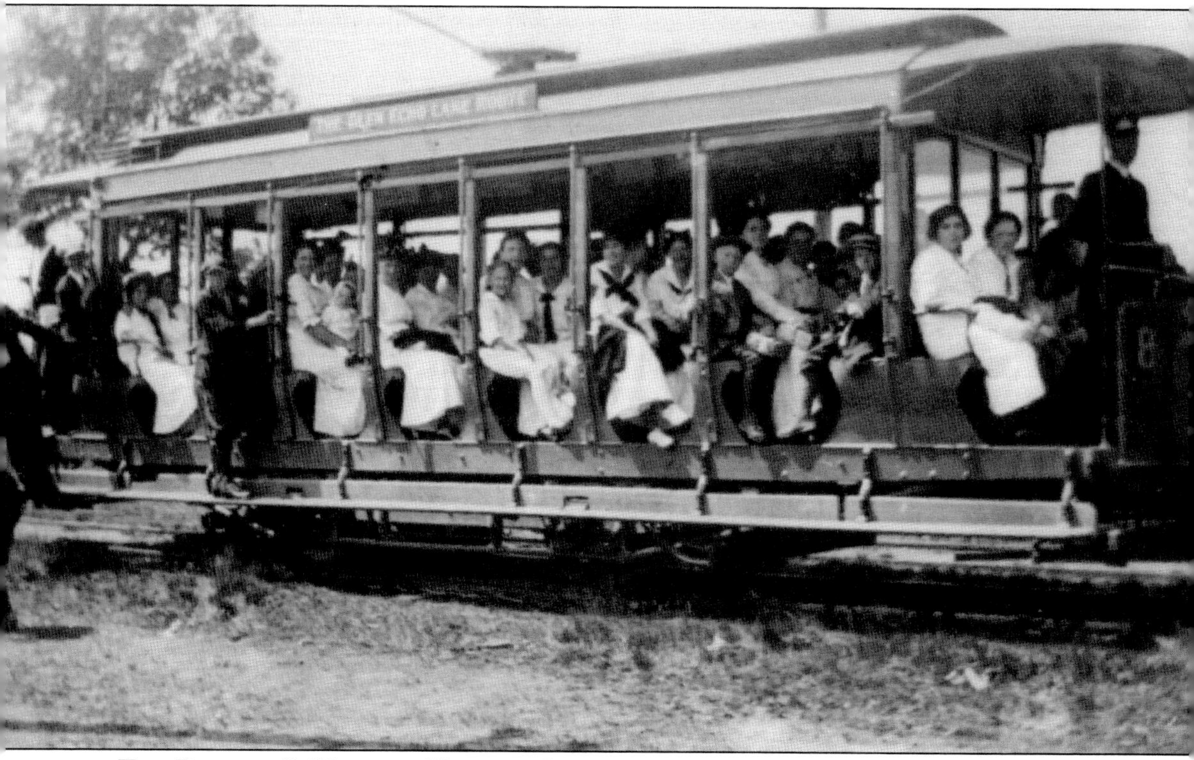

THE BRISTOL & NORFOLK TROLLEY CAR NO. 8 HEADING TO GLEN ECHO PARK IN JULY 1915. This photograph shows a trolley full of members of the Holbrook Methodist Church on their way to Glen Echo Park in Stoughton for their annual picnic party. Bristol and Norfolk Street Railway Trolley ran from November 16, 1901, to July 1923. Bristol and Norfolk also offered trolley service that traveled from Stoughton Square to Morse's Corner in South Easton from 1902 to 1904.

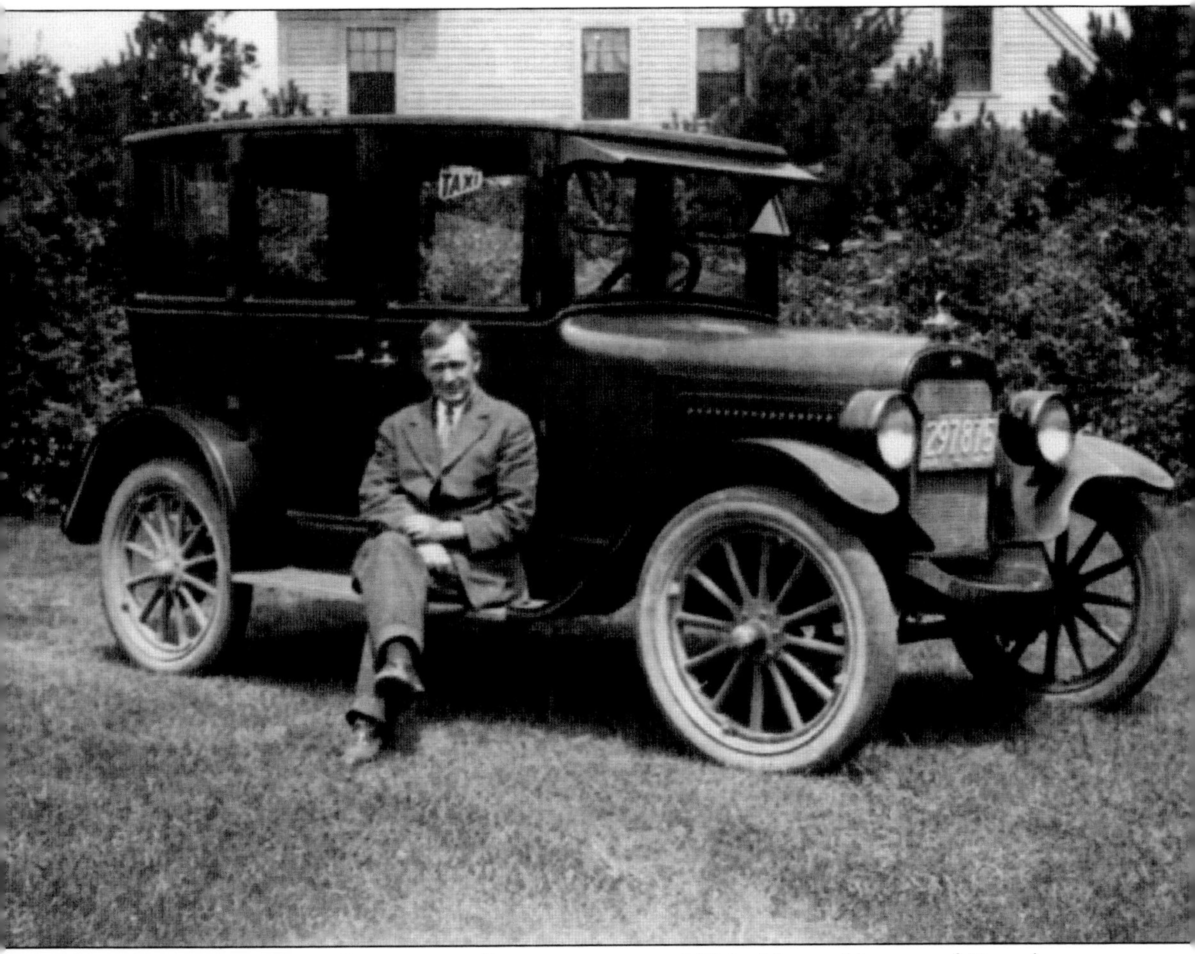

NEAL RICHARDS TAXI SERVICE IN STOUGHTON, C. 1930. Henry Hansen of Stoughton started the first taxi service in Stoughton in 1922 to bring his customers to his new store at 602 Pleasant Street.

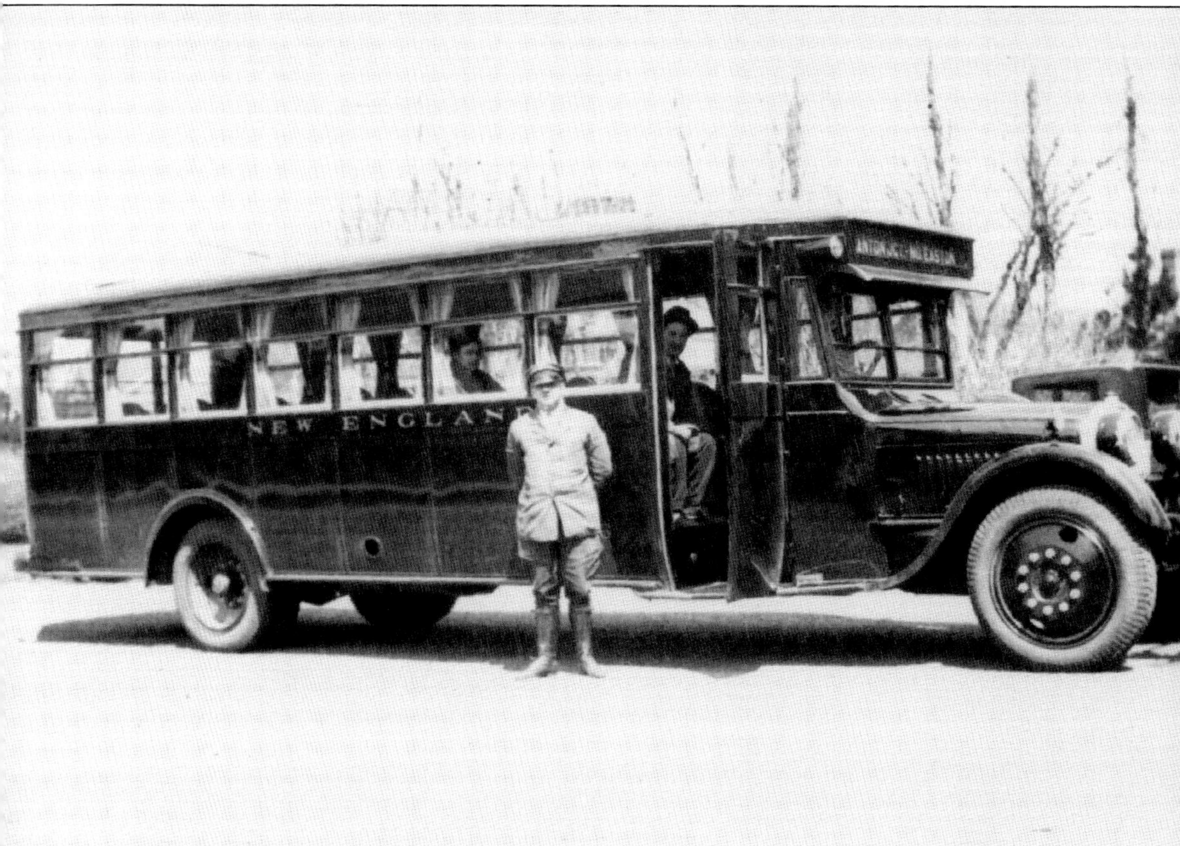

The Arrival of Bus Service, 1933. Bus service arrived in Stoughton in 1933 after trolley service ended. This photograph, taken by John Cyrns Stiles, shows the Canton Junction bus. Seated inside, nearest to the door, is Harrison Cummings.

Five

Stoughton Town Buildings

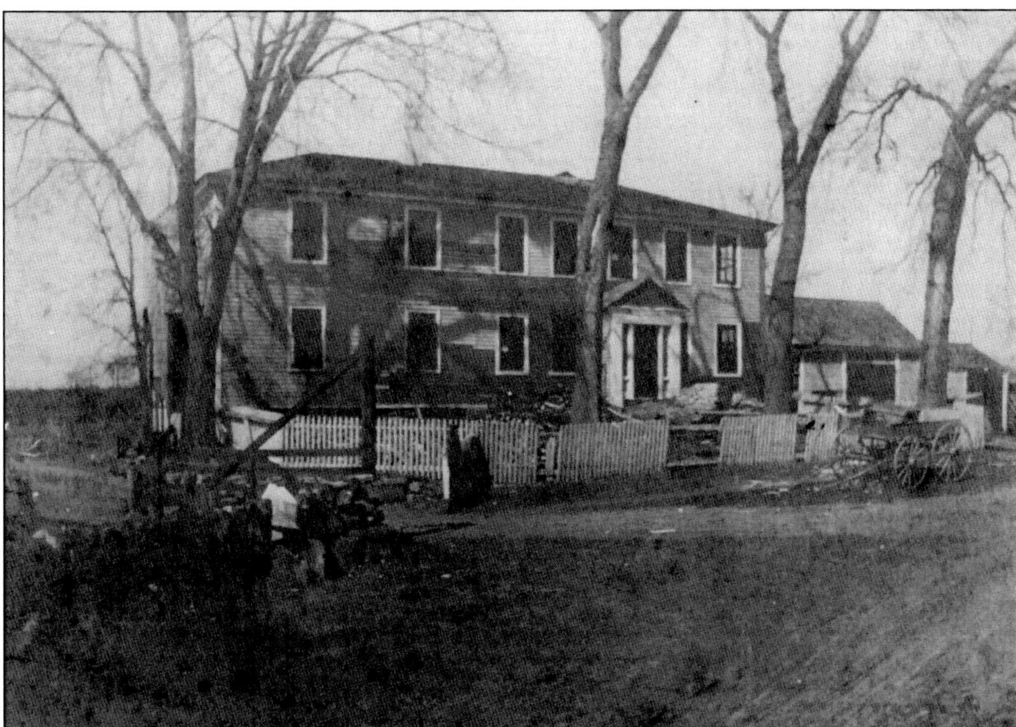

The Stoughton Poor Farm on School Street in Stoughton. The Stoughton Almshouse served the community for many years during the 19th century. This old building was burned on October 7, 1898. The building that replaced it was torn down in the 1940s, when the almshouse closed. The cemetery for the almshouse is marked with no gravestones and is located off School Street.

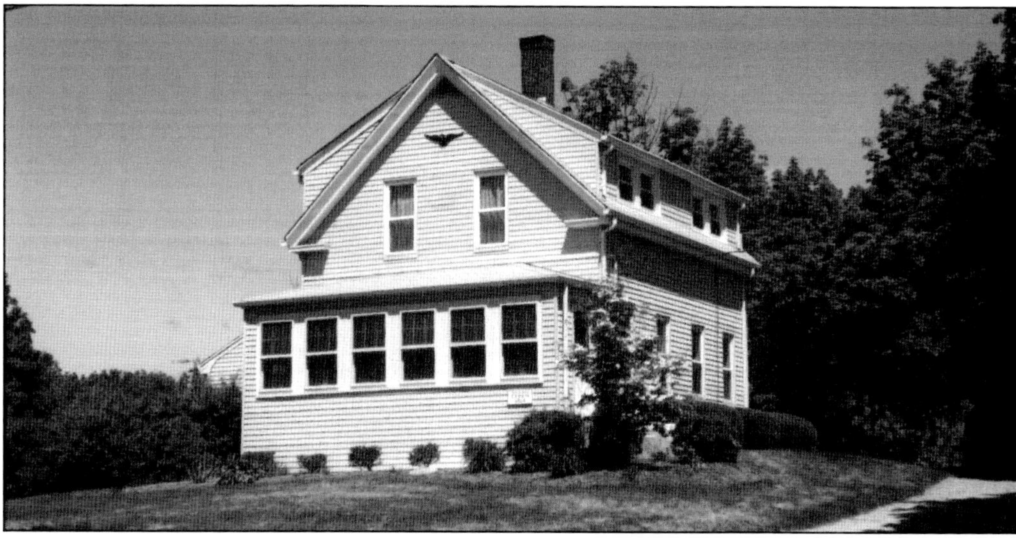

The Building Used for the First Post Office in Stoughton in 1814. This building was built by Wallace Capen and was located along the route of the old South Boston and Taunton Turnpike Corporation. On August 8, 1814, Aaron Gay was appointed the first postmaster of Stoughton. He was listed as the owner of this building in 1831. The building is also referred as the Wallace Capen place and is located at 769 Turnpike Street. (Author's collection.)

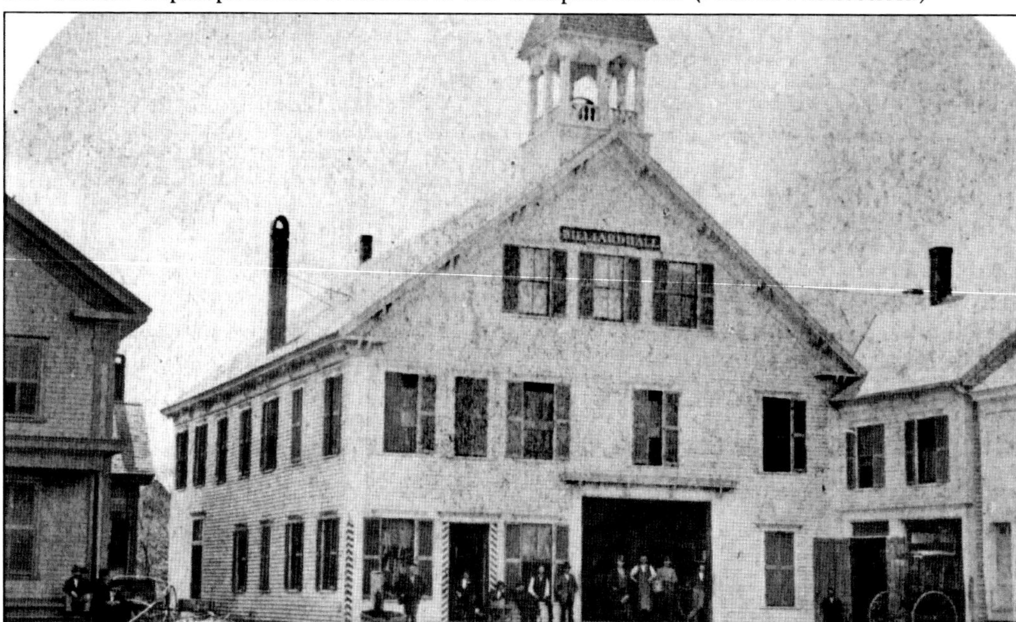

Atwood's Hall and Stable, Built in 1869 near the Corner of Washington Street and Railroad Avenue. Horse stables were located on the ground floor, and minstrel shows were performed often in the second-floor hall. On the third floor was a billiard hall. Stoughton town offices utilized the hall for town meetings in Atwood's since 1870. The town offices had been moved from Chemung Hall in the vestry of the First Parish Universalist Church after the fire of the first Stoughton Town House on Pleasant Street in 1848. Atwood's Hall and the nearby block were totally destroyed by fire on February 27, 1880.

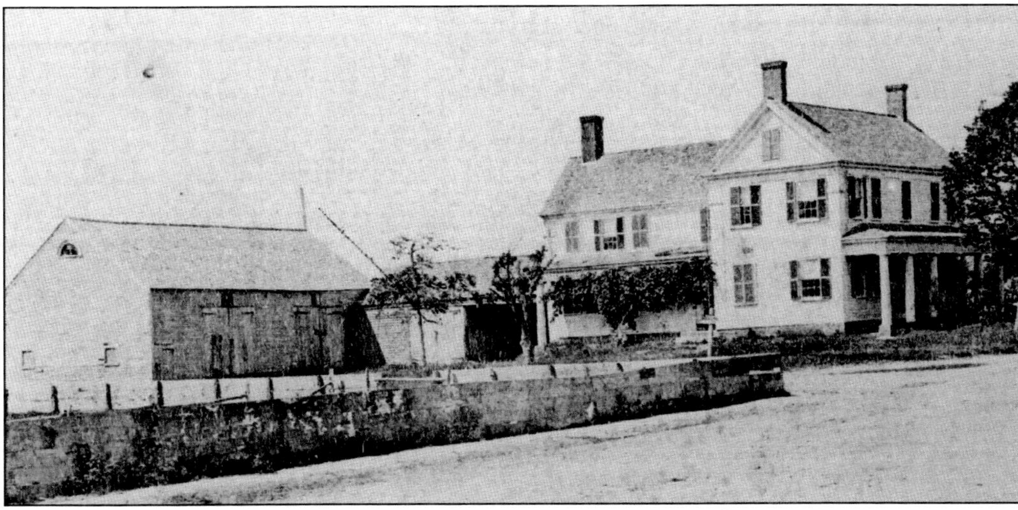

THE HOUSE AND FARM OF DEA. ROBERT PORTER (1798–1876), BEFORE 1881. Porter was president of the Musical Society of Stoughton from 1853 to 1876. The town purchased the land, and Robert Porter's house was razed to make room for the Stoughton Town Hall. Porter was a builder of roads. He was responsible for the causeway connection of West and Highland Streets over Ames Pond, as well as developing a great deal of the roads in Stoughton Square.

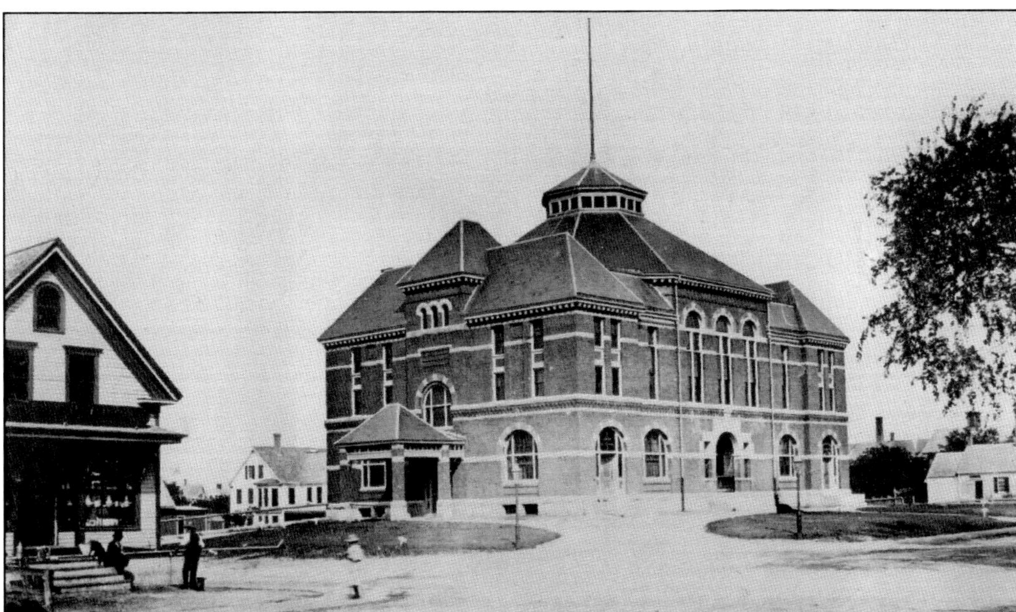

THE STOUGHTON TOWN HALL, AT THE CORNER OF PEARL AND PORTER STREETS. Construction began on April 29, 1880, by contractor S.J.F. Thayer and architect Joseph W. Coburn & Company of Boston. The town house and great hall were dedicated on November 22, 1881, at a cost of $50,621. This building also housed the Stoughton Public Library until 1903, the Stoughton Post Office until 1910, the Stoughton Fire Department until 1927, and the Stoughton Police Department until 1959. The portico on the Porter Street side of the building and the flagpole were later removed. The building saw renovations in 1927, 1938, and 1987.

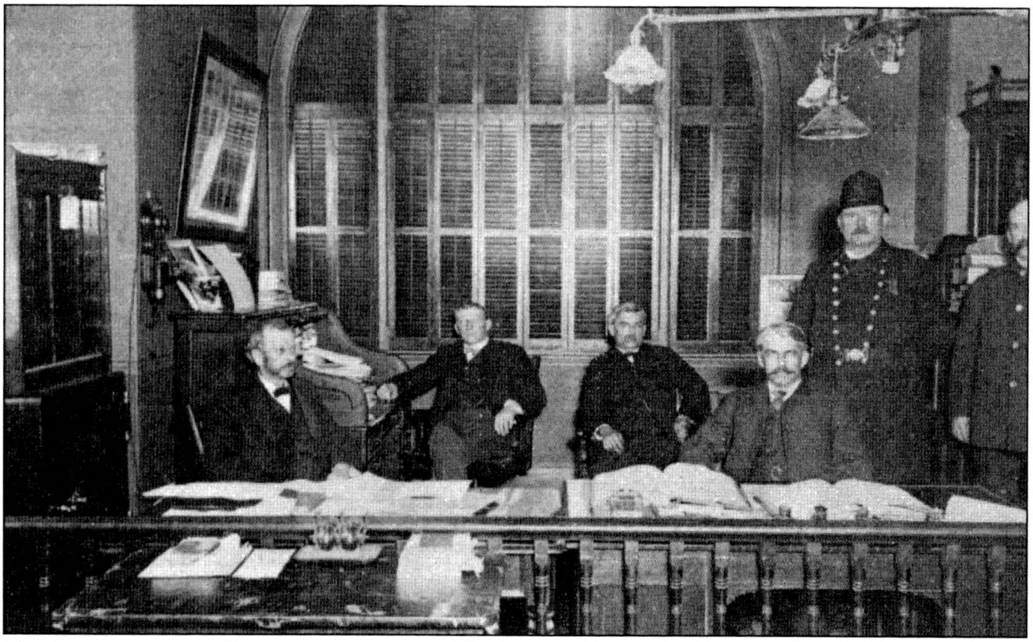

THE INSIDE OF THE STOUGHTON TOWN HALL, C. 1900–1905. Pictured from left to right are the following: (front row) George W. Pratt, James A. Capen, town clerk Cornelius Healy, police chief Richard J. Vanston, and fire chief James J. Pye.

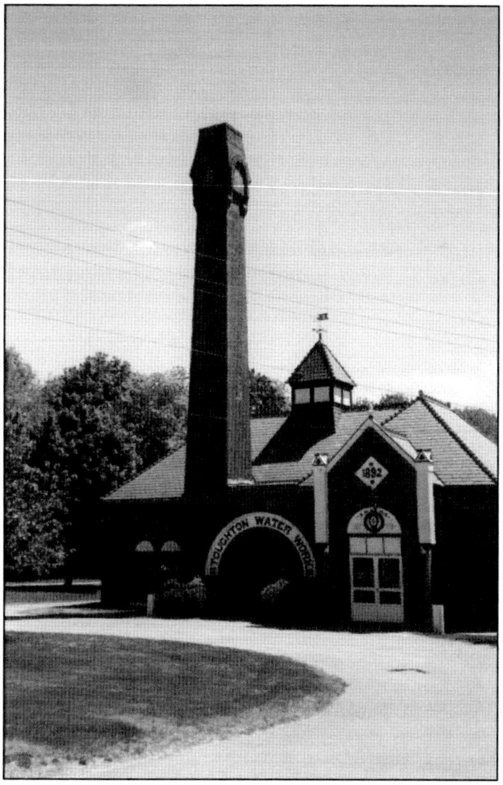

STOUGHTON WATER WORKS PUMPING STATION, AT 1704 CENTRAL STREET, BUILT IN 1892. This plot of land on the northwest corner of Central and West Streets was purchased for $800. This structure was designed by Fergus H. McKain, who designed the Drake School a couple of years earlier. (Author's collection.)

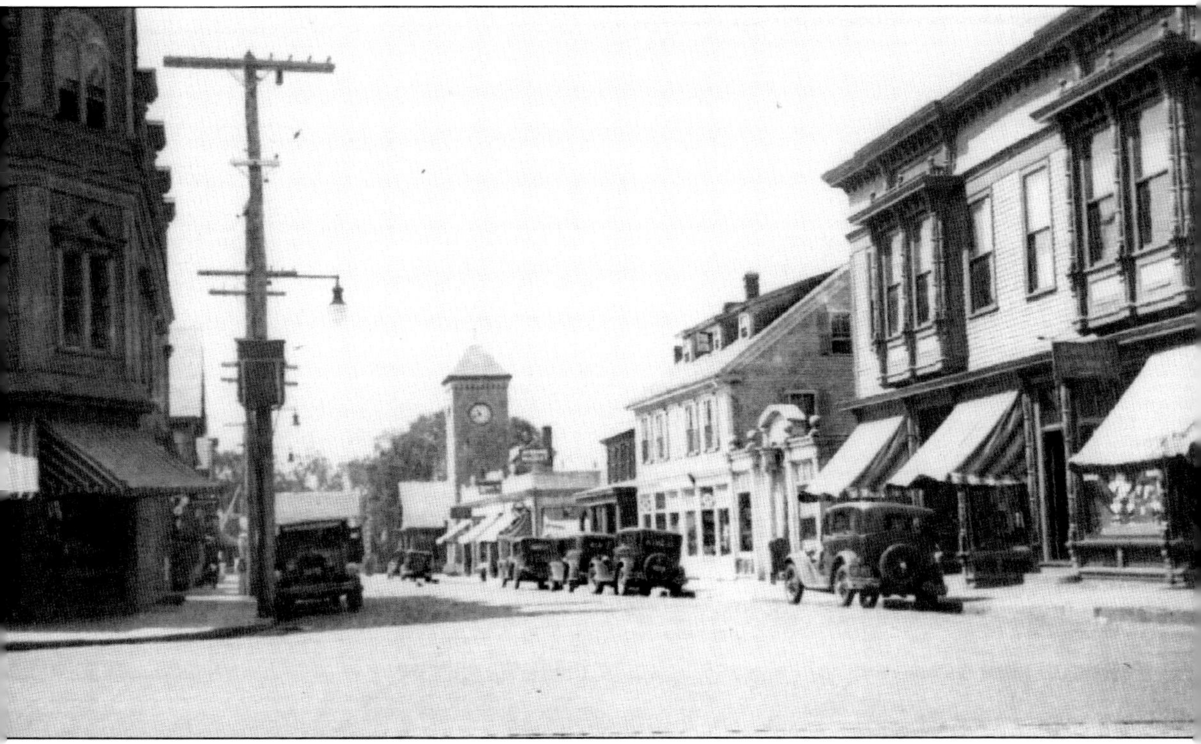

THE WYMAN STREET POST OFFICE. The Wyman Street Post Office is the first building to the left of Swan's Building. This post office was first used in 1910. The post office was relocated from the Stoughton Town Hall, and this location was used until 1939, when the new structure on Park Street was completed. After 1939, this building was used for commercial space and once as a delicatessen. This building and the old hotel beside it were lost to fire in 1960.

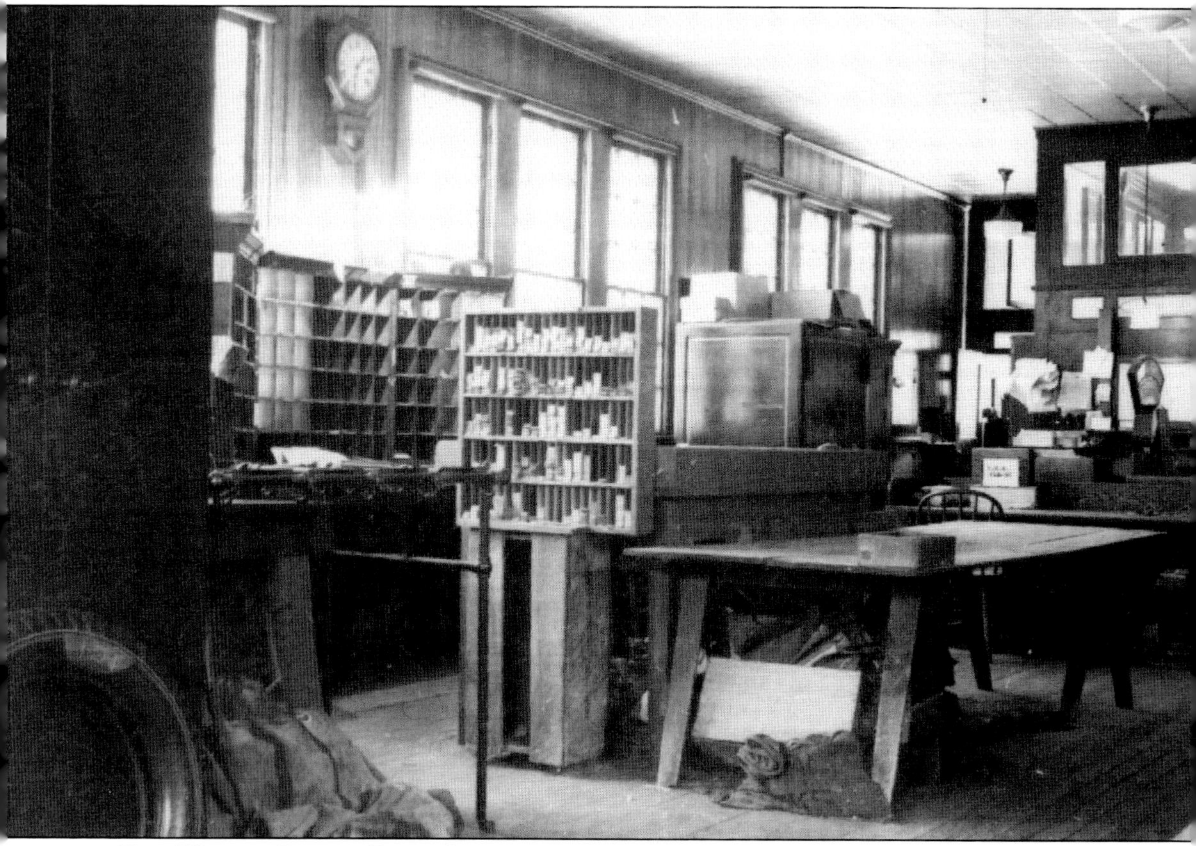

THE WYMAN STREET POST OFFICE BUILDING, C. 1930. This interior view of the Wyman Street Post Office building was taken by post office employee John Cyrns Stiles.

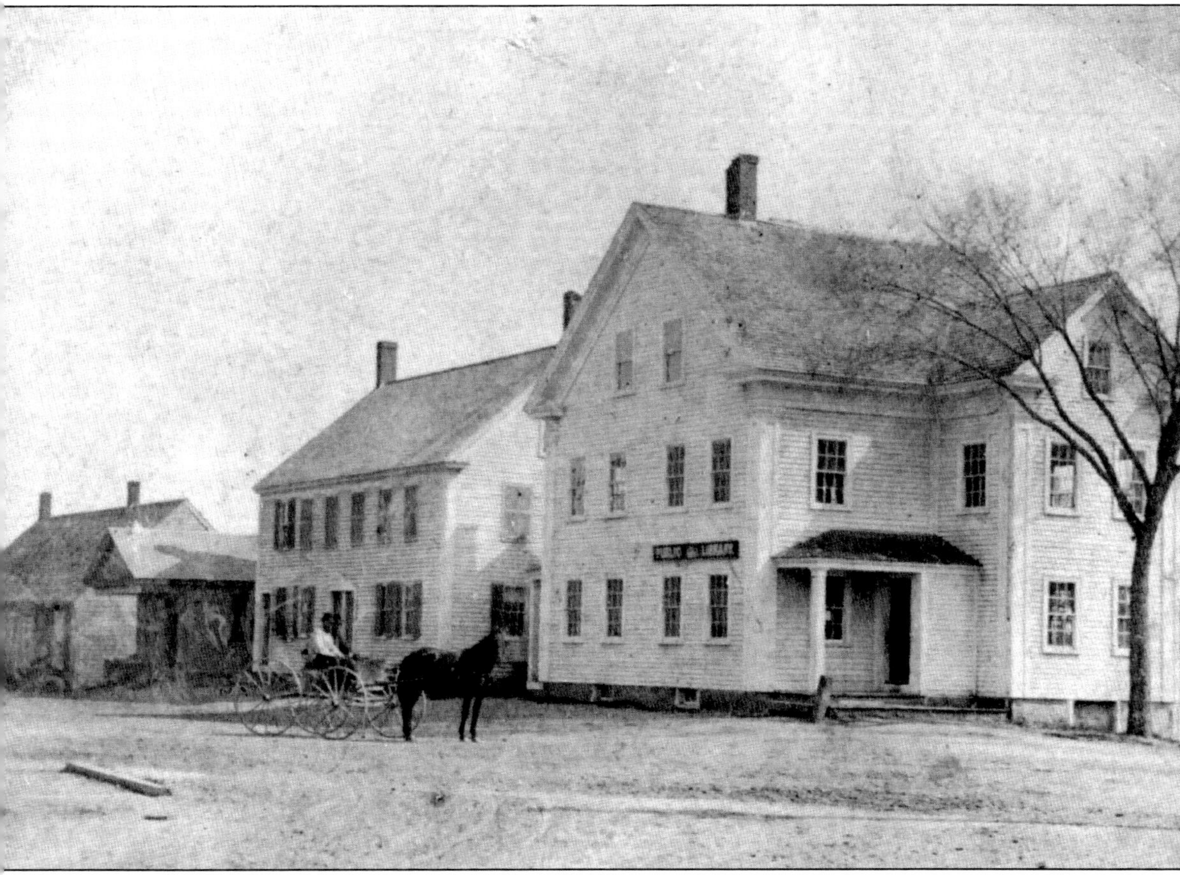

STOUGHTON'S FIRST PUBLIC LIBRARY, LOCATED IN THE OLD GARDNER PETTEE SHOE FACTORY AT MORTON SQUARE. This first library opened its doors on March 17, 1874. Wales French (1847–1916) was the first librarian, serving from 1874 to 1892 and from 1913 to 1916. French was a trustee of the library from 1892 until his death. While working at this location, he served without pay while carrying on his business at the Daniel French Shoe Factory. This building was also the home of the J.E. Drake & Son factory and is currently an apartment house.

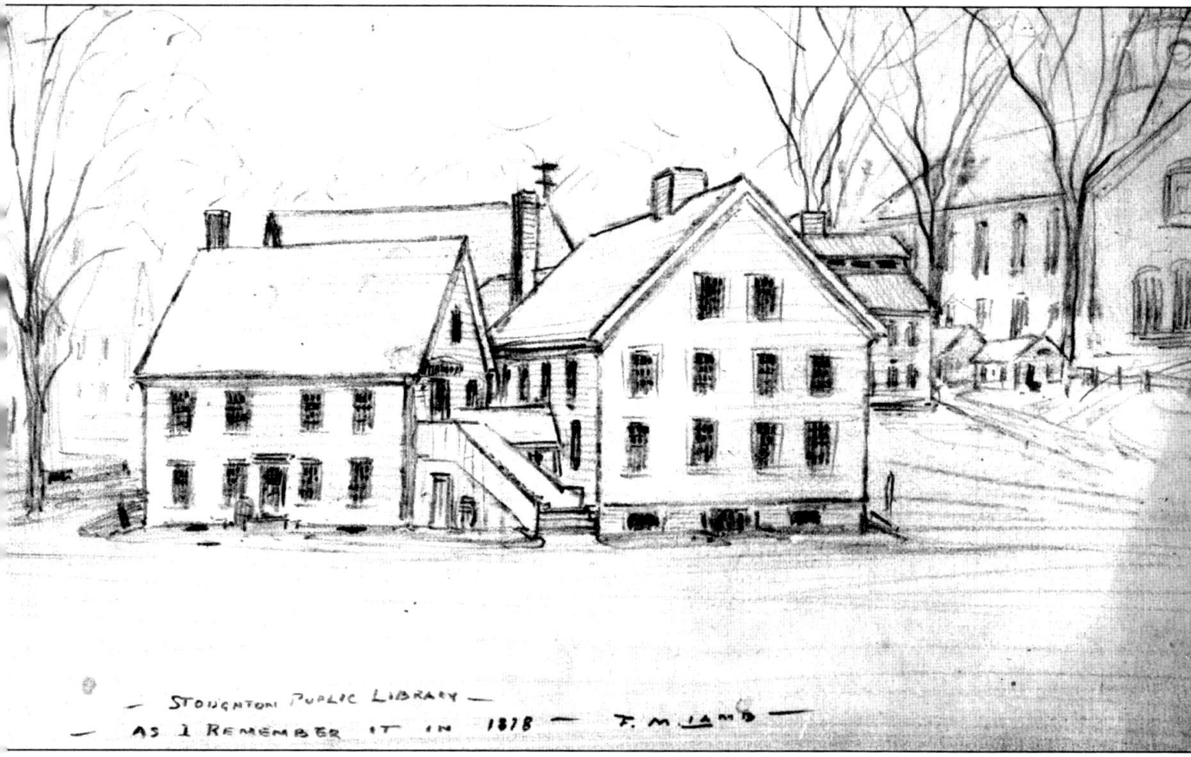

THE OLD LIBRARY'S SECOND HOME. This is F. Mortimer Lamb's drawing of the old library's second home on Washington Street, at the intersection of the present Freeman Street. Owned by Dr. Swan, this structure housed the library from 1875 until the move to the new Stoughton Town Hall in 1882. The building was burned on April 28, 1892. Note the Universalist church on the right.

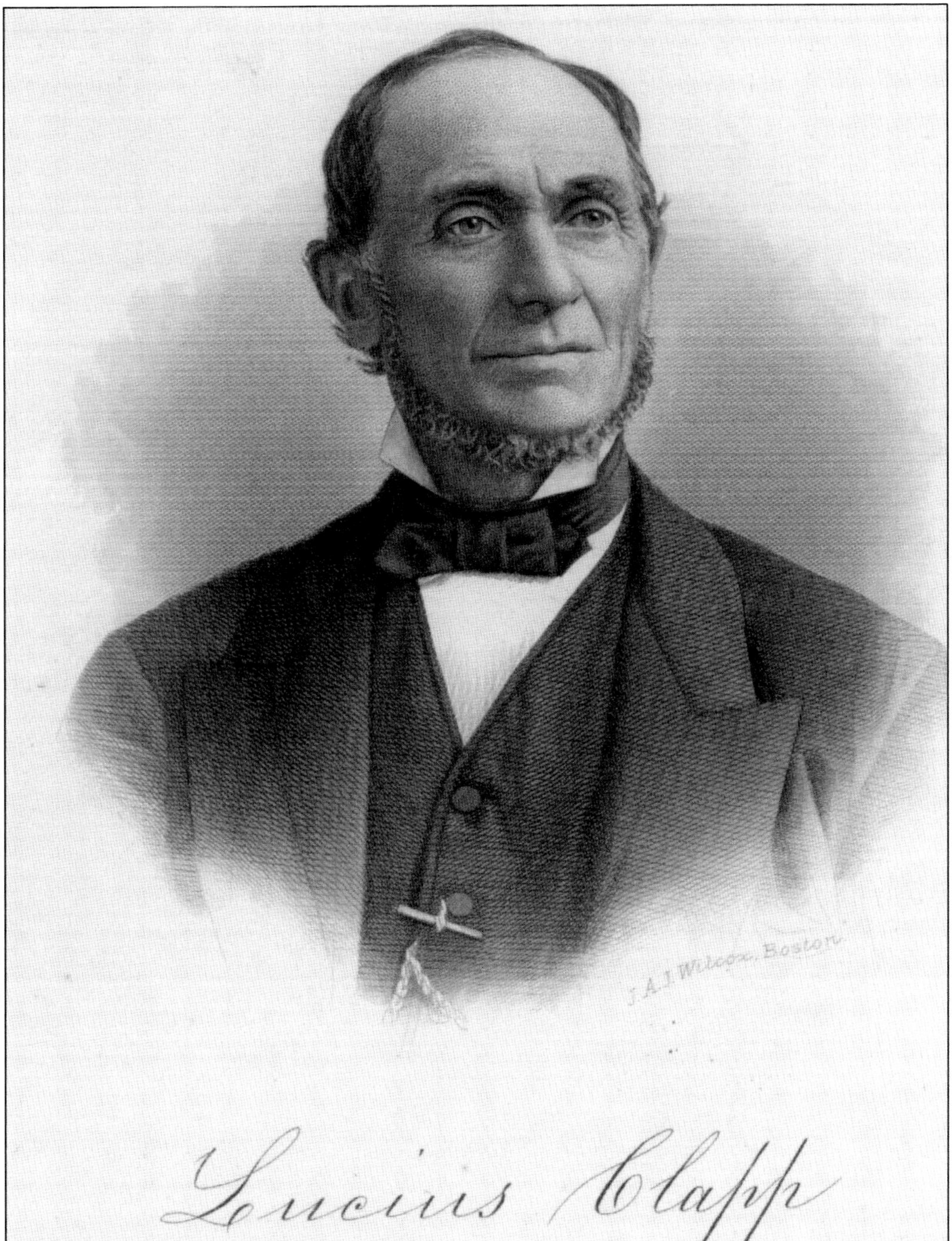

LUCIUS CLAPP (1817–1909). Lucius Clapp was a generous local benefactor. Clapp donated $25,000 for a new library building in 1902. He had previously donated money and books for Stoughton schools and had the Stoughton High School named in his honor. Clapp was born in North Bridgewater (now Brockton) and moved to West Street in Stoughton in 1821. He was a farmer, schoolteacher, and surveyor. He also served as a Stoughton selectman for seven years. He is buried with his family at the Dry Pond Cemetery.

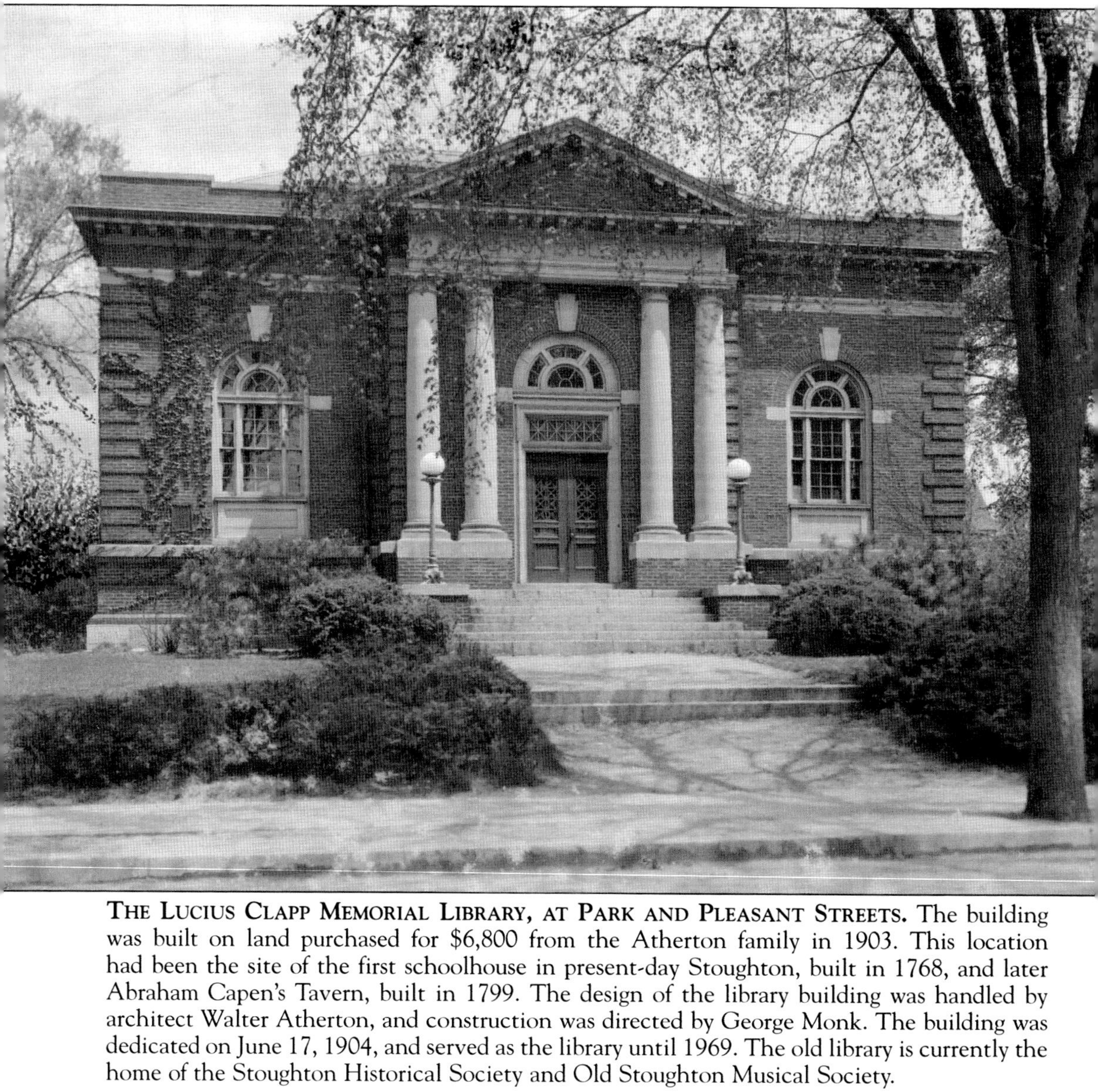

The Lucius Clapp Memorial Library, at Park and Pleasant Streets. The building was built on land purchased for $6,800 from the Atherton family in 1903. This location had been the site of the first schoolhouse in present-day Stoughton, built in 1768, and later Abraham Capen's Tavern, built in 1799. The design of the library building was handled by architect Walter Atherton, and construction was directed by George Monk. The building was dedicated on June 17, 1904, and served as the library until 1969. The old library is currently the home of the Stoughton Historical Society and Old Stoughton Musical Society.

Six

POLICE AND FIRE DEPARTMENTS

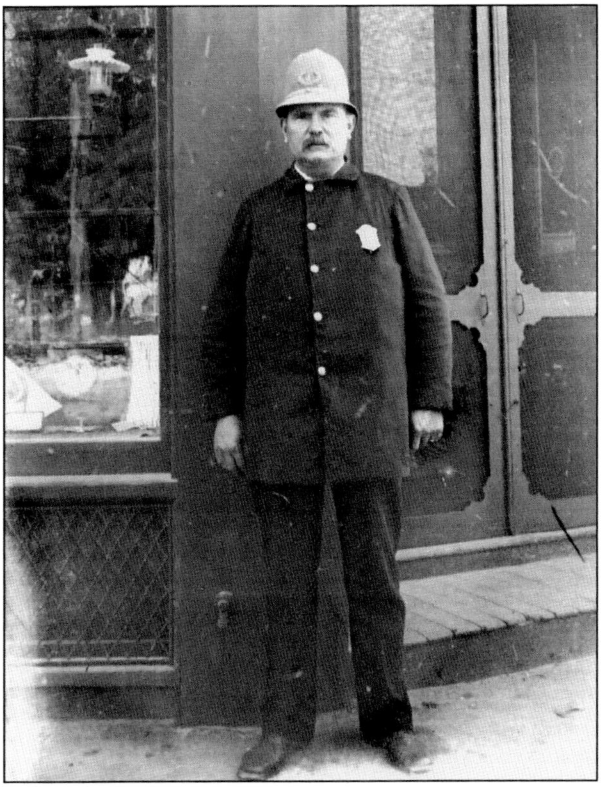

RICHARD J. VANSTON (1855–1925), STOUGHTON CHIEF OF POLICE, 1899–1925. Richard J. Vanston was a member of the Stoughton Fire Department in 1883. He preceded Chief Pye as chief of the Stoughton Fire Department by 11 years. In 1900, there were only two members of the Stoughton Police Department. Chief Vanston was assigned in 1899, and James Pye was the keeper of the police lockup facility.

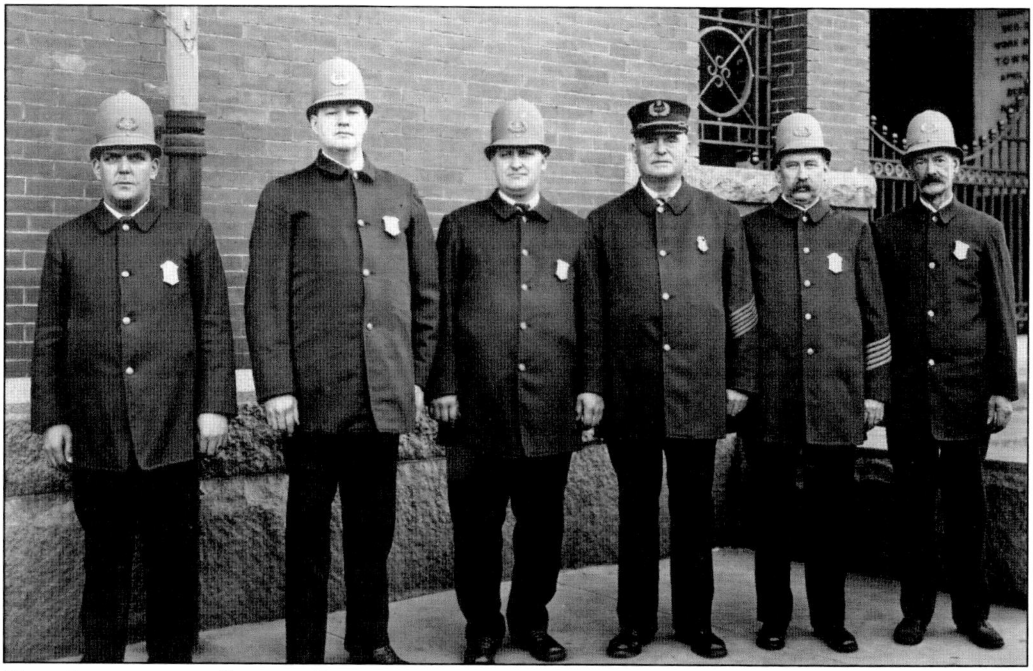

THE STOUGHTON POLICE DEPARTMENT IN FRONT OF THE STOUGHTON TOWN HALL, C. 1915. From left to right are H. Elliott Willis, Daniel F. O'Connor, Anson L. Favor, Chief Richard J. Vanston, James J. Pye, and Charles F. Adams.

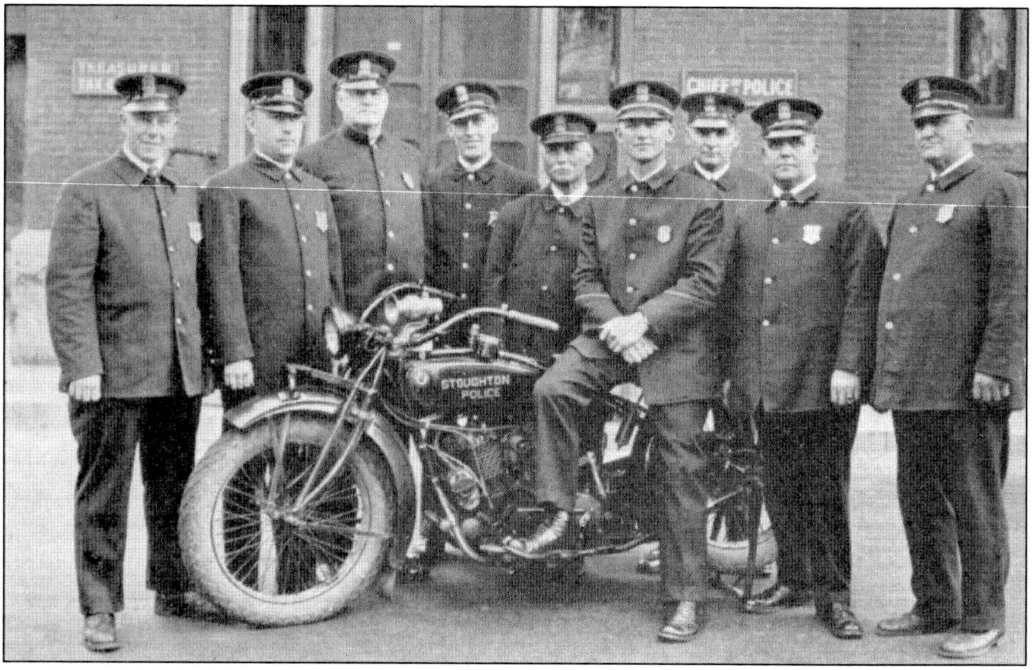

THE STOUGHTON POLICE DEPARTMENT IN FRONT OF THE STOUGHTON TOWN HALL IN 1926. From left to right are Sid Morey; Louis Swanson; Daniel F. O'Connor; Tim Roach; Charlie Shields; Peter J. McGarvey (1896–1976), who served as chief of police from 1925 to 1961; Walter Davis; Elliott Willis; and Anson Favor.

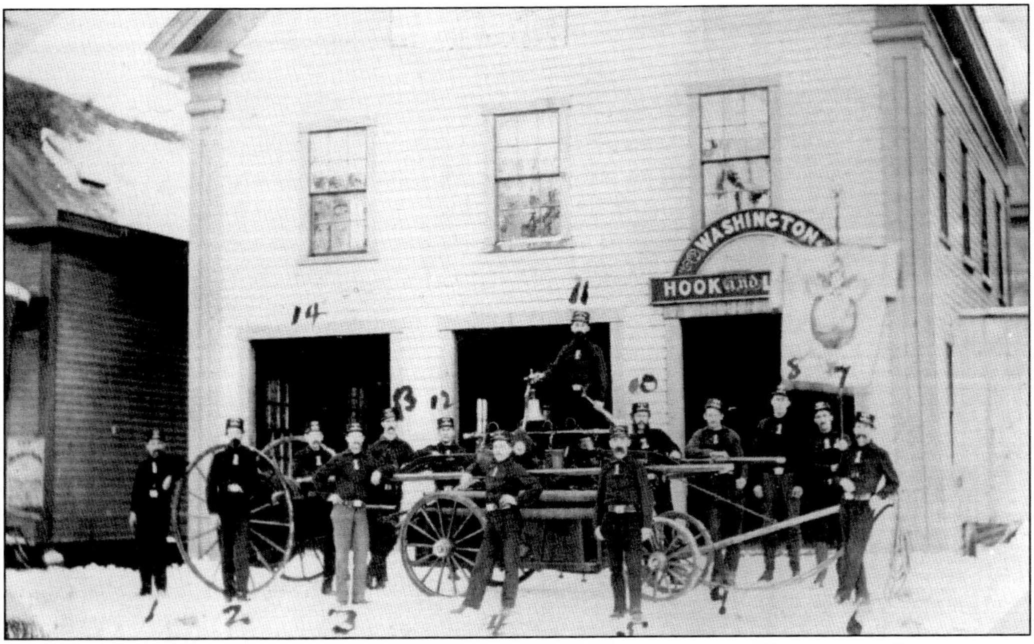

THE EARLY WASHINGTON HOOK & LADDER FIRE DEPARTMENT TEAM AND STATION ON WASHINGTON STREET, C. 1880. This station was constructed between 1853 and 1855 on Washington Street and the entrance to the easterly side of Porter Street. This original building was torn down in 1878 and replaced with a newer structure on the same site. In 1861, the fire department received seven calls and, in 1867, they did not receive a call all year. From left to right are the following: (front row) James Ansel Capen, Howard Kimball, Emery Lane, Fred Hopkins, and James Curley; (back row) Wilbur Mitchell, Morris Ames, Frank E. Hussey, Ellis Drake (standing on engine), Webster Lambert, Warren White, William Taylor, William Graham, and James Daley.

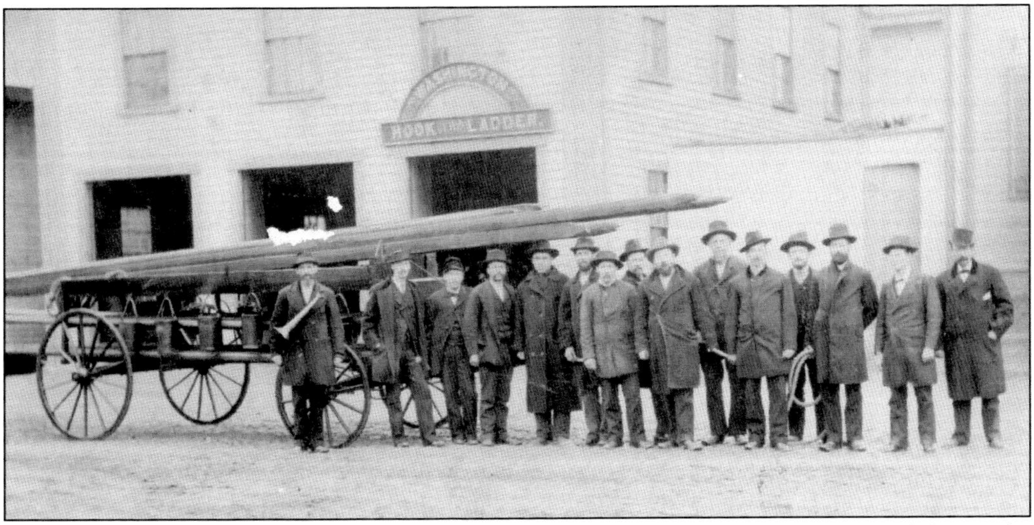

THE WASHINGTON HOOK & LADDER FIRE DEPARTMENT TEAM, C. 1880. From left to right are George Goward, Warner Flanders, Charles Wales, Albert Walker, Elbridge Ross, Andrew Nevins, Arthur L. Holmes, James E. Stevens, George Whitney, Frank Carr, Alden W. Skinner, Alvah B. Colburn, Warren Bird, William DeCosta, and Alphonso Mead.

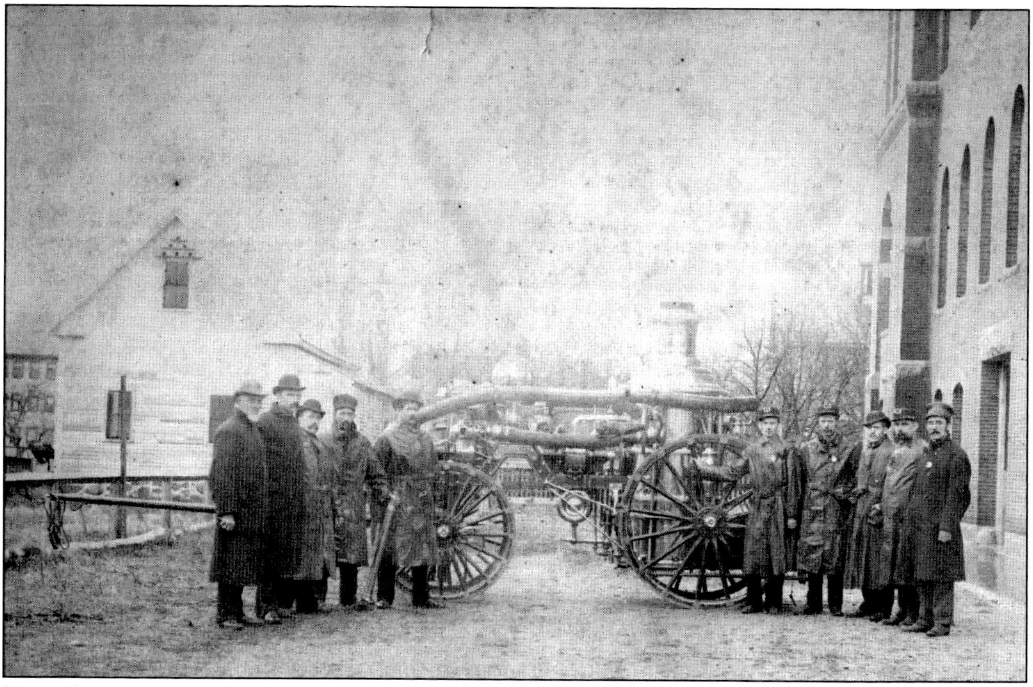

THE STOUGHTON FIRE DEPARTMENT, C. 1905. The Stoughton Fire Department is seen here at the fire station, located underneath the Stoughton Town Hall on Pearl Street. From left to right are David Forsaith (chief of police in 1883), Richard J. Vanston, Mike Smith, Peter Smith, Joe Blanchard, ? Powers, unidentified, Oliver Curtis, Patrick "Patsy" Powers, and Bill Graham.

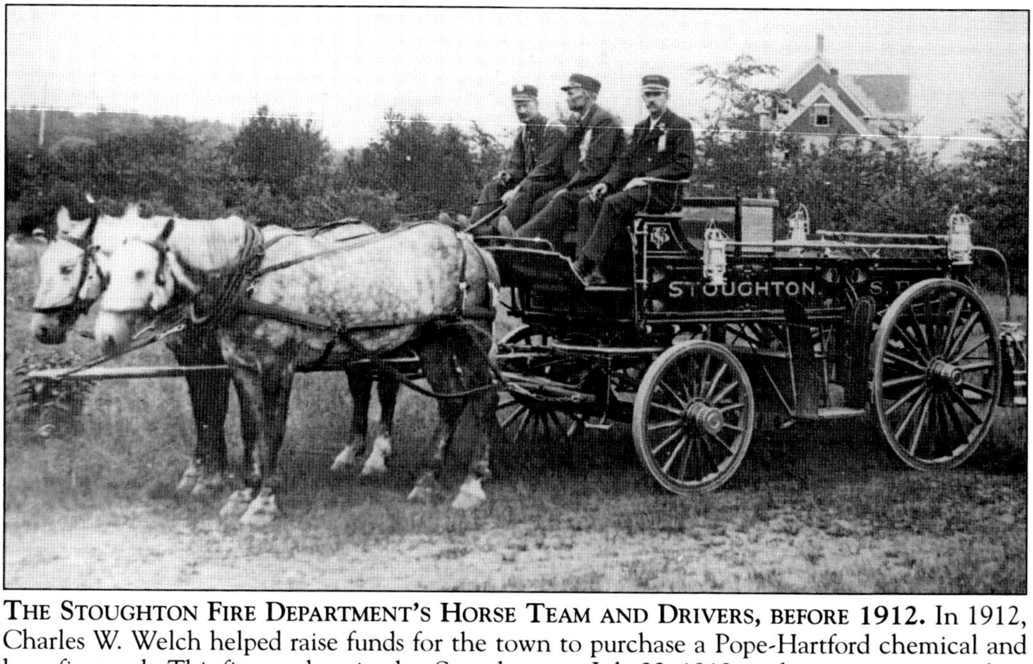

THE STOUGHTON FIRE DEPARTMENT'S HORSE TEAM AND DRIVERS, BEFORE 1912. In 1912, Charles W. Welch helped raise funds for the town to purchase a Pope-Hartford chemical and hose fire truck. This fire truck arrived at Stoughton on July 22, 1912, and was commissioned on August 7, 1912, with Fred H. Pye as driver. At this time, the last pair of horses was sold.

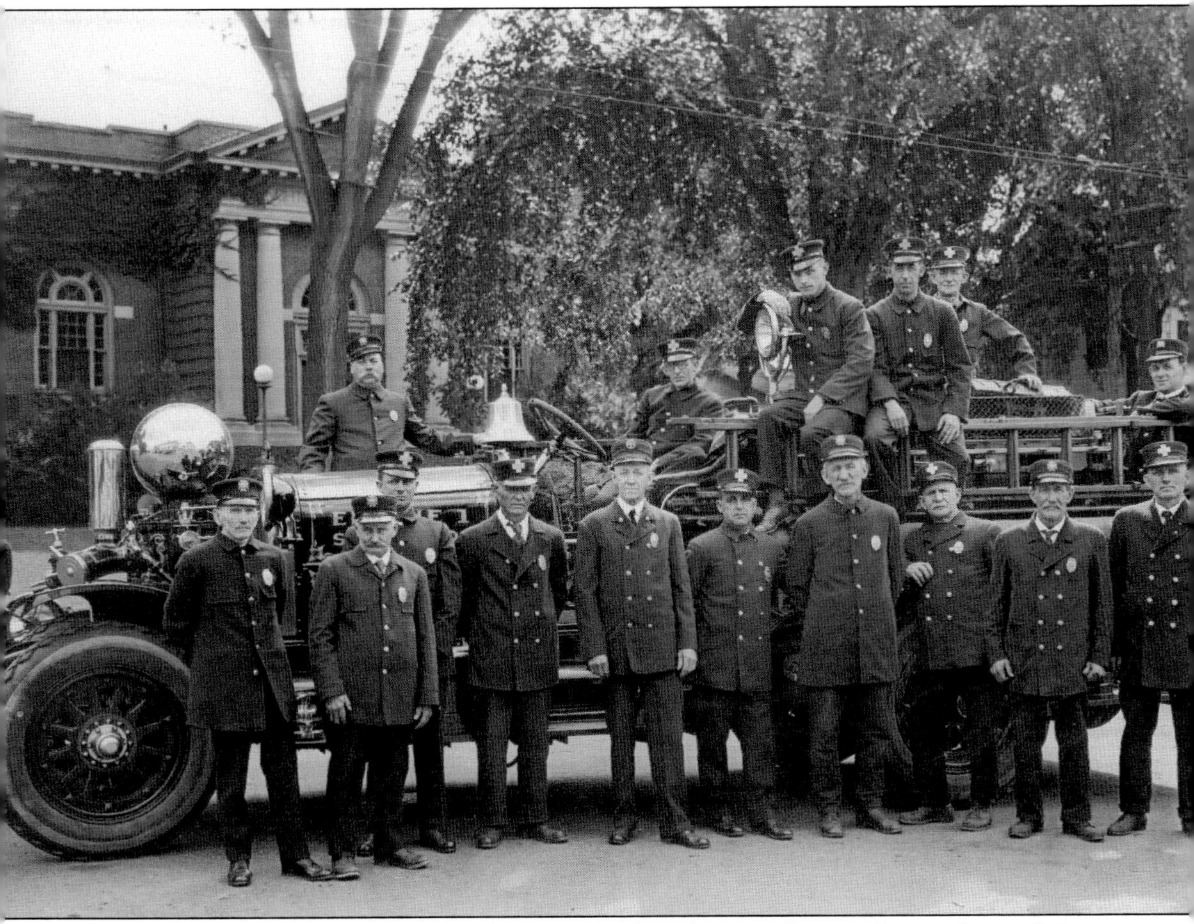

THE STOUGHTON PUMPER PURCHASED IN 1921. This photograph was taken in front of the Stoughton Public Library. From left to right are the following: (front row) Teddy Darbey, Alva Gould, James W. Graham, Frank Phillips, Assistant Chief Henry Bird, Harry Chavis, John McGarvey, Frank Gay, Frank Hussey, and Ernest Holmes; (back row) Spencer Billings, Fred Pye, John Condon, Lewis Foster, James A. Graham, and John Pye. In the background on the left is Duncan Flemming on his Stoughton Police Department motorcycle.

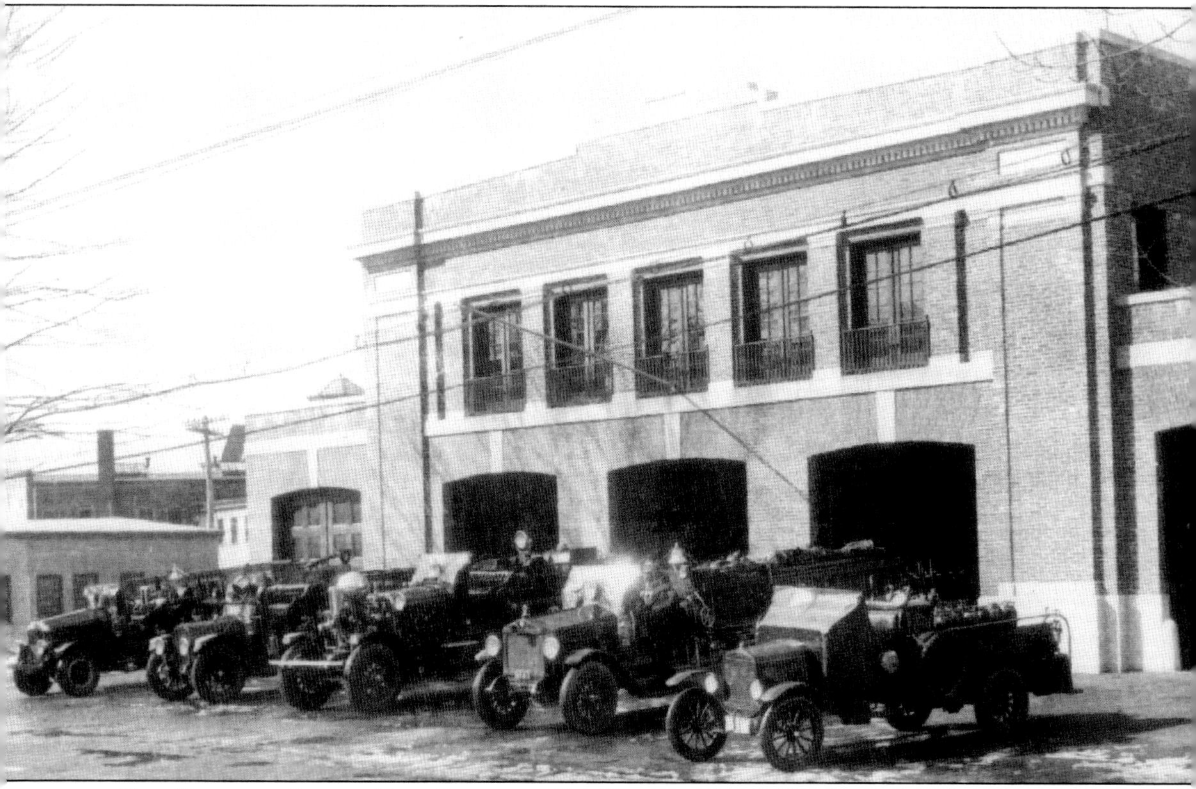

THE FREEMAN STREET FIRE STATION. The Freeman Street Fire Station was occupied by the Stoughton Fire Department on June 13, 1927. This station is currently the main fire station in Stoughton.

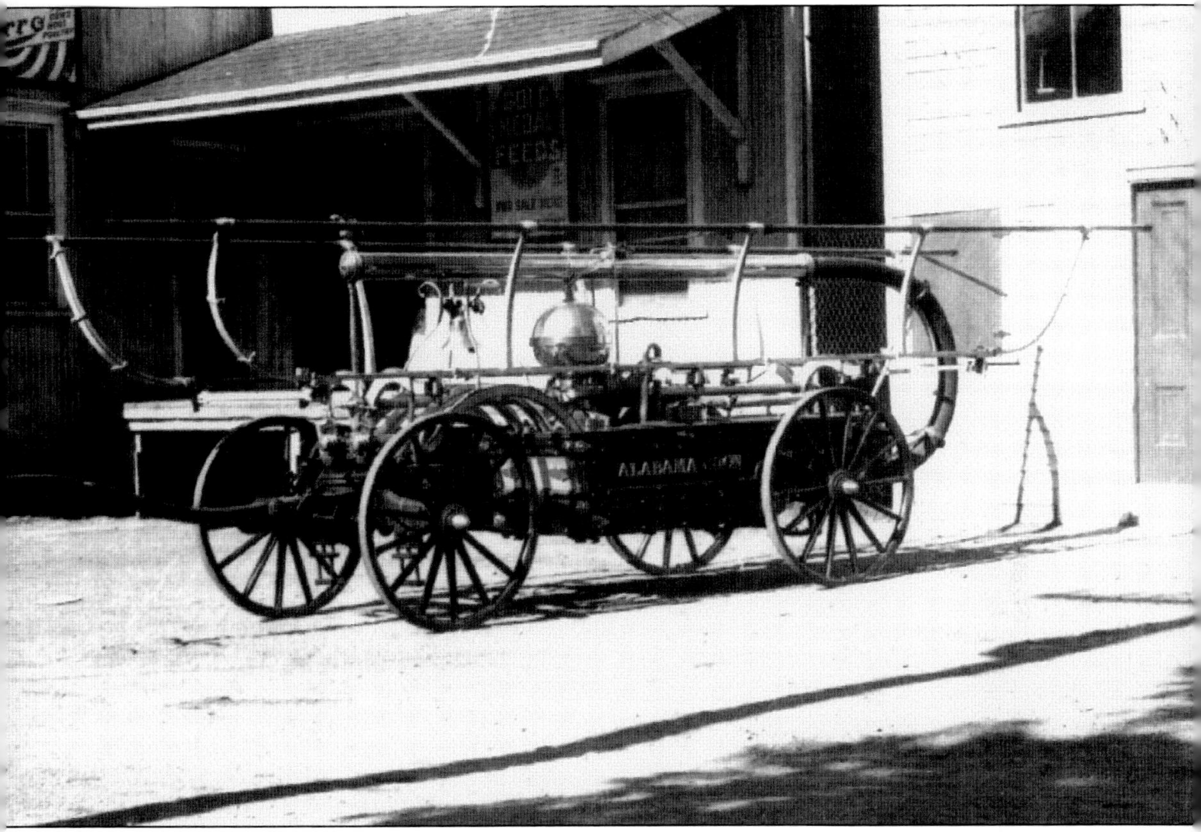

THE CITIZEN NO. 1 HAND TUB OF THE STOUGHTON VETERAN FIREMEN ASSOCIATION ON RAILROAD AVENUE, C. 1910. The Citizen No. 1, also known as the "Alabama Coon," was built in 1859 by the Cowing & Company of Seneca Falls, New York, for the city of Glen Falls, New York. It was later sold to Richmond, Virginia; Augusta, Georgia; Union Springs, Alabama; and Randolph, Massachusetts. Randolph sold the hand tub on November 30, 1901, to the recently formed Stoughton Veteran Firemen Association. They restored the hand tub and won many competitions and league tournaments. The hand tub was sold in the 1940s to Ipswich, Massachusetts. As recently as the 1970s, it was still being used by the Pickering Fire Brigade of Standard, California.

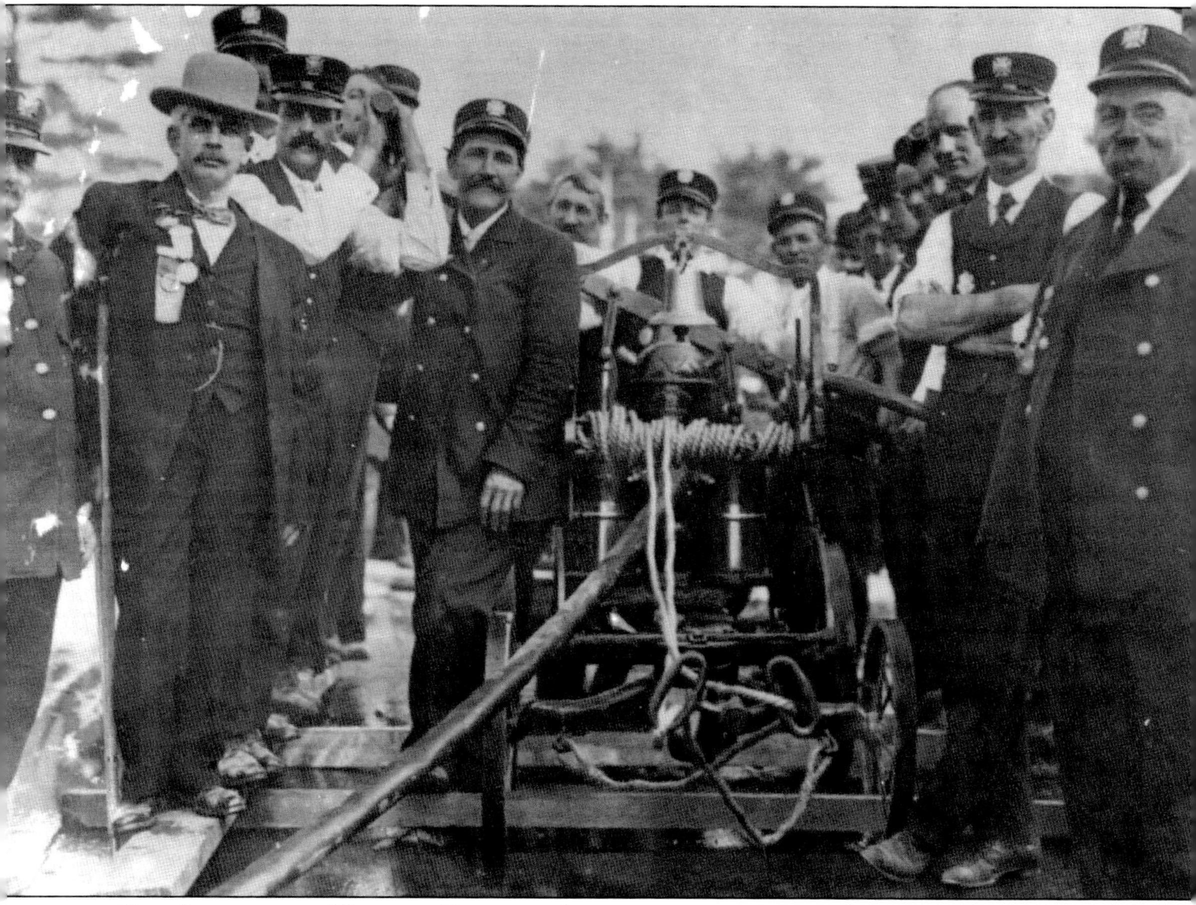

The Stoughton Veteran Firemen Association with the "Alabama Coon" Hand Tub. From left to right are Alvah Gould, Cornelius Healey, unidentified, Harry Chavis, unidentified, Frank Hussey, John McGarvey, Tobe Vanston, Frank Phillips, three unidentified, Frank Gay, Ernest Holmes, Berthier Holmes, and James Curley James Pye. The Stoughton Veteran Firemen Association was formed on November 26, 1901, and purchased the "Alabama Coon" four days later. The association was located in a barn on Railroad Avenue.

Seven

EARLY STOUGHTON VETERANS

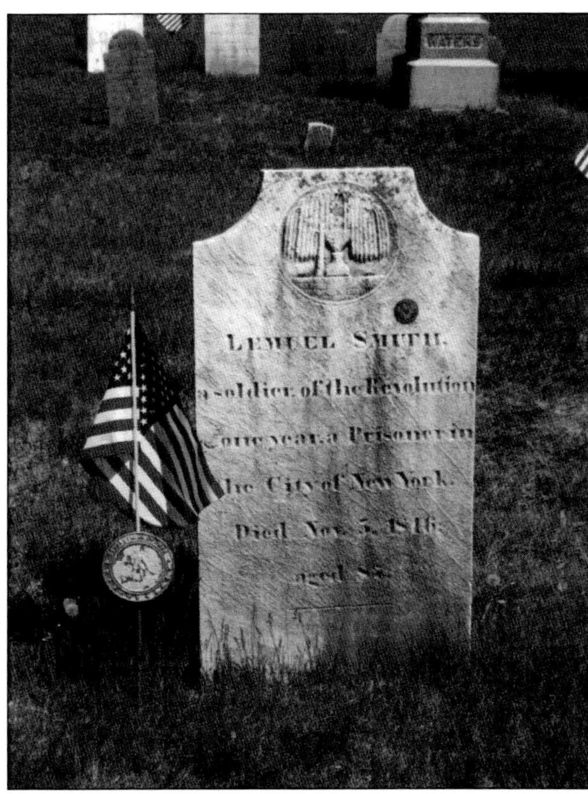

THE GRAVESTONE OF LEMUEL SMITH (1759–1846), AT DRY POND CEMETERY. The inscription reads, "A soldier of the Revolution, & one year a Prisoner in the City of New York." Smith had enlisted in the Revolutionary War at the age of 16. After his release from New York, he walked the distance back home to Stoughton. He lived on the corner of Bay Road and Highland Streets in Stoughton and is buried with other Revolutionary War soldiers at the Dry Pond Cemetery. (Author's collection.)

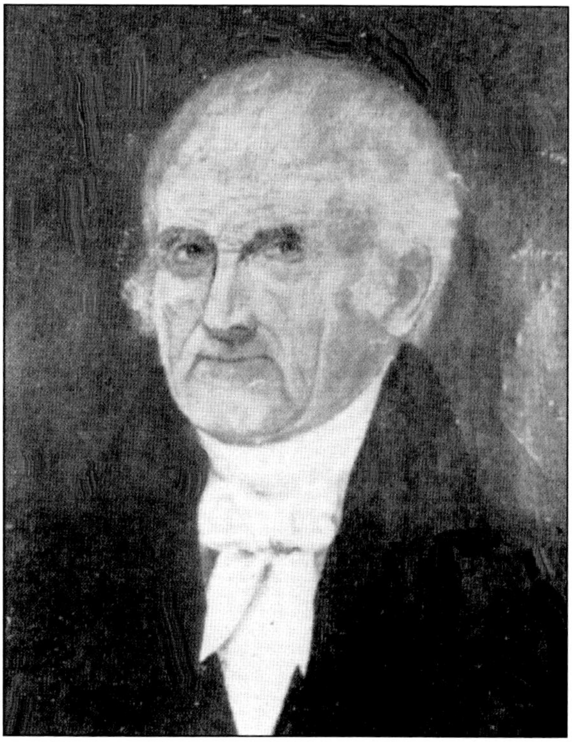

JAMES CAPEN (1756–1853), THE LAST REVOLUTIONARY WAR SOLDIER FROM STOUGHTON. Capen was born at Stoughton and resided on his farm on Pleasant Street. He was a private in Capt. Simeon Leach's company, Col. Benjamin Gill's regiment, which marched from Stoughton to Braintree on March 21, 1776, when the British ships were in the harbor. He served again with Capt. Robert Swan's company, Col. Benjamin Gill's regiment, which marched from Stoughton on December 19, 1776, to Castle Island. Capen was receiving a government military pension when he died in Stoughton on February 24, 1853, at the age of 96. Capen was the father of the artist Ansel Capen (1796–1884), who drew this portrait of him. (Author's collection.)

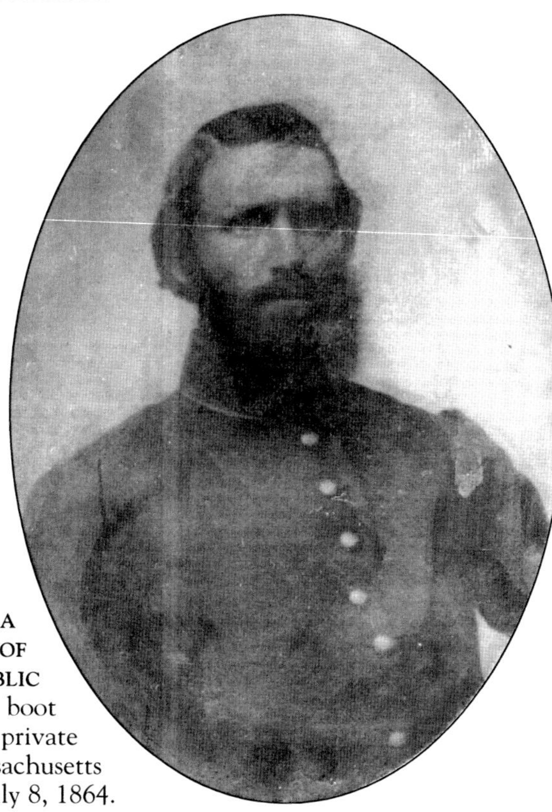

JONATHAN K. PORTER (1831–1907), A CIVIL WAR VETERAN AND MEMBER OF POST 72, GRAND ARMY OF THE REPUBLIC (GAR), IN STOUGHTON. Porter was a boot maker in Stoughton when he enlisted as a private on June 26, 1861, Company H, 12th Massachusetts Infantry, and mustered out at Boston on July 8, 1864.

EDSON J. ANGIER (1832–1893), A CIVIL WAR VETERAN AND MEMBER OF POST 72, GAR, IN STOUGHTON. Angier was a boot maker residing in Randolph before he enlisted in Sergeant Company E, 35th Massachusetts Infantry, as a private on July 24, 1862. He was promoted to full second lieutenant on September 8, 1864, and was discharged on December 10, 1864.

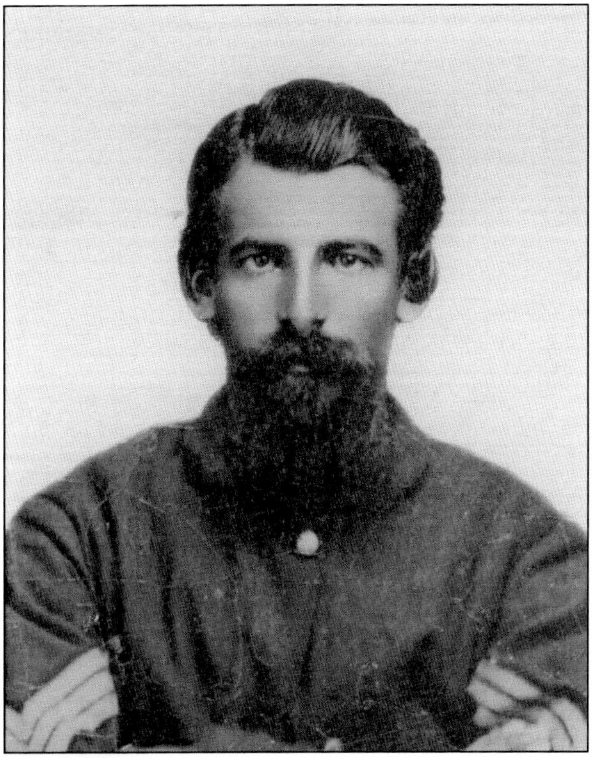

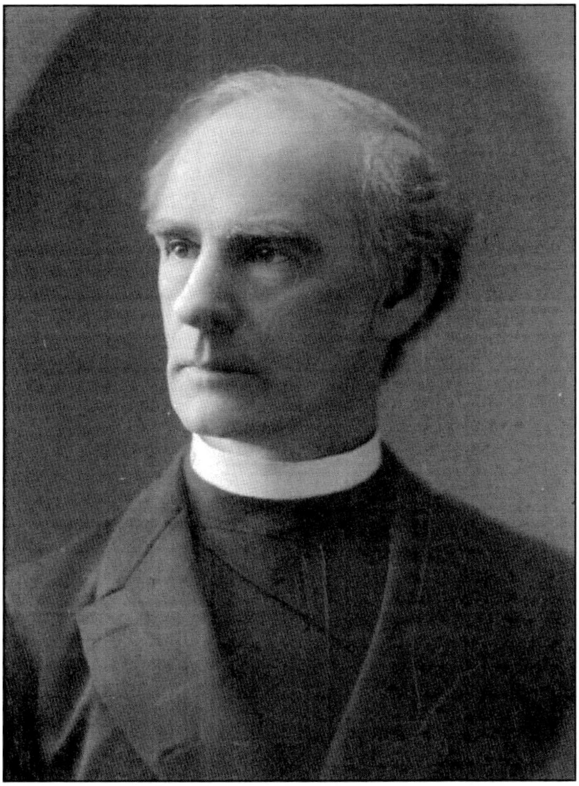

REV. ALBERT ST. JOHN CHAMBRE (1839–1911). Rev. Albert St. John Chambre enlisted on April 30, 1861, as the chaplain for the 8th New Jersey Infantry and resigned his post on March 19, 1863. He became the namesake of Stoughton's Post 72, GAR, on December 10, 1868. He was the minster of the Universalist church in Stoughton from 1864 to 1872.

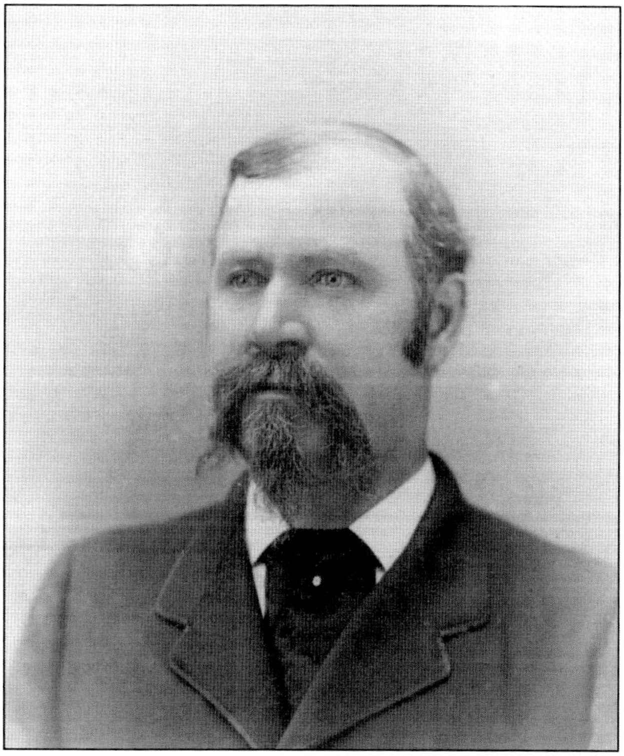

MAJ. GEORGE WENDELL DUTTON (1836–1925). Dutton enlisted while a machinist in Stoughton and was given the rank of captain on June 11, 1861, of Company K, 9th Massachusetts Infantry. He was promoted to full major on August 26, 1862. He was further promoted on July 20, 1863, as full captain of Company C, 10th Veterans Relief Corps, and was finally mustered out of service on June 30, 1866. He served as the guard for Dr. Mudd, who was standing trial as a conspirator in the assassination of Pres. Abraham Lincoln. Dutton was a member of Post 72, GAR.

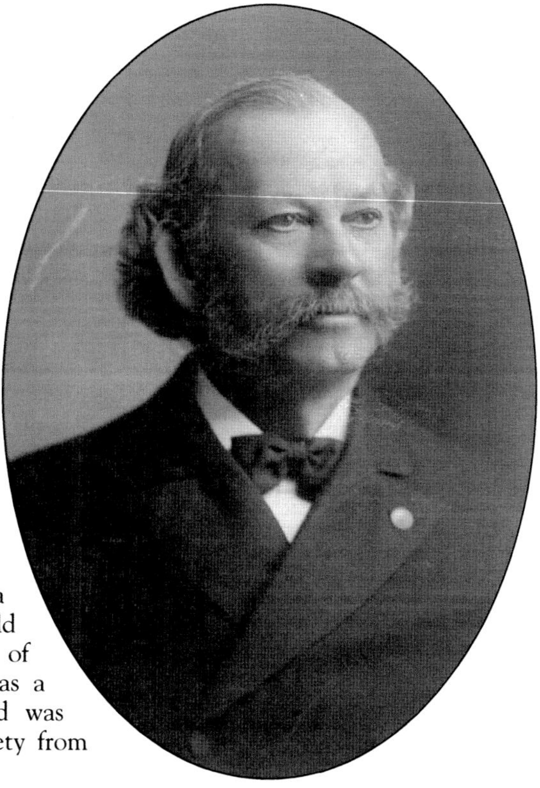

GEORGE WILLIAM PRATT (1843–1927). Pratt enlisted from his birthplace at Chelsea on September 1, 1862, as a private in Company H, 43rd Massachusetts Infantry. This regiment was mustered out at Readville on July 30, 1863. Pratt was past commander of Post 72, GAR, which he joined as a member on May 1, 1883. He would later hold the position as commander of the State of Massachusetts GAR Post. He also served as a selectman for Stoughton for 20 years and was president of the Stoughton Historical Society from 1922 until his death.

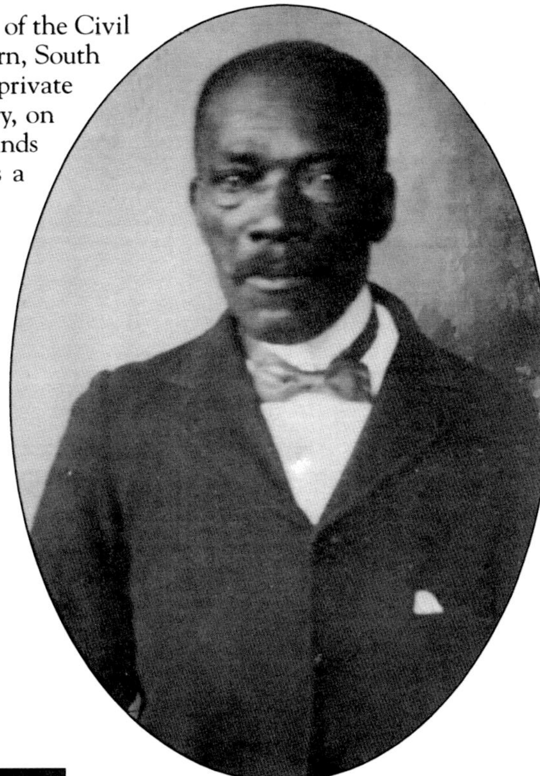

SAMUEL SHARP (1841–1923). At the time of the Civil War, Sharp claimed his residence as Newbern, South Carolina, and was a farmer. He enlisted as a private in Company D, 55th Massachusetts Infantry, on May 27, 1863, and was discharged for wounds at Worcester on May 25, 1865. Sharp was a member of Post 72, GAR.

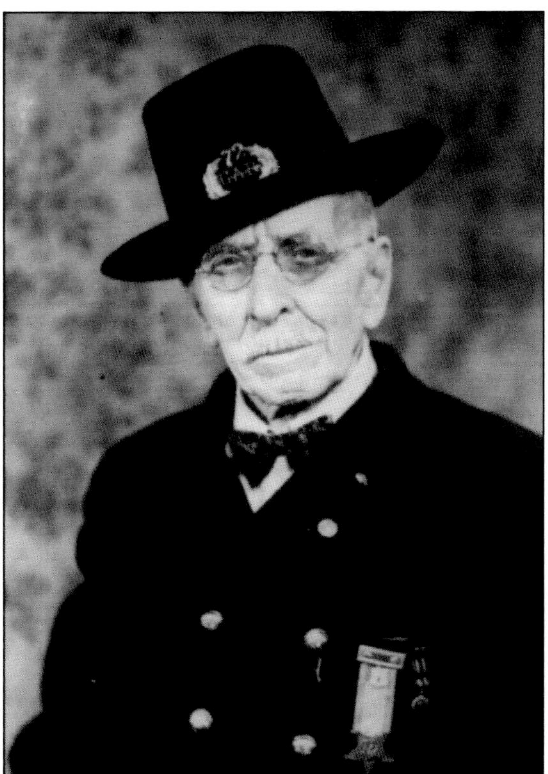

COMDR. CHARLES A. MILES (1846–1940). Miles was Stoughton's last veteran of the Civil War and the last member of Post 72, GAR, founded 77 years before.

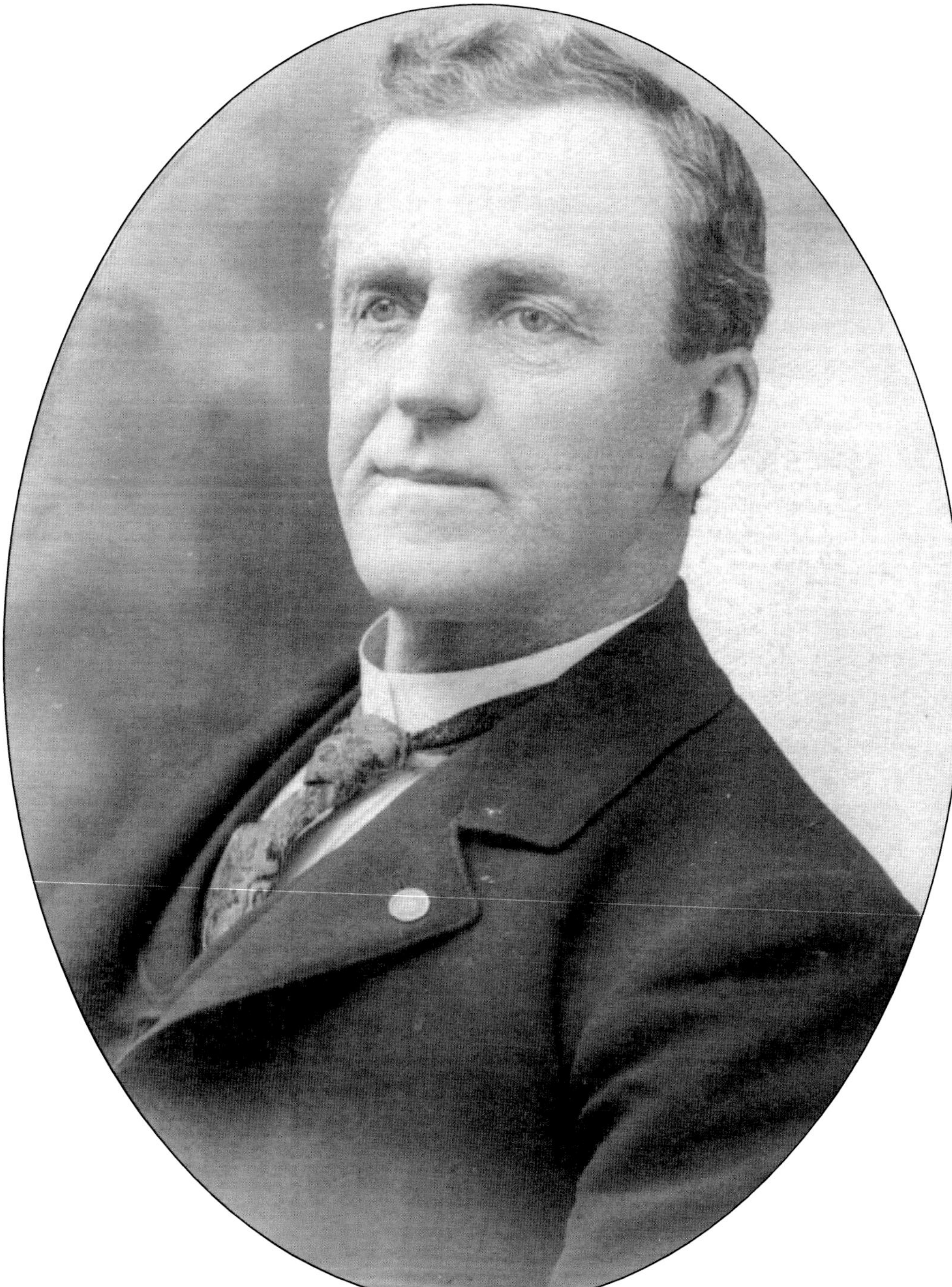

MARCUS MORTON PORTER (1841–1921). Porter enlisted as a private on October 15, 1862, in Company G, 47th Massachusetts Infantry, and was mustered out on September 1, 1863. He was a member of Post 72, GAR. Porter became a member of the Old Stoughton Musical Society in 1893 and served as the society's president from 1911 to 1913.

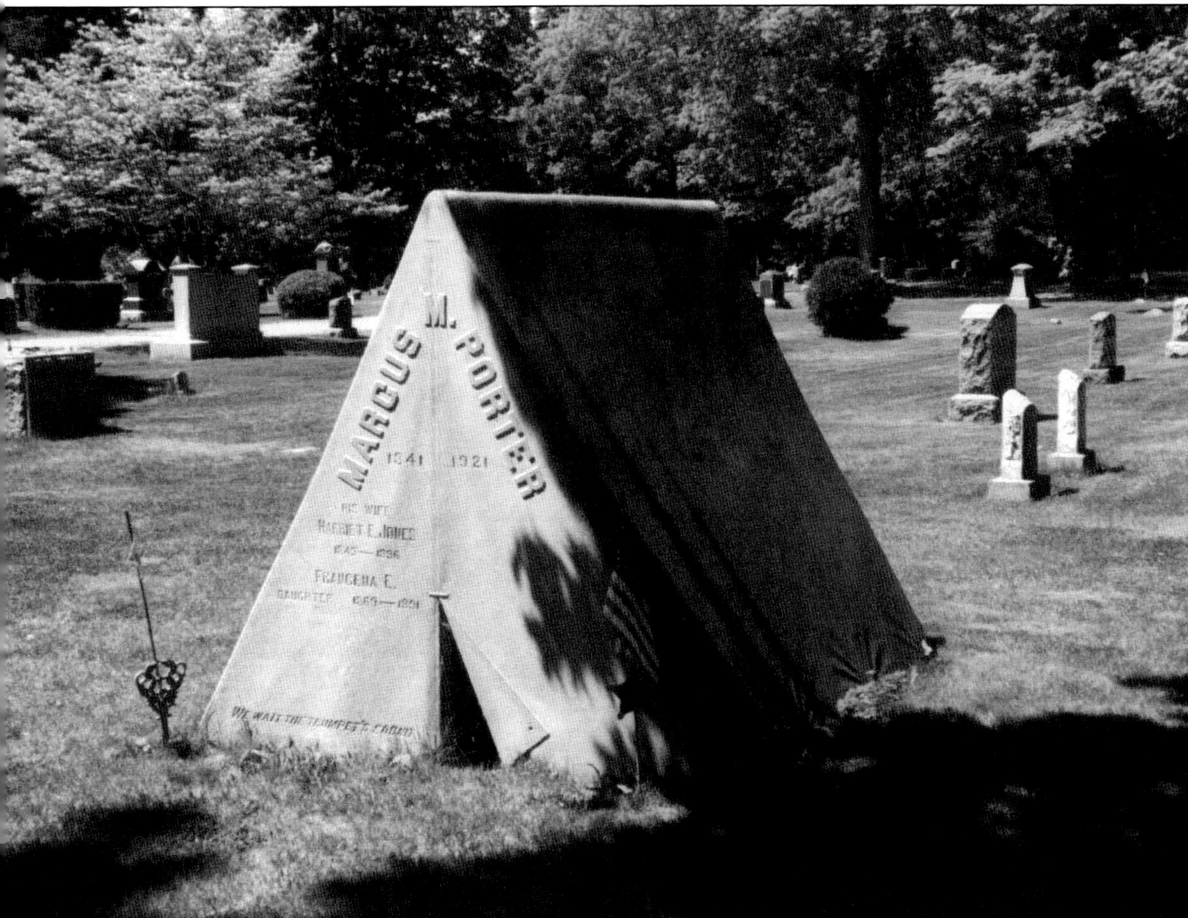

THE GRAVESTONE OF MARCUS PORTER AND FAMILY, AT THE EVERGREEN CEMETERY. This unique granite gravestone is in the shape of a Civil War A-frame tent. Porter's wife, Harriet E. (Jones) Porter (1843–1896), and their daughter Francena E. Porter (1869–1891) are interred here. (Author's collection.)

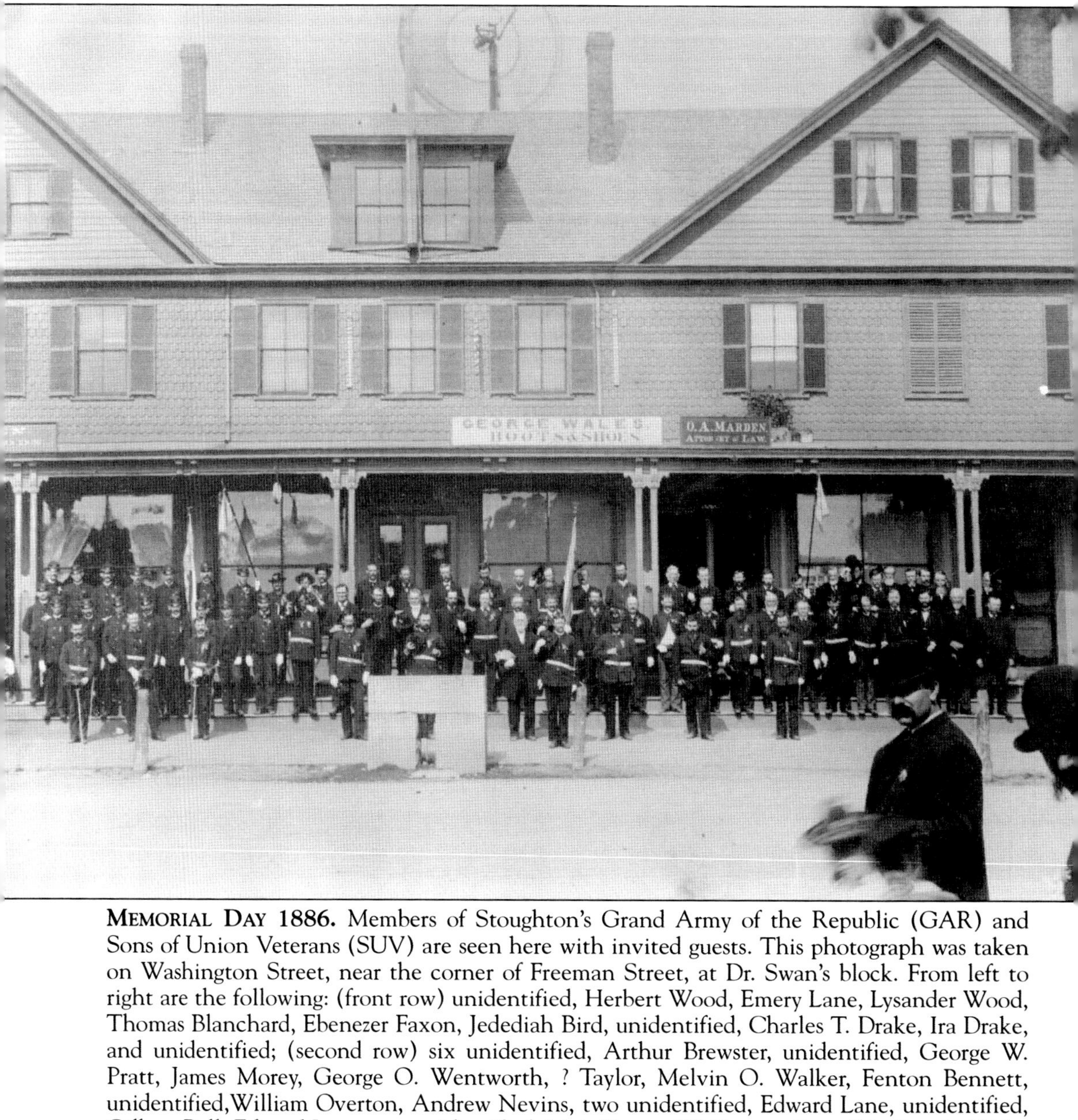

MEMORIAL DAY 1886. Members of Stoughton's Grand Army of the Republic (GAR) and Sons of Union Veterans (SUV) are seen here with invited guests. This photograph was taken on Washington Street, near the corner of Freeman Street, at Dr. Swan's block. From left to right are the following: (front row) unidentified, Herbert Wood, Emery Lane, Lysander Wood, Thomas Blanchard, Ebenezer Faxon, Jedediah Bird, unidentified, Charles T. Drake, Ira Drake, and unidentified; (second row) six unidentified, Arthur Brewster, unidentified, George W. Pratt, James Morey, George O. Wentworth, ? Taylor, Melvin O. Walker, Fenton Bennett, unidentified,William Overton, Andrew Nevins, two unidentified, Edward Lane, unidentified, Gilbert Bell, Edward Lunt, two unidentified, Maj. George W. Dutton, Rev. C.L. Rotch, Elisha C. Monk, and George F. Walker; (back row) Alvah Colburn, five unidentified, Conrad Bryant, unidentified, Herbert Holmes, unidentified, Frank Raymond, Howard Kimball, unidentified, James Hall, Altheus Brewster, James McKenny, ? Fisher, unidentified, ? Dyer, Thomas McHugh, Tisdale Drake, Edgar Hawes, Henry Collins, Abel Farrington, Henry C. Kimball, Rev. C.R. Tenney, William DeCosta, unidentified, Rev. Samuel B. Patterson, J.B. Gifford, three unidentified, and James W. Richardson.

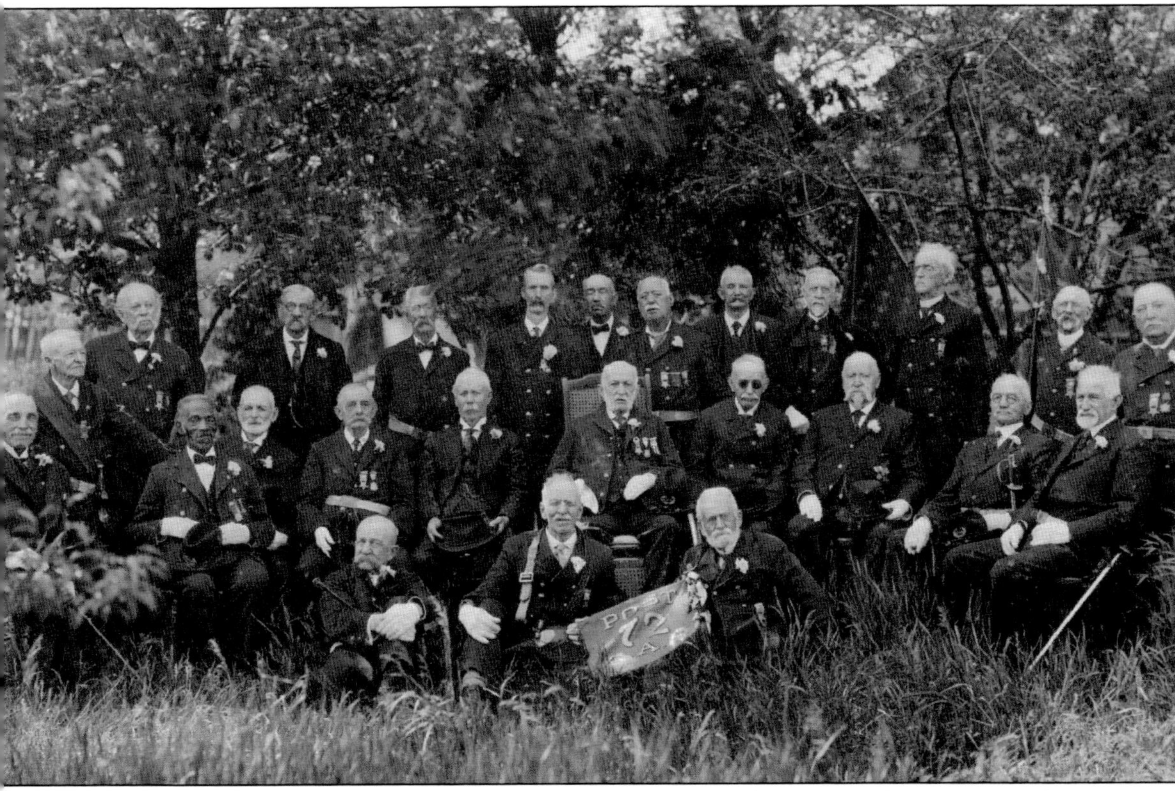

STOUGHTON'S POST 72, GAR. Unidentified members of Stoughton's Post 72 pose *c.* 1915.

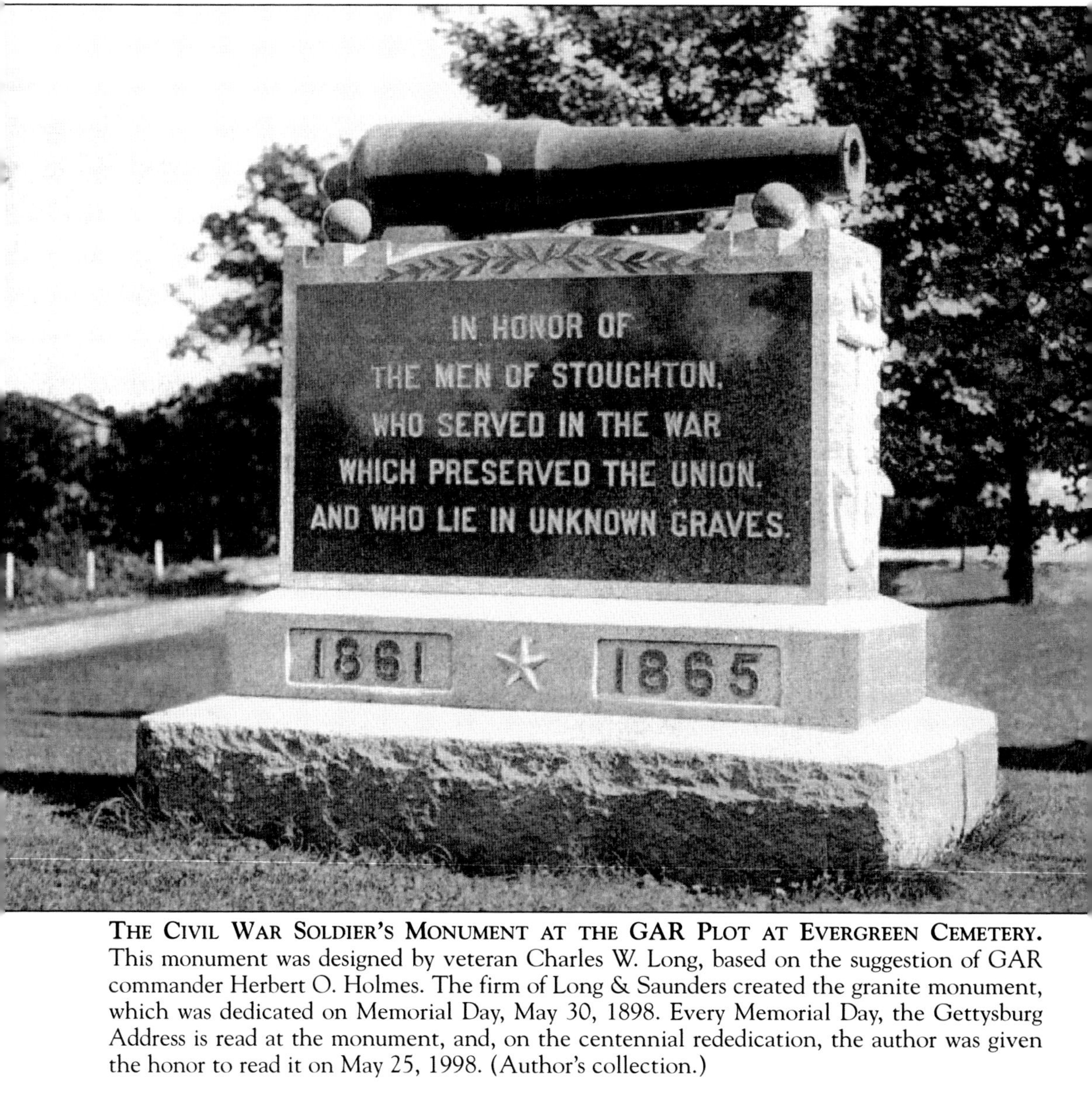

THE CIVIL WAR SOLDIER'S MONUMENT AT THE GAR PLOT AT EVERGREEN CEMETERY. This monument was designed by veteran Charles W. Long, based on the suggestion of GAR commander Herbert O. Holmes. The firm of Long & Saunders created the granite monument, which was dedicated on Memorial Day, May 30, 1898. Every Memorial Day, the Gettysburg Address is read at the monument, and, on the centennial rededication, the author was given the honor to read it on May 25, 1998. (Author's collection.)

Eight

Stoughton Factories

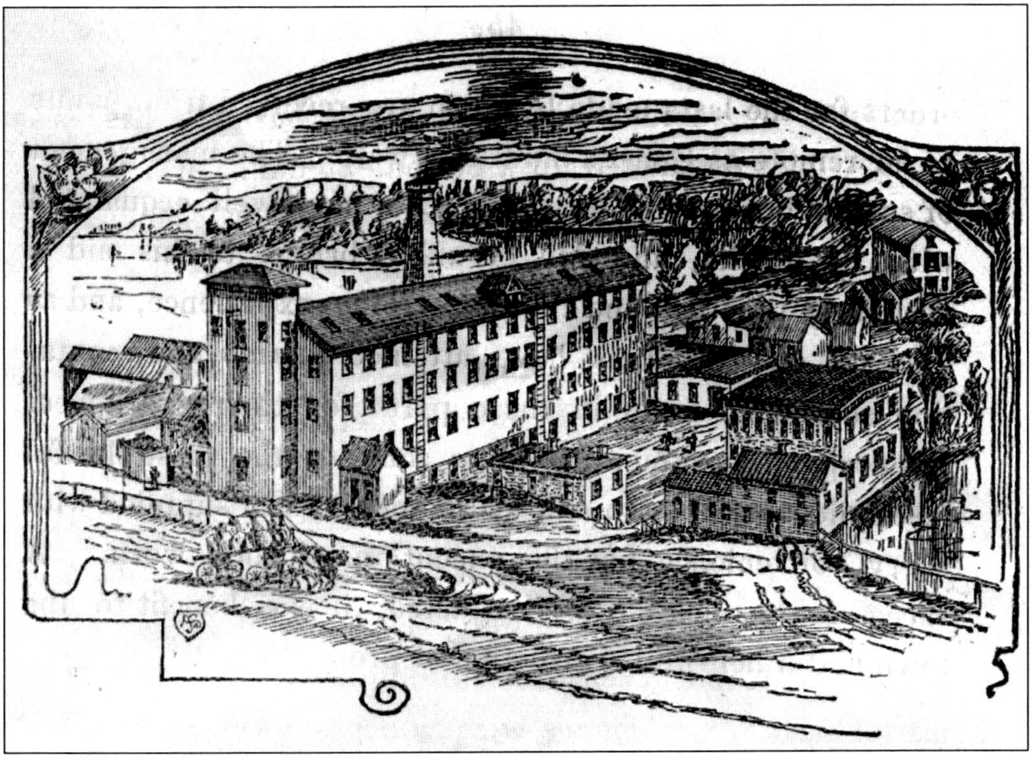

The French & Ward Factory in West Stoughton, c. 1890. This factory was located on Central Street across from the present Helen Hansen Elementary School. Col. Charles French purchased these mills in 1857 from Leonard Hodges, who operated a satinet mill there and was a founder of the Gay Cotton Manufacturing Company in 1813. Colonel French later teamed with Henry Ward and established the French & Ward Woolen Mills. This later became French & Ward Mills in West Stoughton.

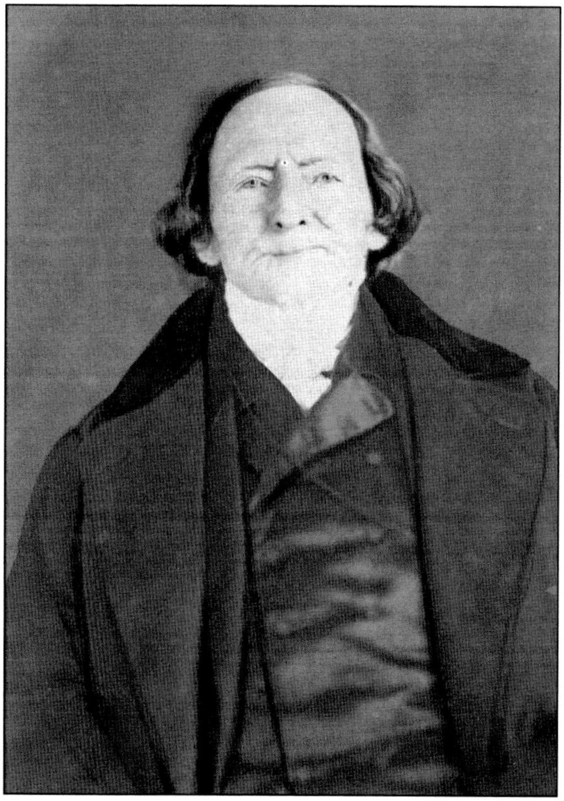

Col. Consider Southworth (1775–1863). Southworth was one of the primitive shoe manufacturers in the early 19th century. He was said to have purchased the right to peg shoes, which was a new invention. He served as colonel in the Stoughton Militia, which was called into active service in the War of 1812; however, they were never called into action. He was an early member and past master of the Rising Star Lodge of Masons (1814–1815). In 1823, he started a cotton-thread factory and, later, a factory that produced cotton cord of various colors used to finish the tops of boots and shoes. These cords were made by the Southworth family until 1857, after the invention of the sewing machine. The Southworth factory made the first cotton cord ever manufactured in Massachusetts solely by waterpower.

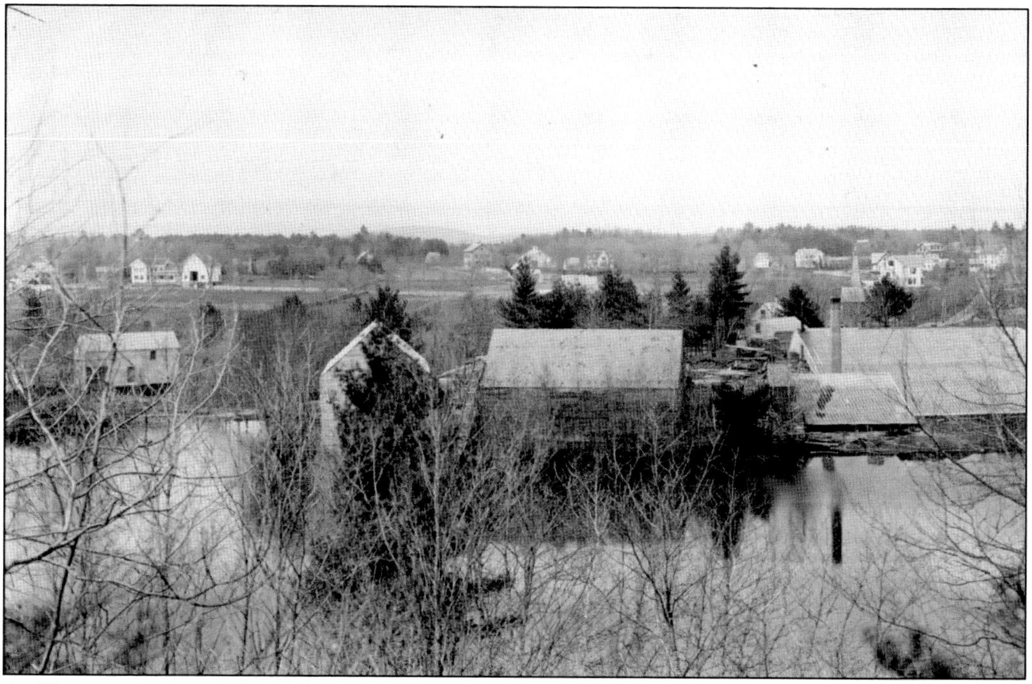

A View from the Hill behind Consider Southworth's Pond in West Stoughton. Southworth's mills can be seen in the foreground. In the distance are Central and Canton Streets.

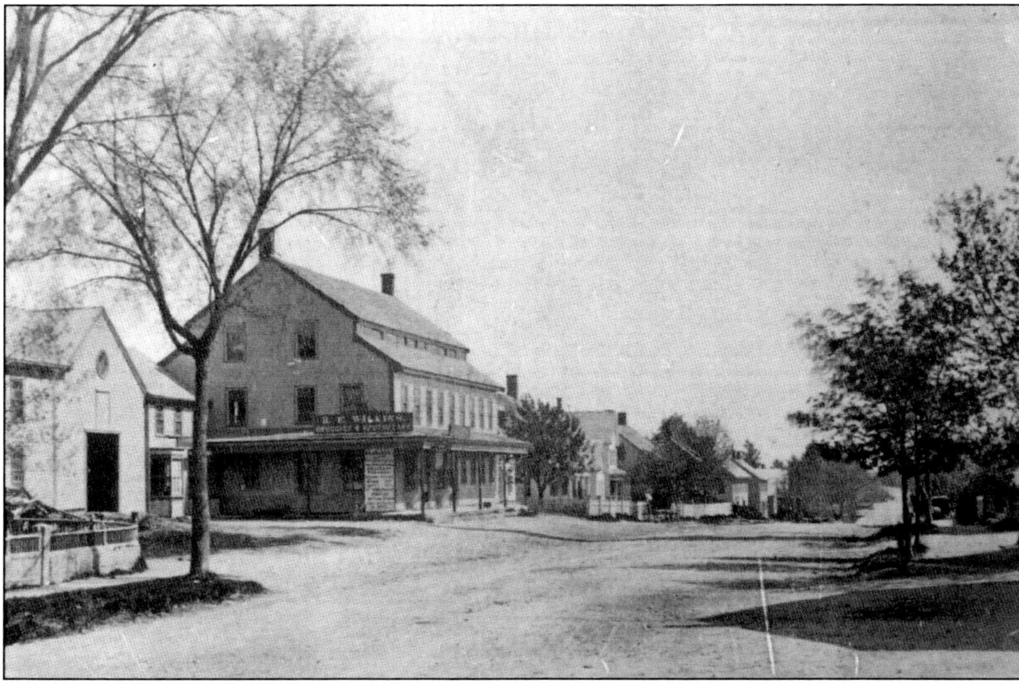

A View down Washington Street Showing the Old Boot Factory and Barn of Martin Wales on the Left. This was later occupied by Henry E. Wilkins Drug Store, as seen in the photograph. George Wales ran his boot and shoe company, occupying the upper story, *c.* 1870. The factory structure was later converted into apartments, which serve its present use.

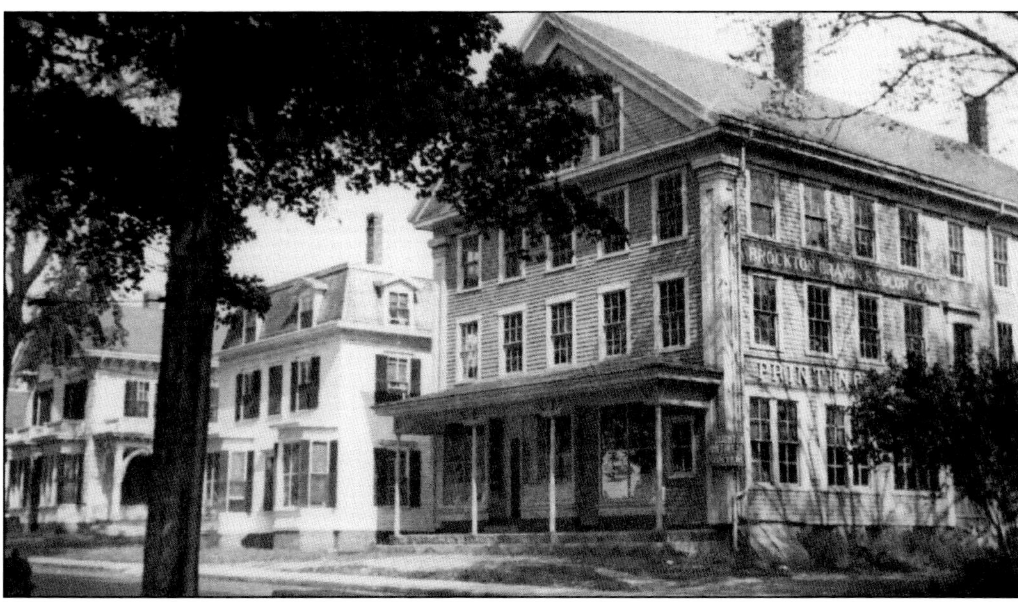

The James & Nathaniel Atherton Boot Manufacturing Shop, on Pleasant Street. This structure was built in 1851. It later housed the Stoughton News Sentinel and the Brockton Crayon Company. The building was razed in 1943, and the Randolph Saving Bank now occupies the site.

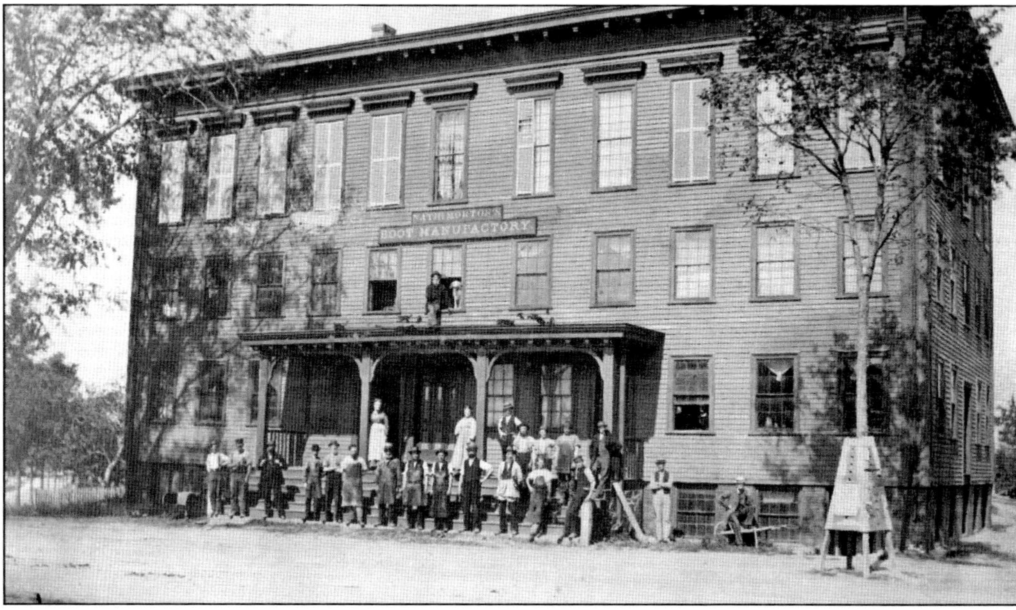

NATHANIEL MORTON'S FACTORY AT MORTON SQUARE, C. 1875. This building, constructed in 1858, was the second factory of Nathaniel Morton. The original location was the west side of the railroad tracks at the intersection of Summer and Wyman Streets. The Rising Star Masonic Lodge met in this building starting on March 17, 1859. The lodge purchased the factory building in 1885 and had it moved across the railroad tracks in the late 1880s by oxen. The building was razed in 1979 after the lodge moved out.

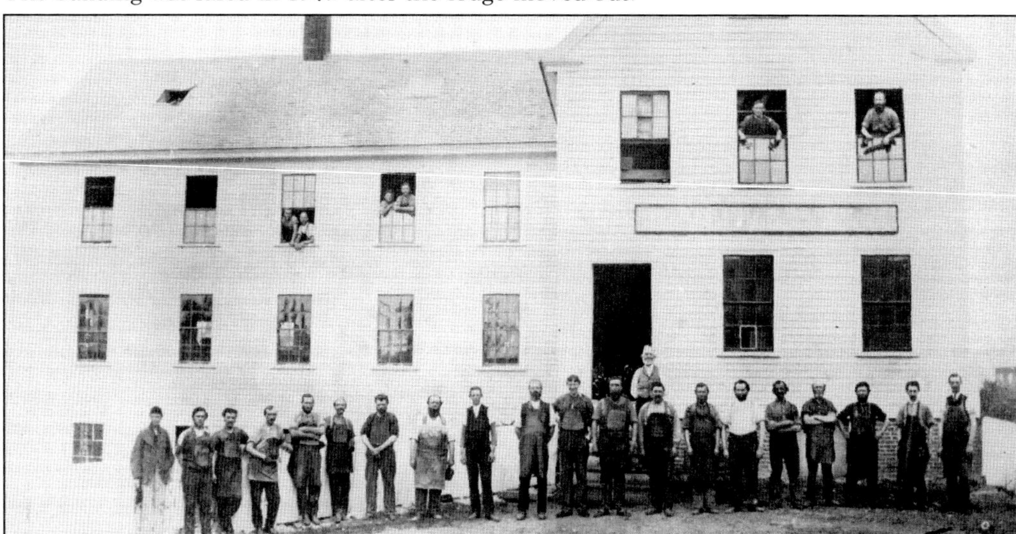

EMPLOYEES AT THE DANIEL FRENCH BOOT AND SHOE FACTORY, C. 1872. From left to right are the following: (front row) unidentified, Loring Tilden, Leon Babb, Horatio Snow, Ben Hall, James McMellen, Bill Hayden, Charles Hill, Eben Williamson, John French, Thomas Vanston, Israel Lamb, William Taylor, Alden Beals, Henry Staples, John Hooper, Eliphalet Elmes, Enos Gill, Wales French (later the first librarian of the Stoughton Public Library), and Hiram Smith; (standing to the right of the door frame) factory proprietor Daniel French; (in the windows) Tom Bright, Henry Loring, Frank Bell, George Bell, Horace Tower, and ? Spiller.

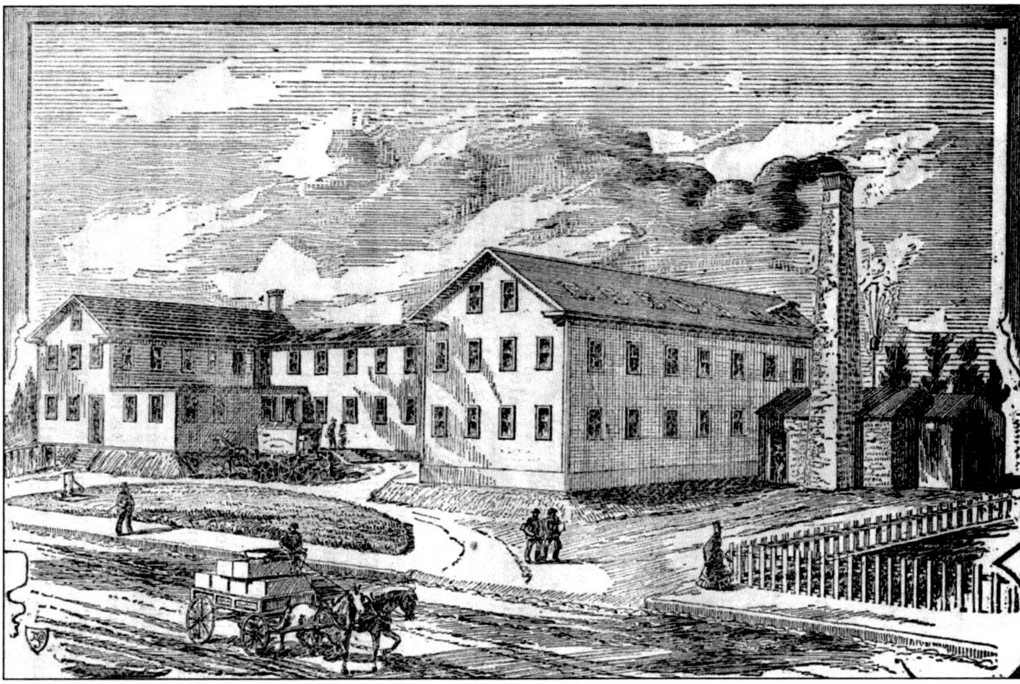

THE UPHAM BROTHERS SHOE FACTORY AT LINCOLN AND PLEASANT STREET, C. 1885. The factory building farthest north on Pleasant Street was built in 1872 and produced men's boots. The factory of H.B. Crane (left) would later be combined to produce this boot.

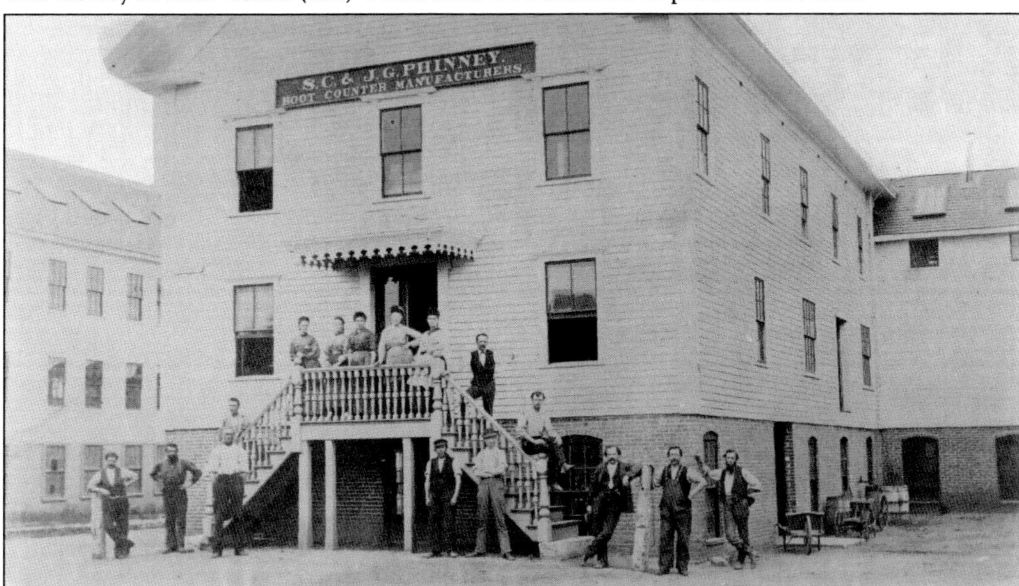

EMPLOYEES OF THE SYLVANUS C. AND JOHN GREENLEAF PHINNEY COUNTER FACTORY, C. 1875. From left to right are the following: (front row) William Welch, Cornelius Healey, Sullivan Burnham, John Howard, Timothy Toomey, Sylvanus C. Phinney (proprietor), Edward Lane, and Al Reed; (back row, on stairs) Henry Stearns, Hattie Loring, two unidentified, Mary Hurley, Maggie Leary, John Greenleaf Phinney (proprietor), and Emery Lane. Many buildings from this old factory are still to be seen on Summer Street.

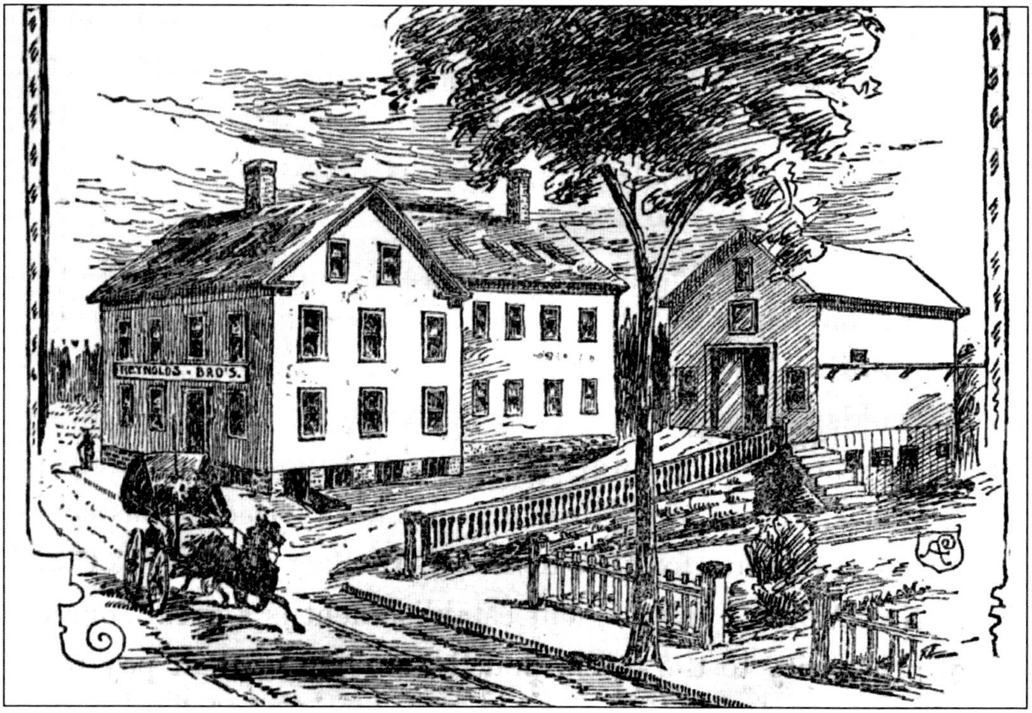

THE REYNOLDS BROTHERS SHOE SHOP IN STOUGHTON, c. 1885. This factory was located on the corner of Lincoln and Washington Streets.

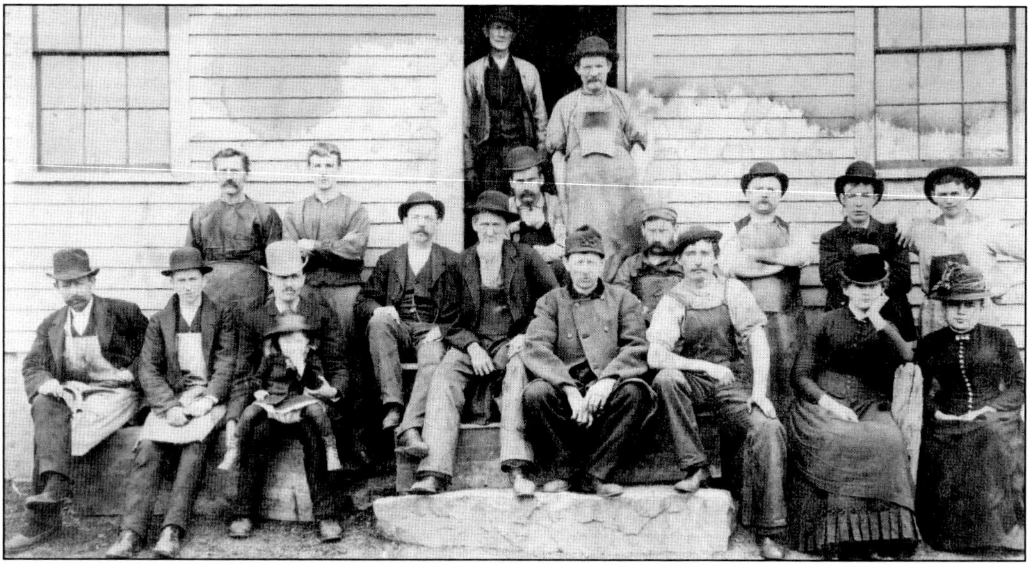

EMPLOYEES OF THE REYNOLDS SHOE SHOP, RUN BY ELLERY AND FRANK REYNOLDS. This photograph of employees was taken *c.*1880–1886. From left to right are the following: (front row) Alphoso Mead, William Toomey, Ellery P. Reynolds (holding Stella Reynolds), John Sullivan, David Rumrey, George Rumrey, William Sullivan, Sarah Morey, and Emma Taylor; (back row) Howard Kimball, Maurice Dryer, George Faunce, Brine O'Donnell (in doorway, standing), Tom Roach (standing in front of door), Abel Farrington, John Meade, John Riley, and John Roache.

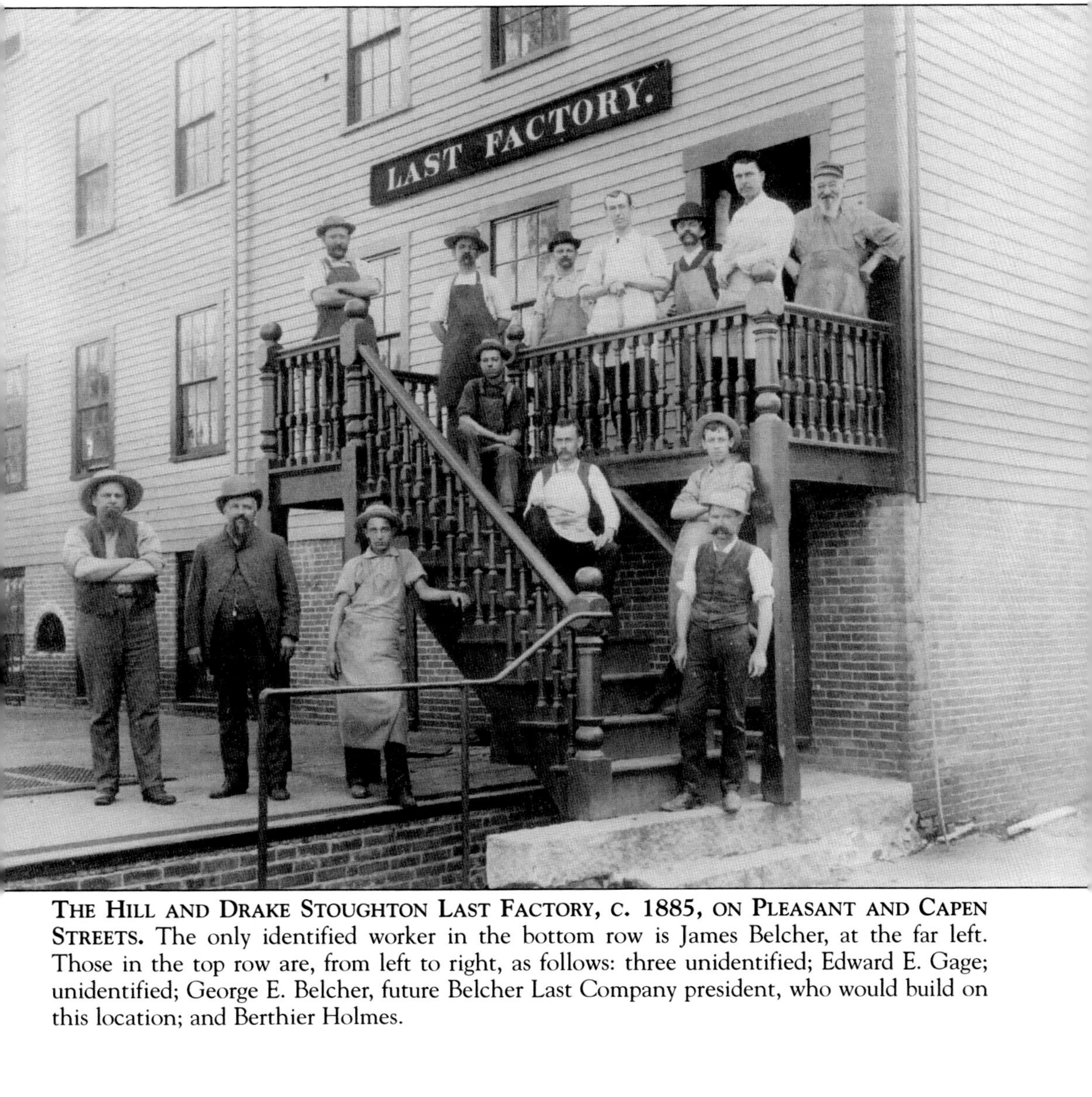

THE HILL AND DRAKE STOUGHTON LAST FACTORY, C. 1885, ON PLEASANT AND CAPEN STREETS. The only identified worker in the bottom row is James Belcher, at the far left. Those in the top row are, from left to right, as follows: three unidentified; Edward E. Gage; unidentified; George E. Belcher, future Belcher Last Company president, who would build on this location; and Berthier Holmes.

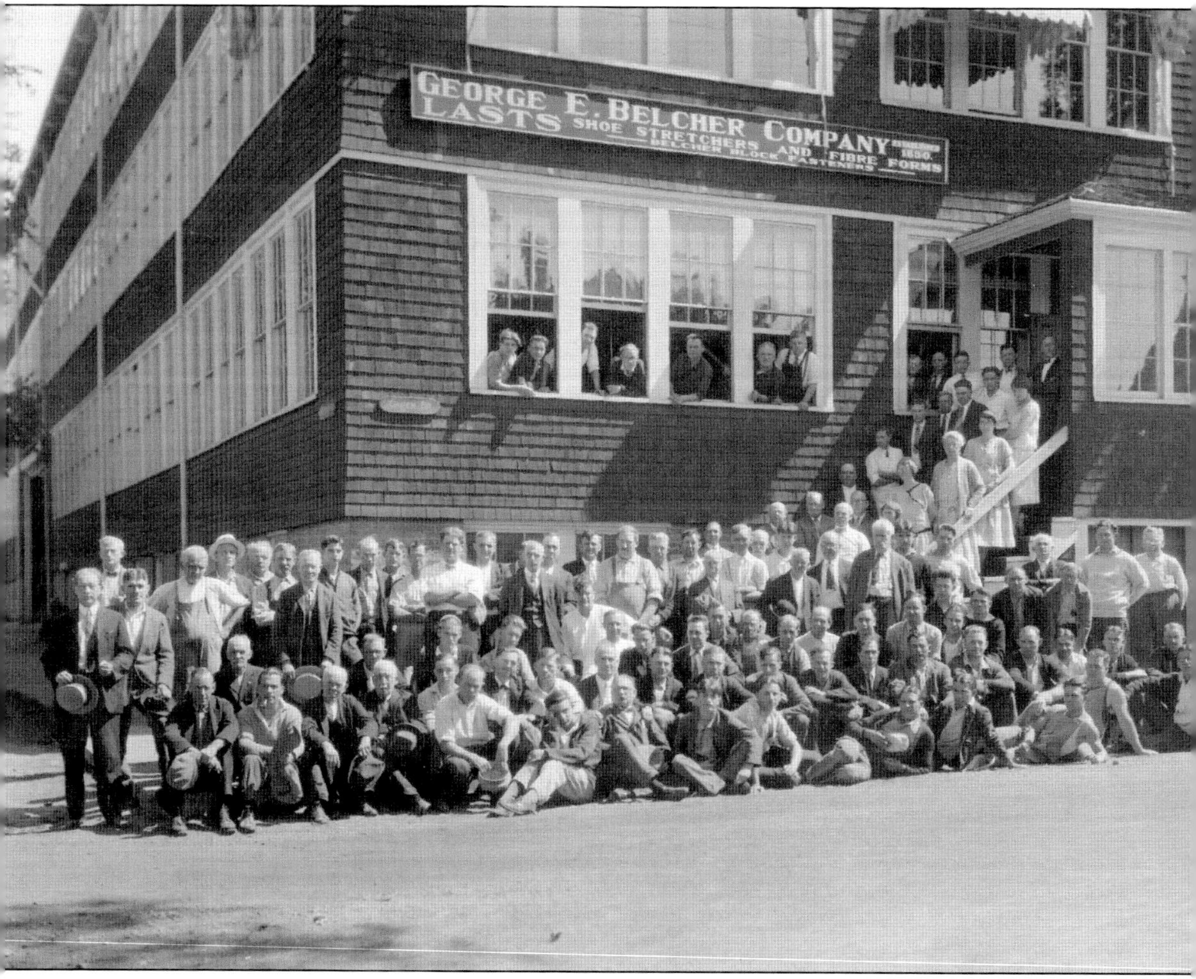

EMPLOYEES OF THE GEORGE E. BELCHER LAST COMPANY. Seen in this view are employees of the George E. Belcher Last Company at the corner of Capen and Pleasant Streets. Belcher built this factory in 1893, after acquiring the Walker & Phinney factory. This photograph was taken c. 1930 by George Adolph Gerard, a Stoughton photographer. Note the sign for Belcher's that reads, "George E. Belcher Company, Established 1850. Lasts, Shoe Stretchers and Fibre Forms, Belcher Block Fasteners."

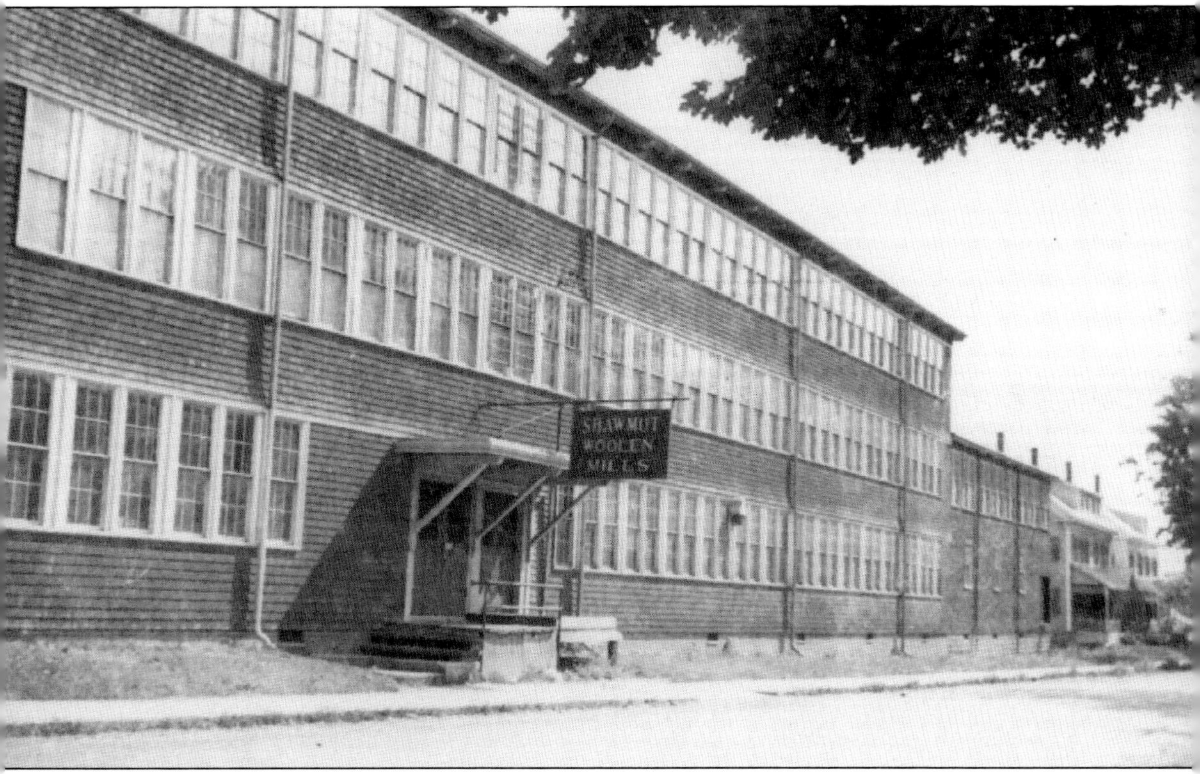

THE SHAWMUT MILLS FACTORY. This factory was built in 1916 on Canton Street.

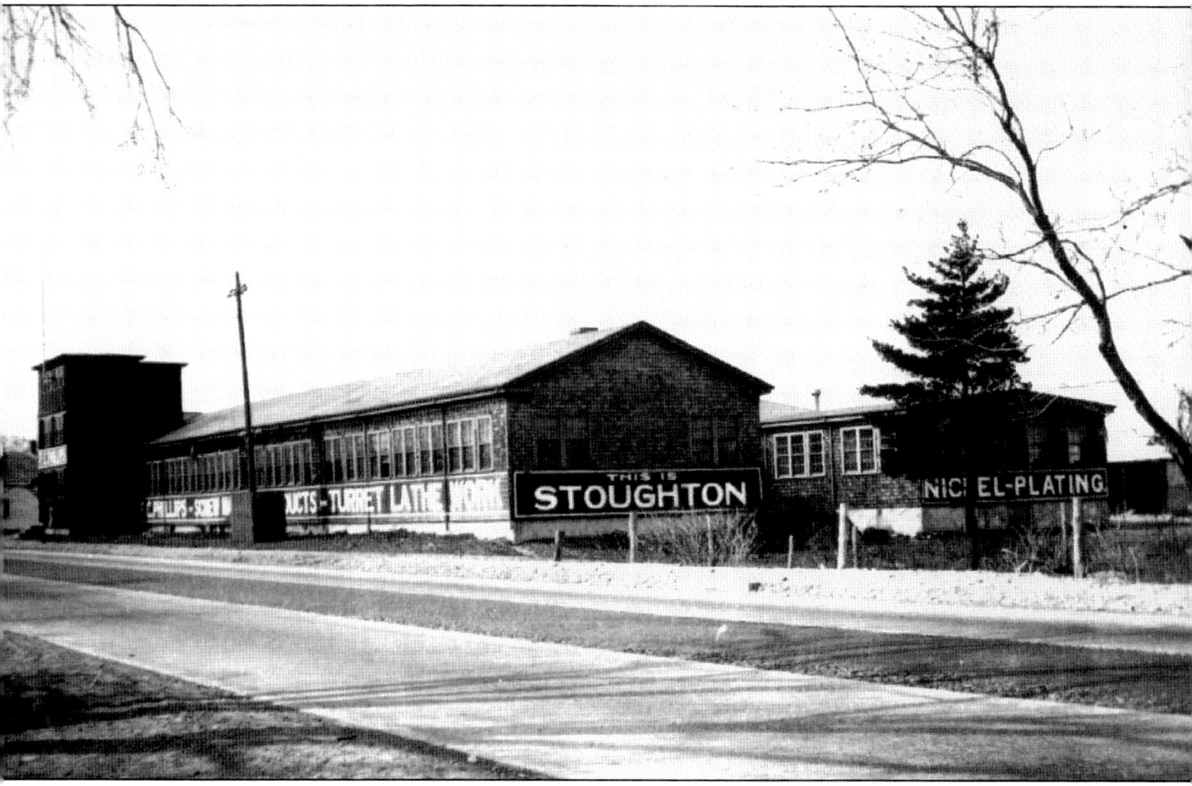

THE F.C. PHILLIPS COMPANY, AT 473 WASHINGTON STREET. The Phillips factory was built in 1916 by the company founder Fred C. Phillips (1884–1963), when he brought his screw machines to Stoughton in 1911. This company became well known for producing detachable golf spikes.

Nine

STOUGHTON BUSINESSES

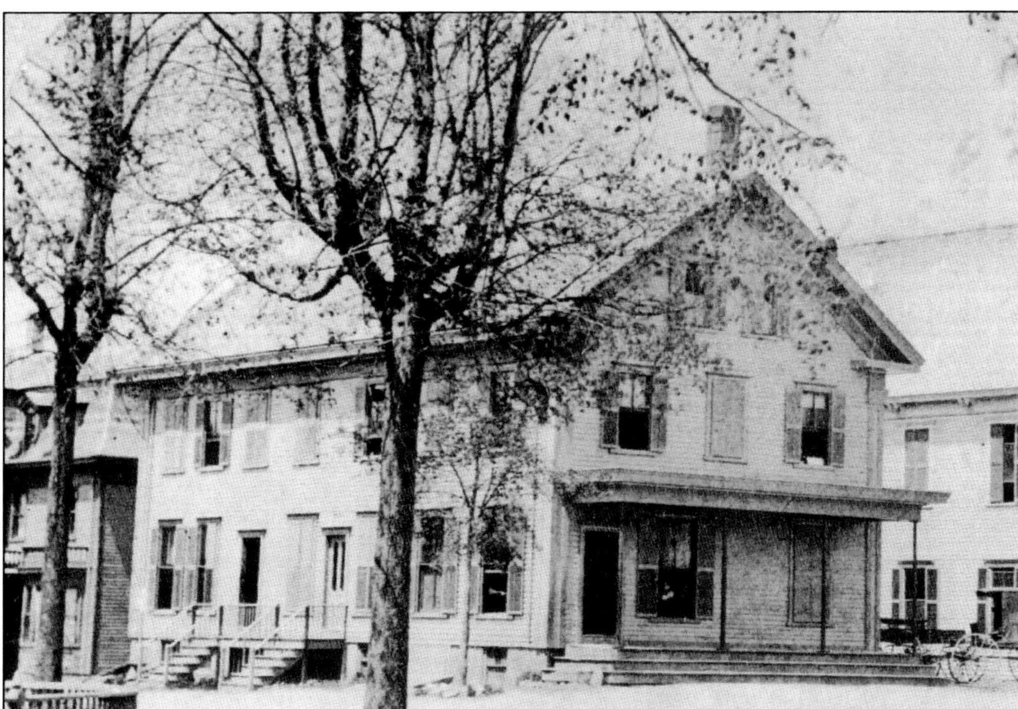

LEONARD DRAKE'S HOTEL AT WASHINGTON STREET AND RAILROAD AVENUE. This hotel was built in 1860 and burned down in the fire of 1880. The original Drake and White Hotel moved to Summer Street in 1858–1859 to make room for the new building.

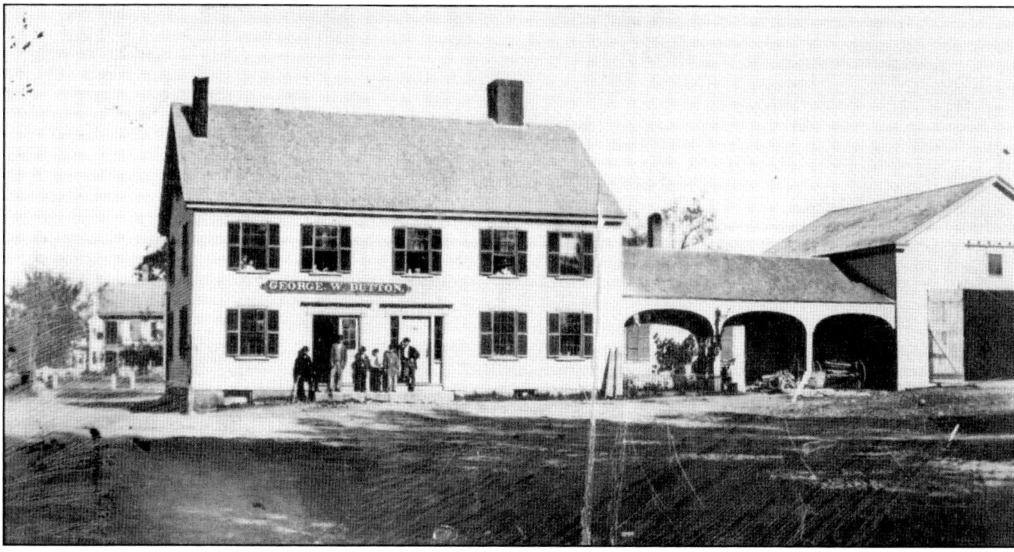

THE LEMUEL DICKERMAN RESIDENCE AND, LATER, FLYNT AND DUTTON STORES. This building, located at Washington Street and what is now Freeman Street, was known as Dickerman's, the Maj. Lemuel Gay place, and the Levi Flint and Company. At the time of this photograph, Maj. George Dutton operated a business here. This building burned to the ground on April 28, 1892, when it was known as Dr. Swan's Block. Afterwards, the house was occupied by Massena H. Ballou, and the store was occupied by Flint and Company. This was the Stoughton Post Office in 1829.

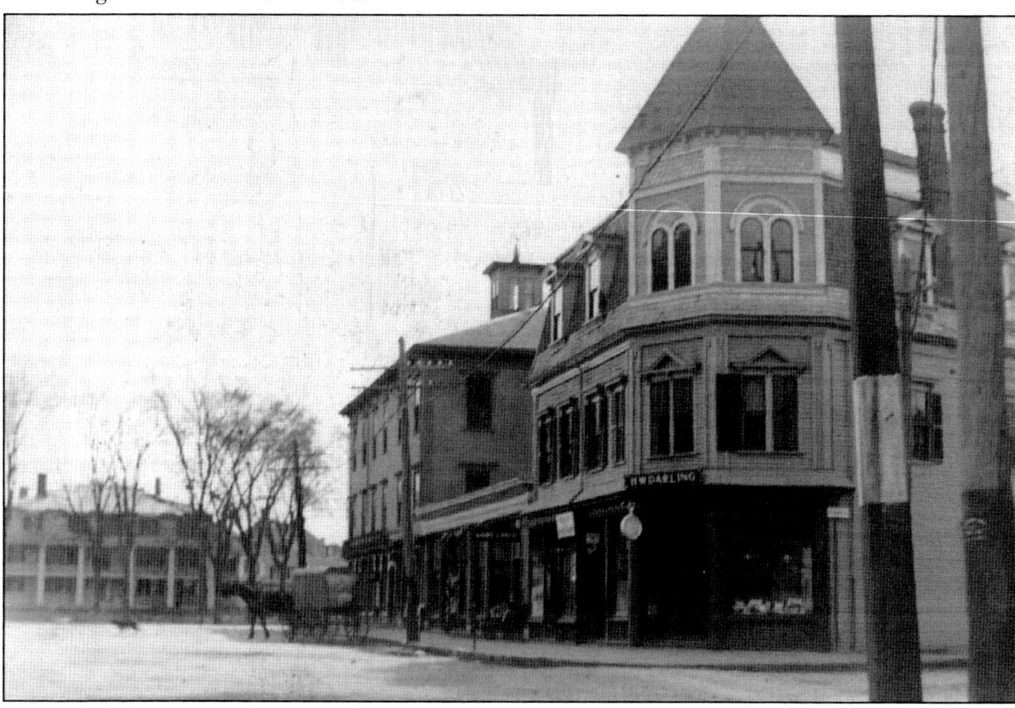

HENRY W. DARLING'S BLOCK, AT THE SOUTHWEST CORNER OF WYMAN AND WASHINGTON STREET. This building was once the home to jeweler Henry W. Darling, who built it in 1885. The structure survived until 1949, when it was razed. (Author's collection.)

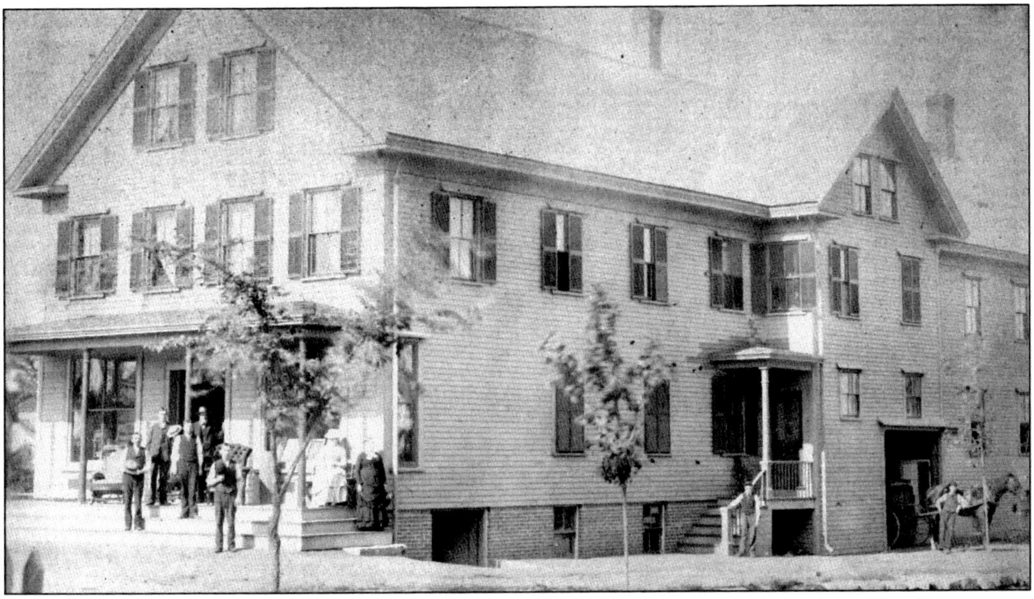

The Withington & Lowe Furniture and Funeral Home, built on Porter Street in 1860. This structure was originally the Phineas M. Withington knife factory, located on Porter Street, near the railroad tracks. In 1860, Withington acquired the business of the late Samuel Clapp, who was an undertaker and furniture dealer in Stoughton. The business later involved his nephew Horace Lowe. Additional partners included Webster Smith and Michael F. Powers. The business became known as Lowe, Smith & Powers until the death of Webster Smith in 1916. From then on, the business operated as the Lowe & Powers Funeral Home. They moved from Porter Street to Monk Street in 1928. It is the oldest family-run business in Stoughton, now operating as Sheehan, Lowe & Powers Funeral Home.

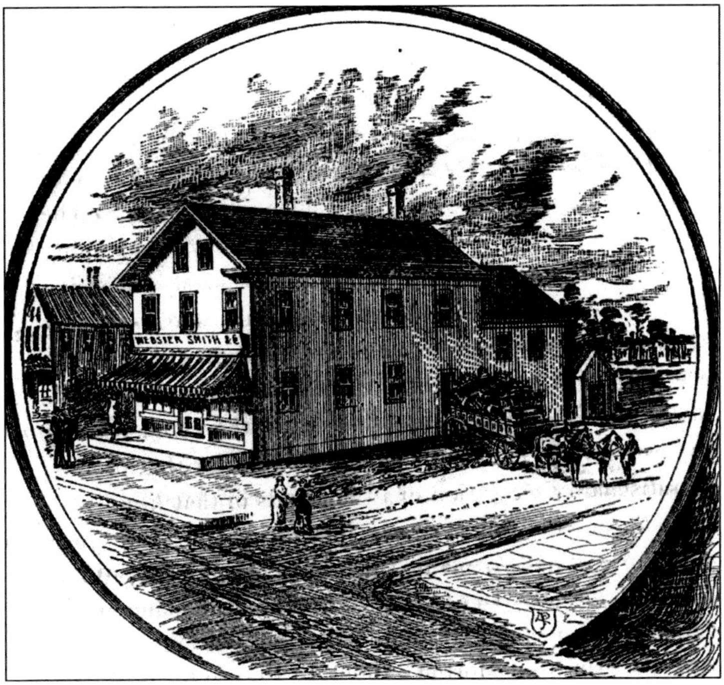

Webster Smith's Building for His Furniture Store and Undertaking Business. Smith built this structure in 1882 and, in 1891, offered competition to Withington & Lowe's undertaking business next door. They later became close business partners. This building, on the northwest corner of Porter and Roses Streets, was the home of Stoughton's famous Town Spa from 1955 to 1986.

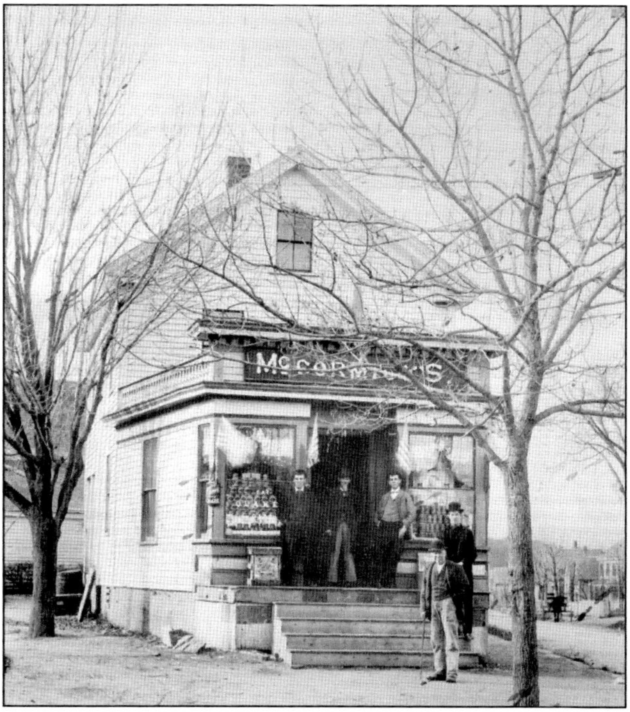

B. McCormick's Store, at the Corner of School and Canton Streets. From left to right are John Jordan, Brine McCormick, Thomas McCormick, Patrick Marron, and Joseph McDonough.

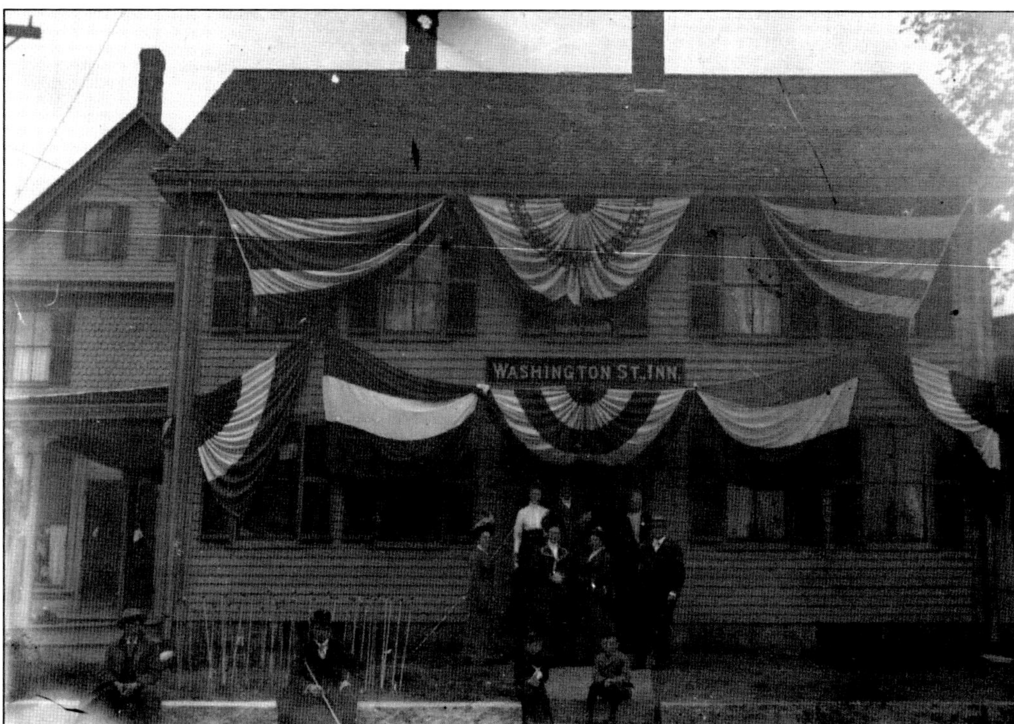

The Washington Street Inn, on Washington Street in Stoughton Square. This photograph shows unidentified visitors to the inn before 1900. The inn would soon after be moved to 703 Washington Street.

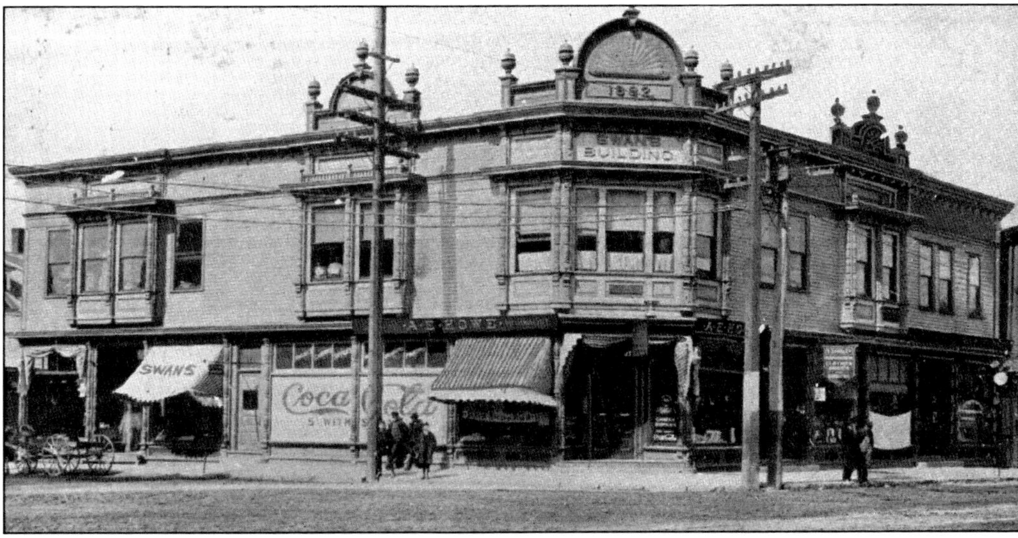

Swan's Building, at the Northwest Corner of Washington and Wyman Streets. This building, constructed in 1892, housed a variety of shops, from candy stores to a liquor store. It also housed Stoughton District Court under Judge Oscar A. Marden, who met on the upper floors. A fire in December 1969 caused this majestic building to disappear from Stoughton Square's landscape. (Author's collection.)

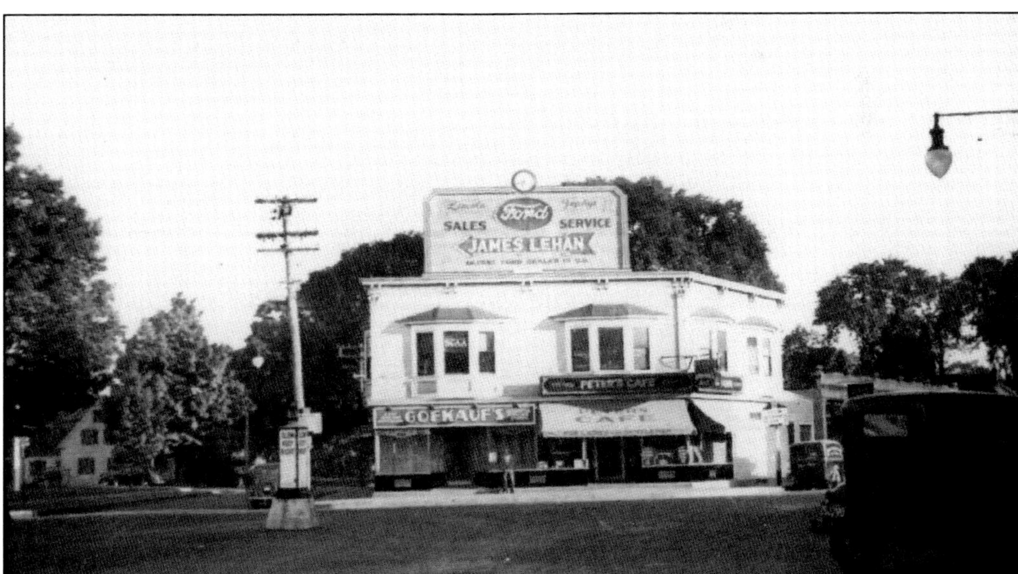

Britton's Block, on the Corner of Pearl and Washington Streets. This structure was built in 1899 by Henry W. Britton of Stoughton. The building has held insurance offices, a bank, a café, and an infamous adult bookstore, which Stoughton residents were able to remove. On this location once stood the home of James Swan, before it was removed after 1892.

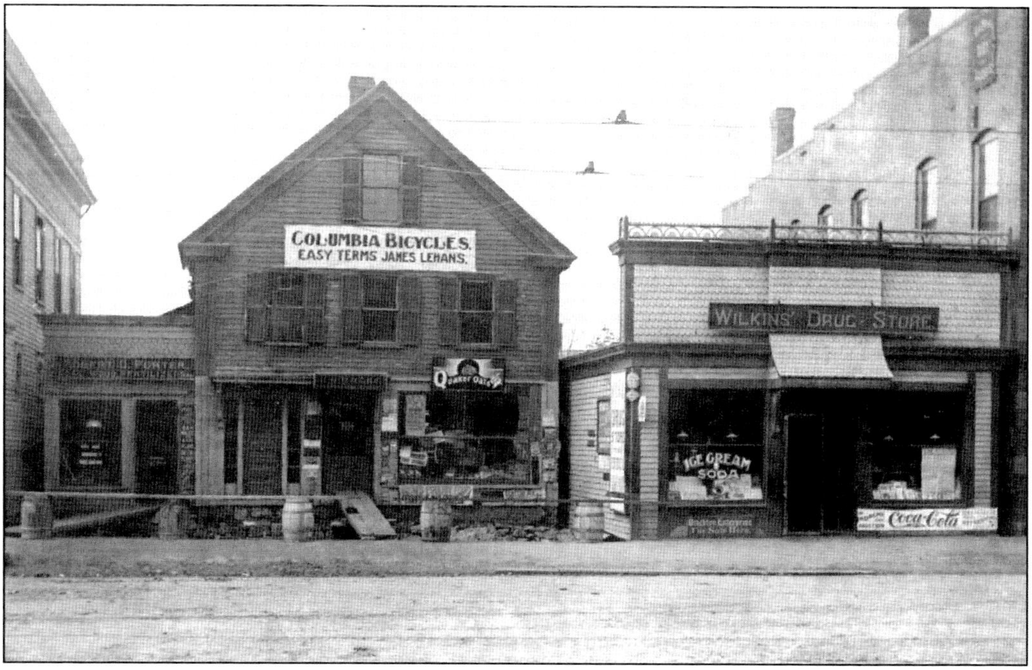

JAMES LEHAN'S BICYCLE SHOP, IN THE OLD LUCAS HOUSE ON WASHINGTON STREET. From left to right are Robert Porter's Coal Office, James Lehan's Columbia Bicycle Shop, and Wilkins Drug Store after 1886. James Lehan's bicycle shop would be his first success with promoting transportation.

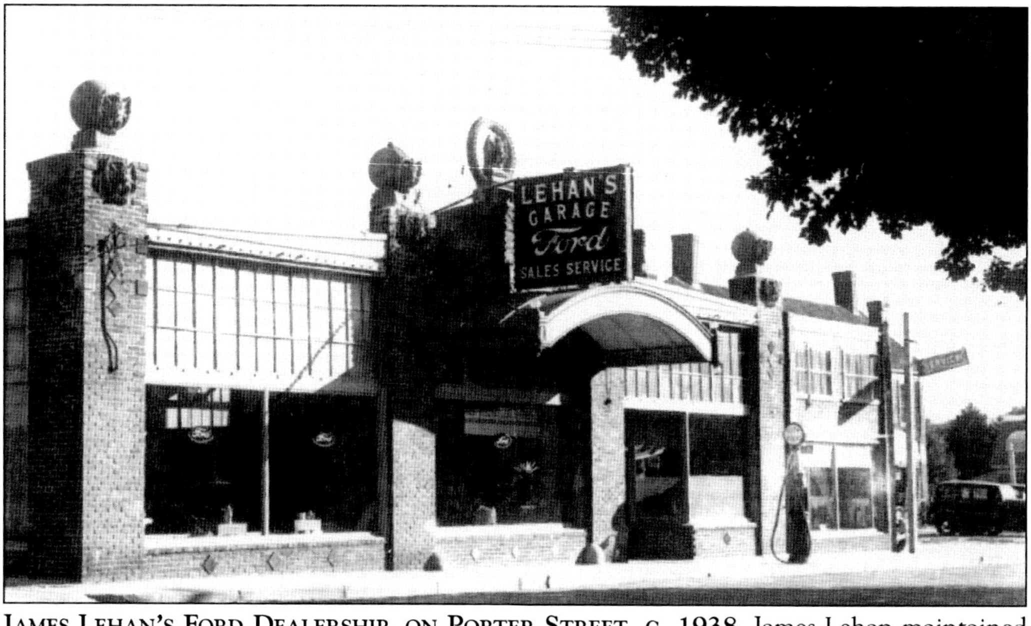

JAMES LEHAN'S FORD DEALERSHIP, ON PORTER STREET, C. 1938. James Lehan maintained the oldest running Ford dealership in America. He sold his first automobile to Henry W. Britton of Stoughton in 1904. In 1916, Lehan's built its first dealership and garage on Porter Street behind Monk's Cash Store. This location would remain the same until the 1970s. The U.S. post office would be built on the site.

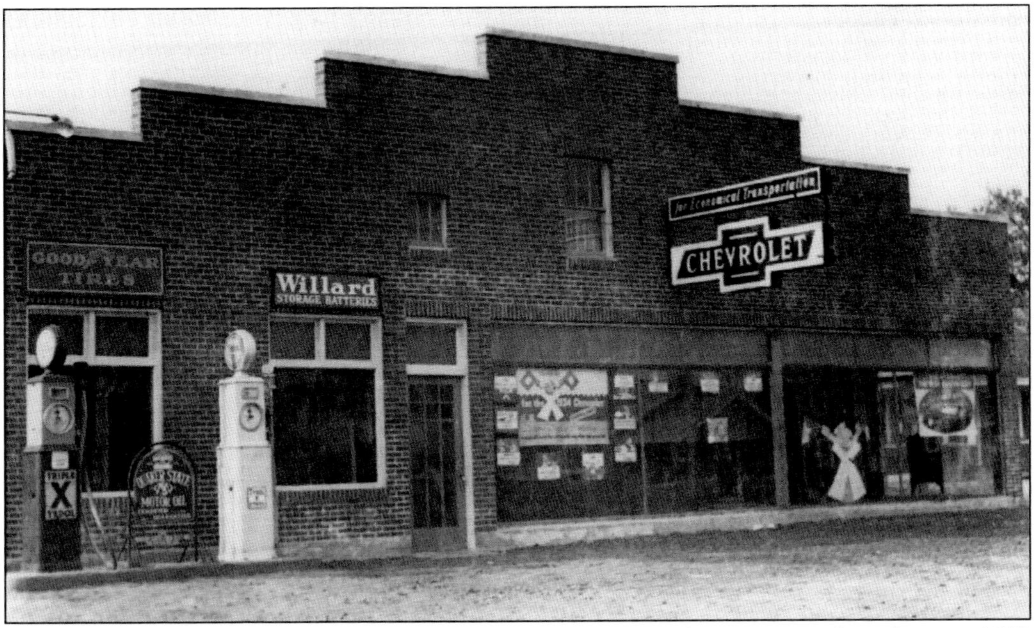

THE FRANK AND FRED SIMONDS CHEVY DEALERSHIP AND SHOWROOM. Seen here *c.* 1930 is Frank and Fred Simonds Chevy dealership, at 950 Washington Street in Stoughton. This former dealership is now home to Route 138 Auto Body.

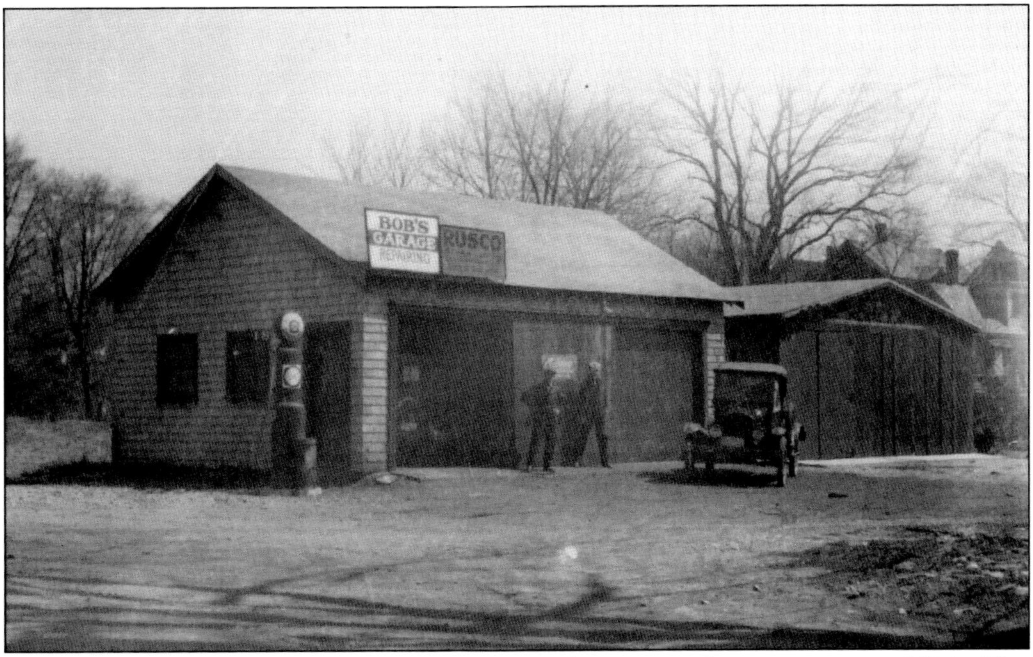

ROBERT IVALDI'S REPAIR GARAGE, ON MONK STREET IN STOUGHTON, C. 1930. This business, run in this small garage, was later moved to Canton.

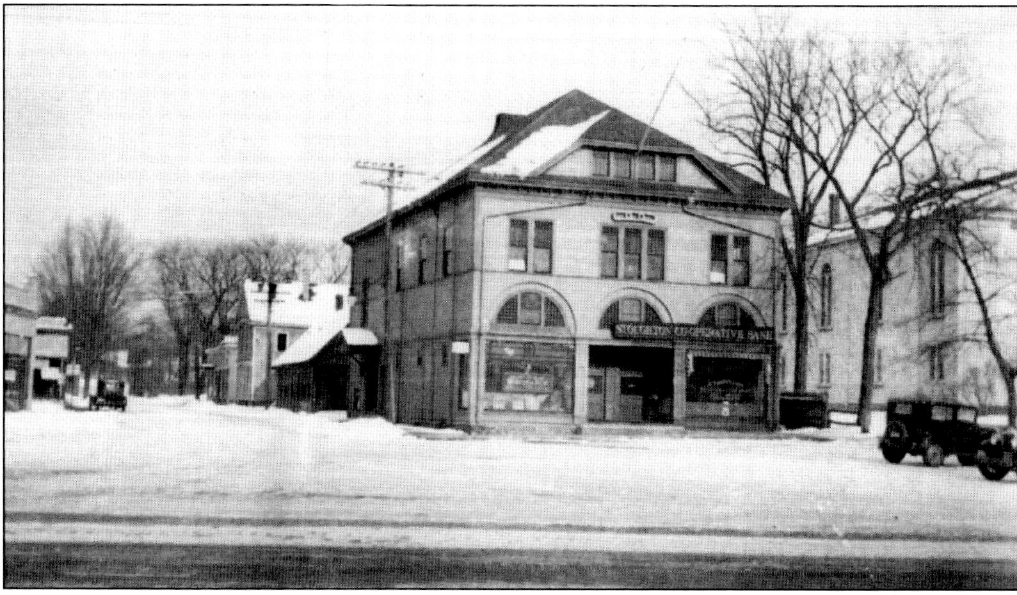

The Independent Order of Odd Fellows Block and Holbrook's Store, Built in 1892 at the Corner of Freeman and Washington Streets. This building was home to the Odd Fellows of Stoughton, instituted in 1845. At the time of this photograph, the Stoughton Cooperative bank was located in this building, which is now the Pacheco hardware store.

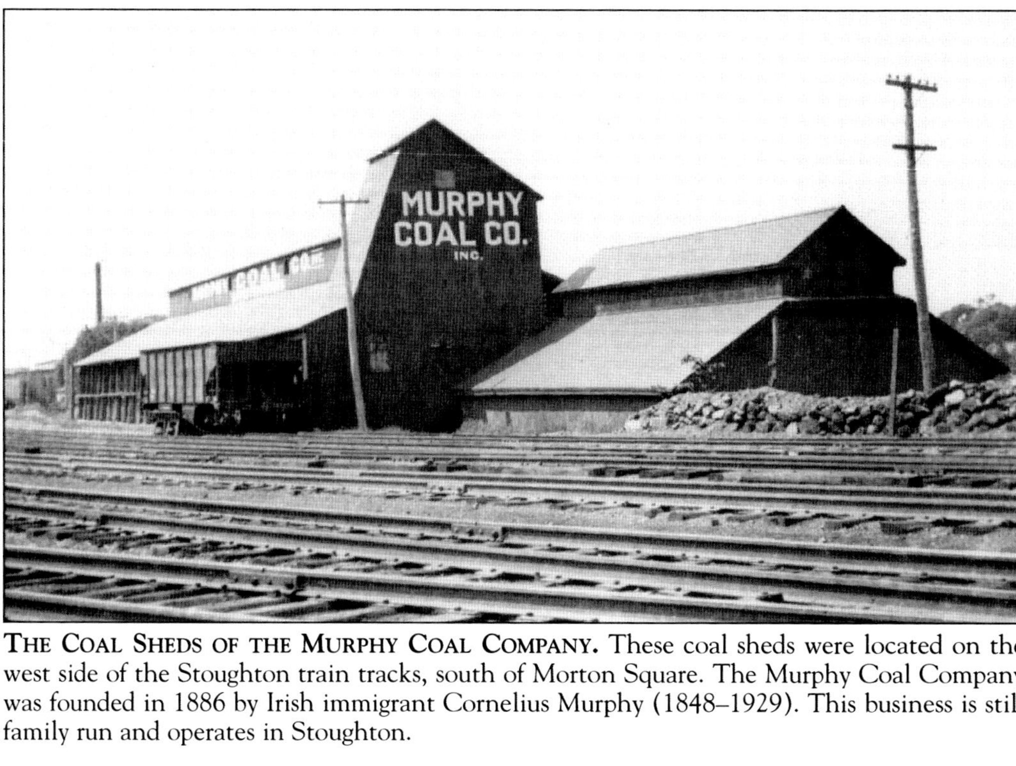

The Coal Sheds of the Murphy Coal Company. These coal sheds were located on the west side of the Stoughton train tracks, south of Morton Square. The Murphy Coal Company was founded in 1886 by Irish immigrant Cornelius Murphy (1848–1929). This business is still family run and operates in Stoughton.

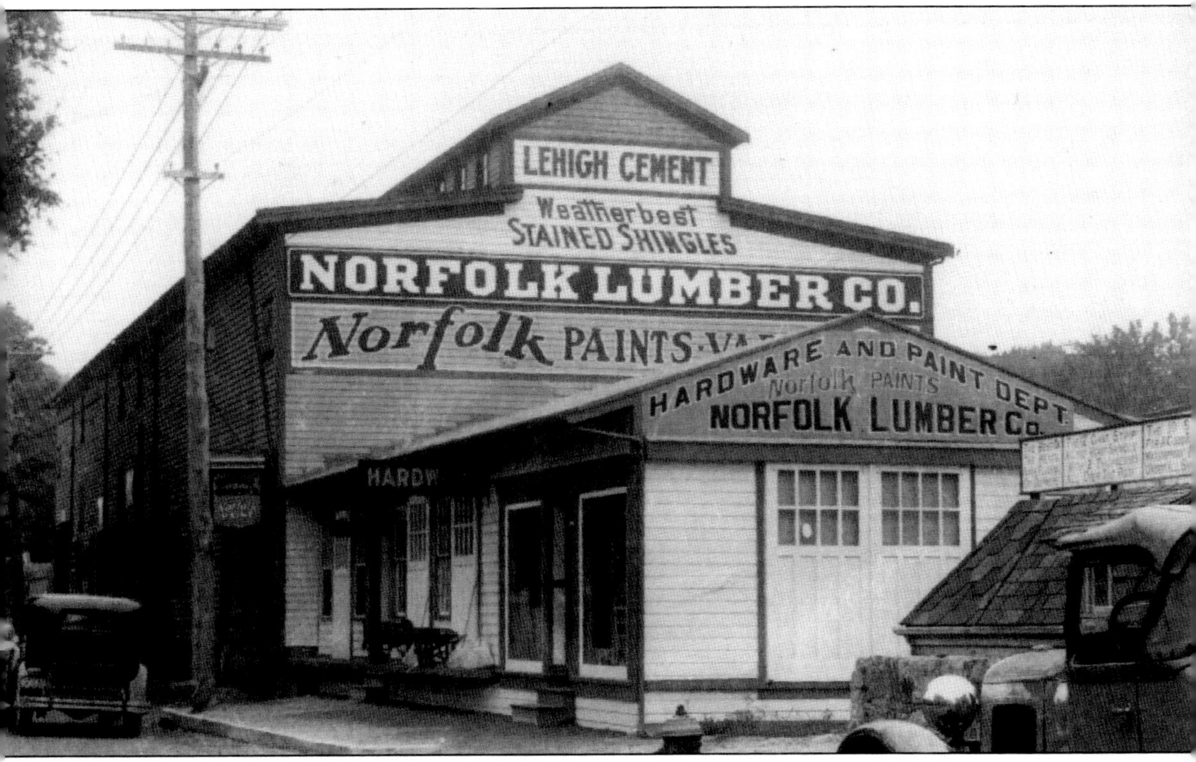

THE NORFOLK LUMBER COMPANY, AT CANTON AND PORTER STREETS. A lumber company operated on this site for many years, owned by Ellery P. Clapp, Charles Dodge, and Henry Lyons. This structure burned down in the late 1960s, like other Stoughton landmarks.

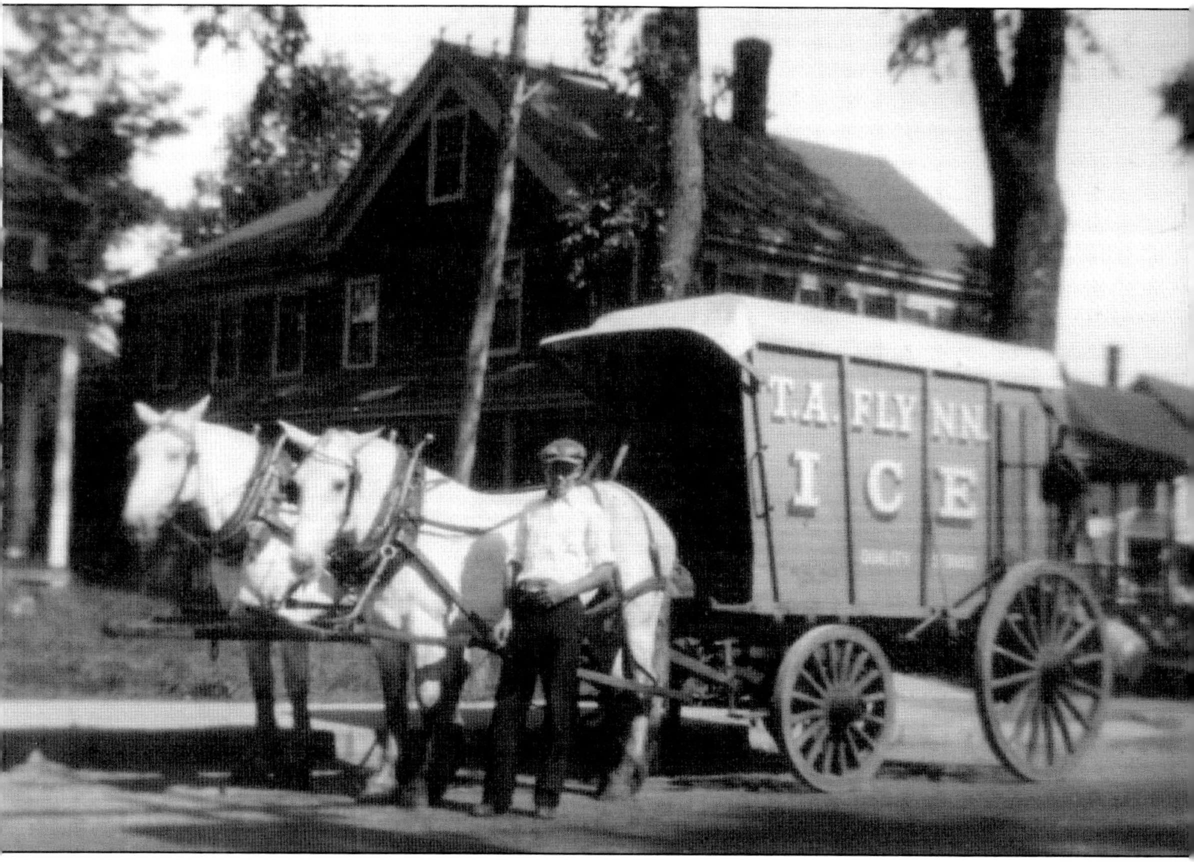

T.A. Flynn's Ice Truck in Front of the Old Washington Street Inn in the 1940s. This was one of the last horse-drawn businesses conducted in Stoughton.

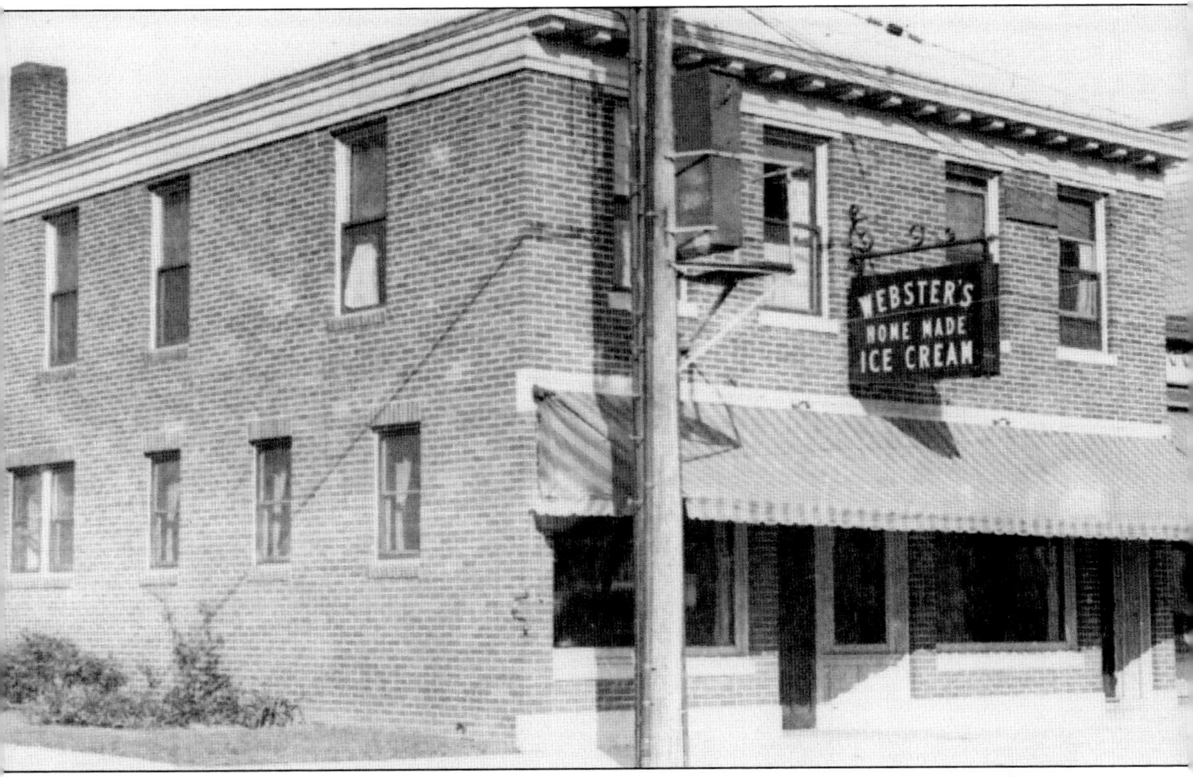

WEBSTER'S ICE-CREAM SHOP, ACROSS FROM THE STOUGHTON TOWN HALL ON PEARL STREET. Many Stoughton residents will fondly remember having an ice cream in Webster's shop. A candy store also run by the Websters was located next door.

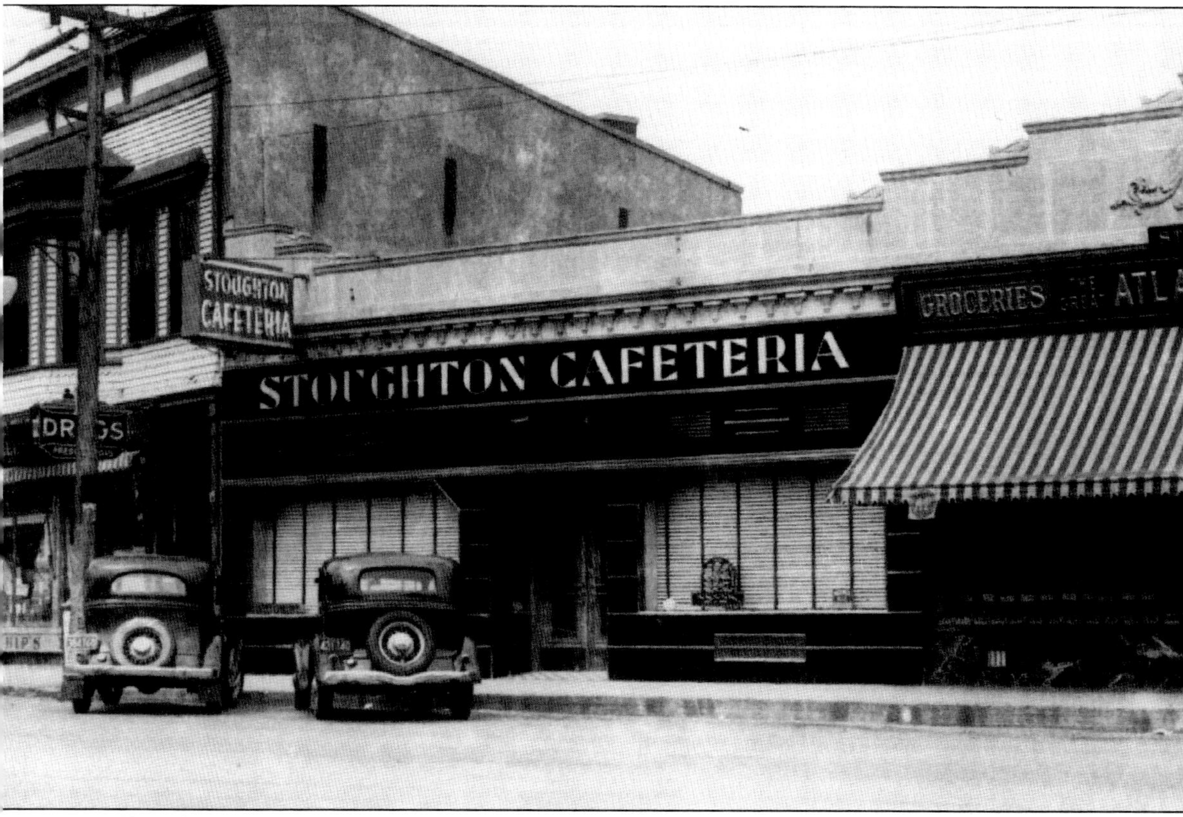

THE STOUGHTON CAFETERIA IN STOUGHTON SQUARE, C. 1940. This is one of the many photographs taken by the late John Cyrns Stiles of Stoughton from his Fotokraft studio across the square. This location has long been a site of restaurants in Stoughton Center.

Ten

STROLLING AROUND STOUGHTON

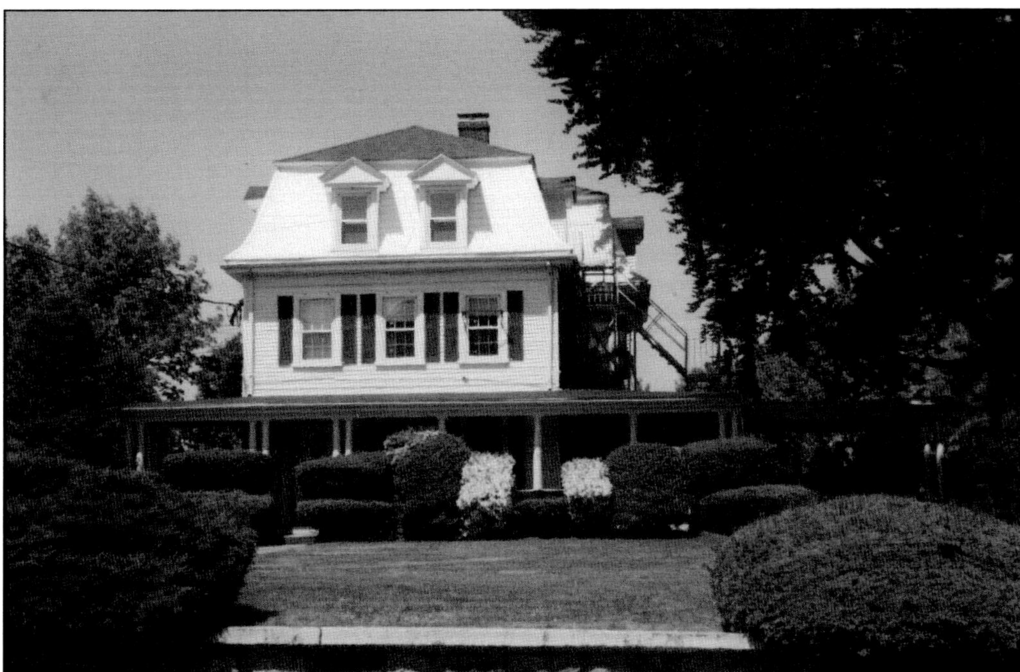

THE HOUSE OF GEORGE QUINCY CLIFFORD ON CENTRAL STREET. Clifford was president of the Belcher Last Company in 1912, when he set off for a business trip to Europe. He would board the RMS *Titanic* at Southampton, England, and perish in the icy waters of the Atlantic on April 15, 1912.

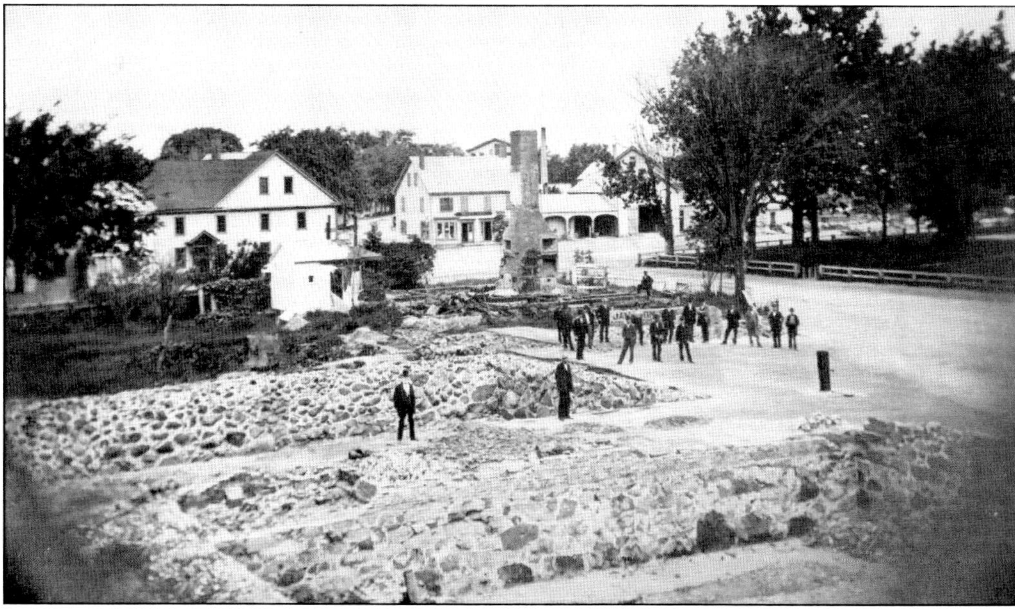

RUINS FROM THE GREAT STOUGHTON FIRE OF FEBRUARY 27, 1880. This view is looking northeast. Notice that Joseph Swan's store on the opposite side of Wyman Street is not harmed. To the left of the ruined chimney is the store of Levi Flint at the future site of Freeman Street. The church green of the Universalist church can be seen to the right.

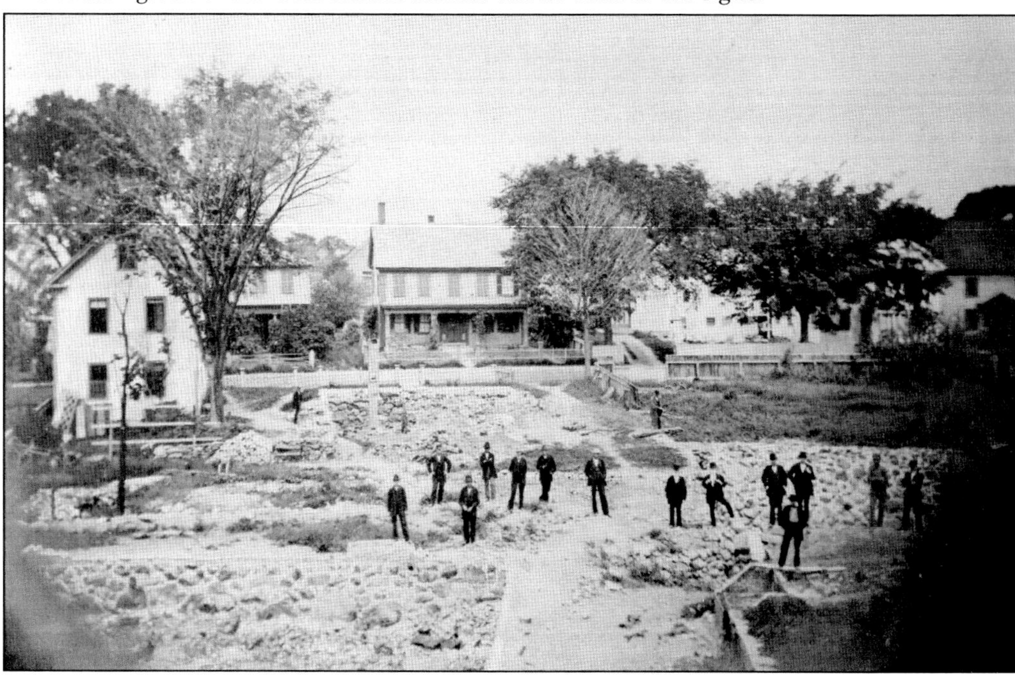

MEN STANDING IN THE RUINS OF THE 1880 FIRE. Wyman Street can be seen in the background with some standing structures. Some individuals can be identified. They are, from left to right, as follows: two unidentified, William Sheehan, unidentified, Matthew Nally, unidentified, Horace Mann, Nathan Bird, Lemuel Whiting, five unidentified, and Jesse Holmes in the background.

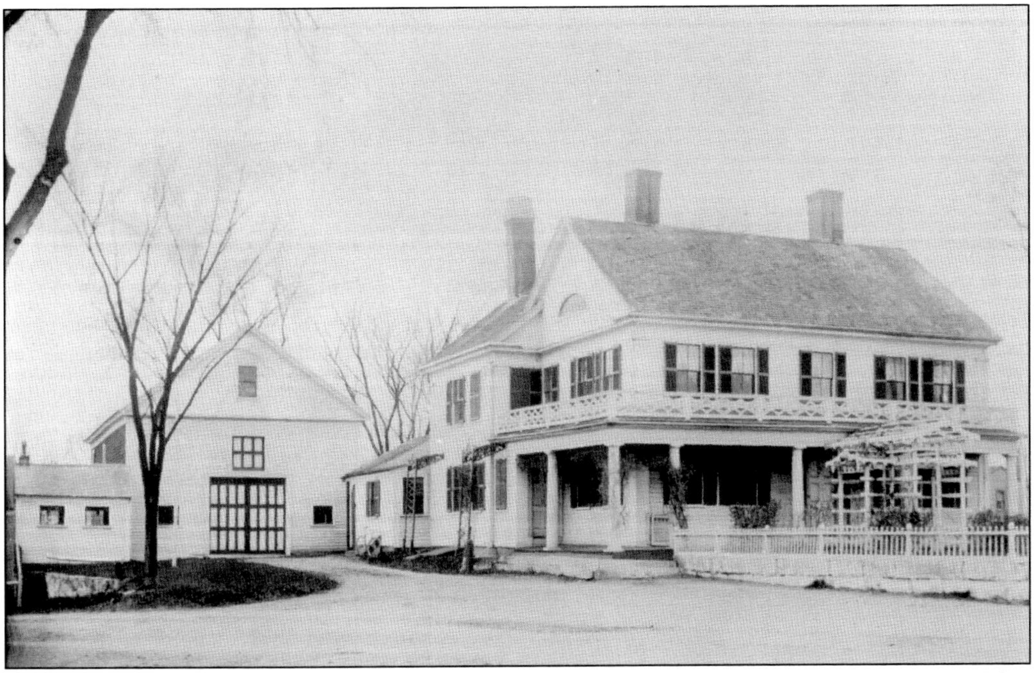

The Mansion House of Nathaniel Morton, Built in 1837 at Morton Square. This building would be transformed into a factory and later become the home to New England Furniture. Nathaniel Morton's boot factory would later become the home of Rising Star Lodge, when they purchased it and moved it across the tracks in 1885.

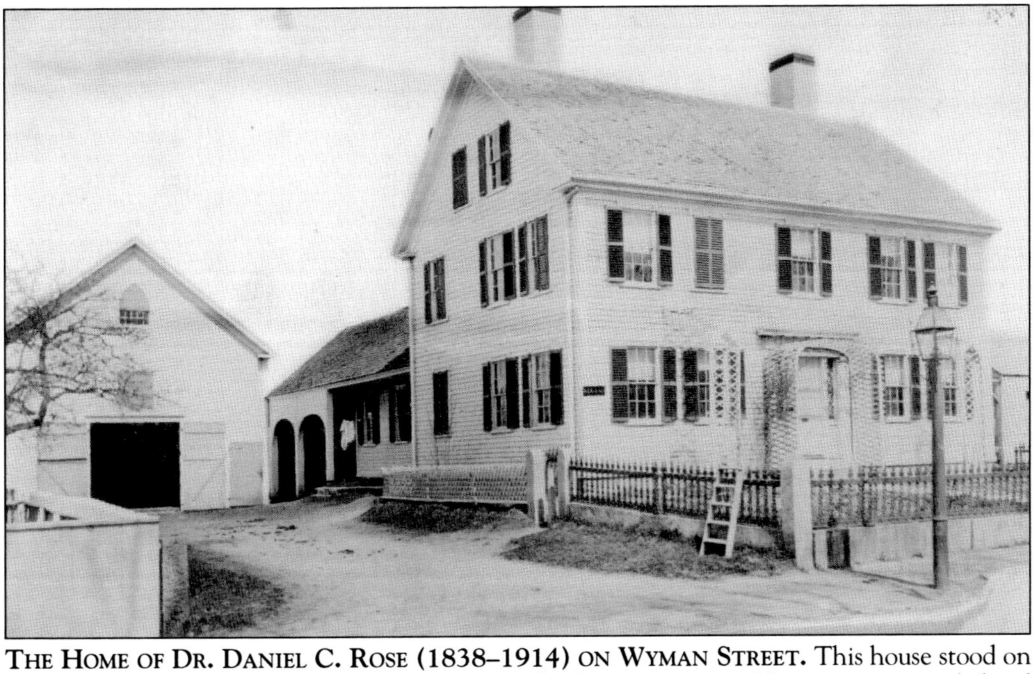

The Home of Dr. Daniel C. Rose (1838–1914) on Wyman Street. This house stood on the present site of the Stoughton train station. The house was moved by oxen to a site behind the Stoughton Town Hall on Rose Street. This house was previously the home of Dr. Simeon Tucker, who replaced Dr. Peter Adams as Stoughton's physician.

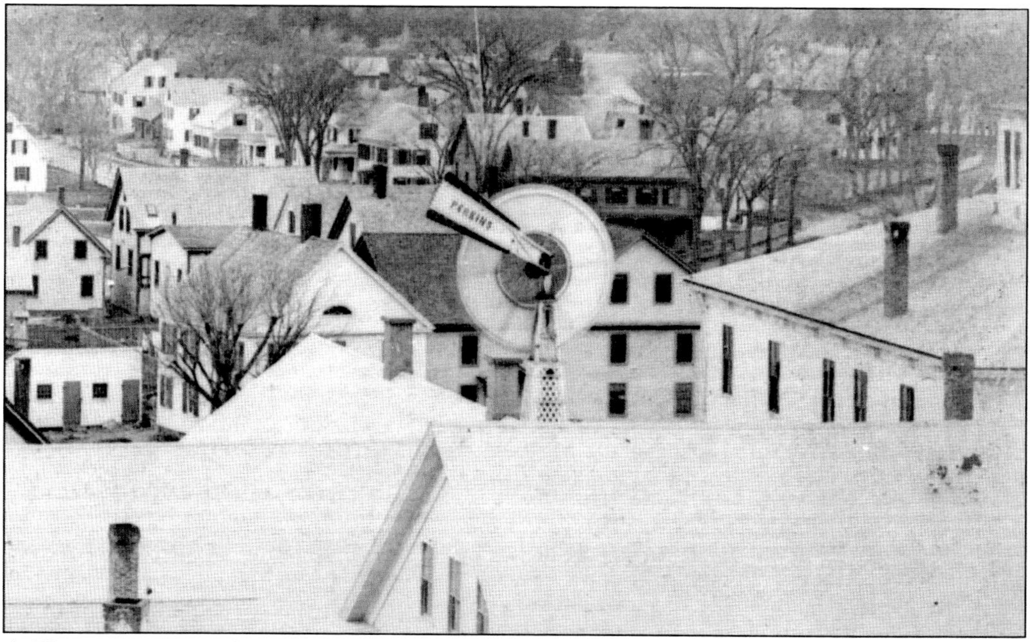

A VIEW FROM THE STEEPLE OF THE FIRST CONGREGATIONAL CHURCH ON WASHINGTON STREET. This view is looking north toward the intersection of Pearl and Washington Streets in 1885. The building above the windmill in the center is the current site of Britton's Block, where the former house of James Swan can still be seen.

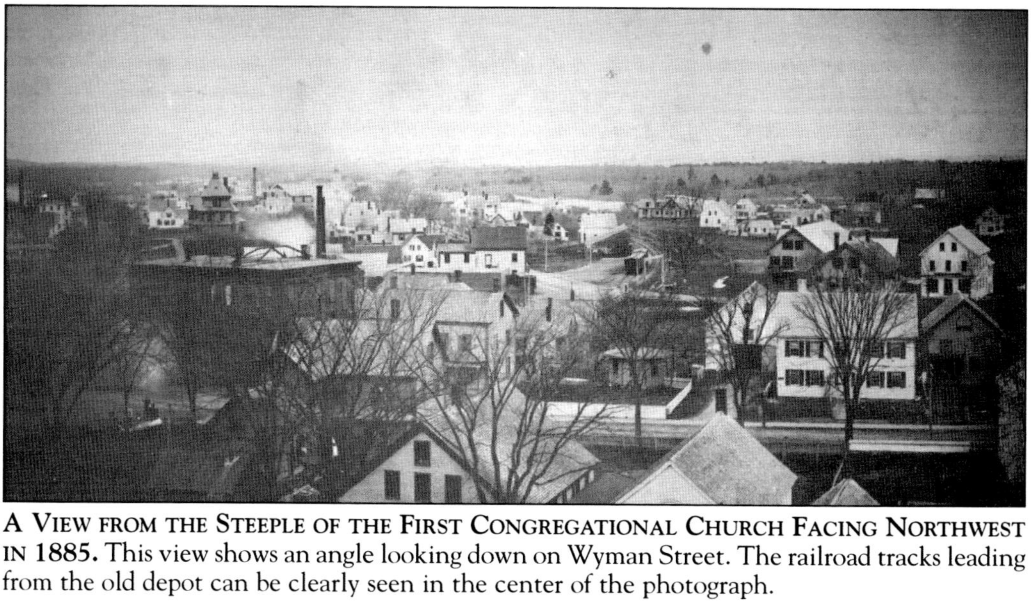

A VIEW FROM THE STEEPLE OF THE FIRST CONGREGATIONAL CHURCH FACING NORTHWEST IN 1885. This view shows an angle looking down on Wyman Street. The railroad tracks leading from the old depot can be clearly seen in the center of the photograph.

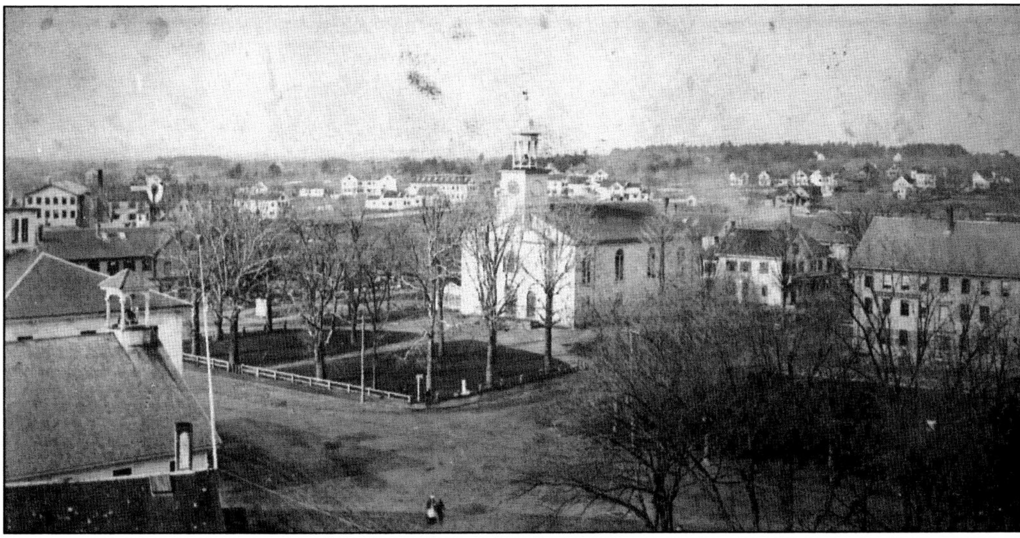

A VIEW FROM THE STEEPLE OF THE FIRST CONGREGATIONAL CHURCH LOOKING NORTHEAST IN 1885. This angle clearly shows the Universalist church and church green. Atherton's Boot Manufactory can be seen at the far right, and Atwood's new market can be seen to the left.

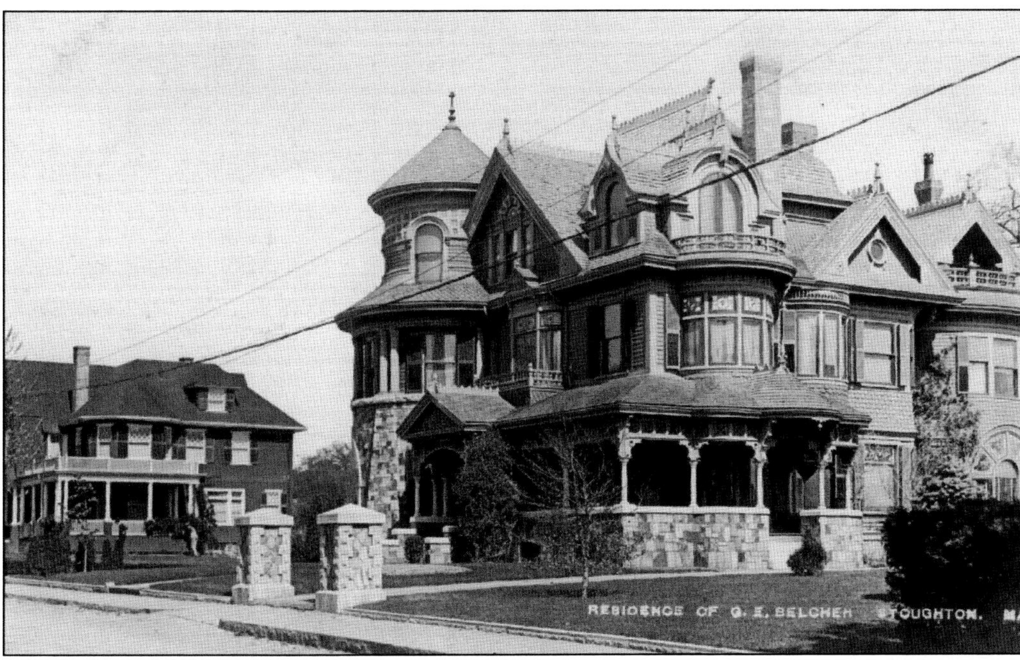

THE HOME OF GEORGE E. BELCHER, ON SEAVER AND CAPEN STREETS. Owned by factory owner George E. Belcher, this is one of the most magnificent homes in Stoughton. The detail inside is as extraordinary as the outside. Belcher purchased this house and extensively renovated it.

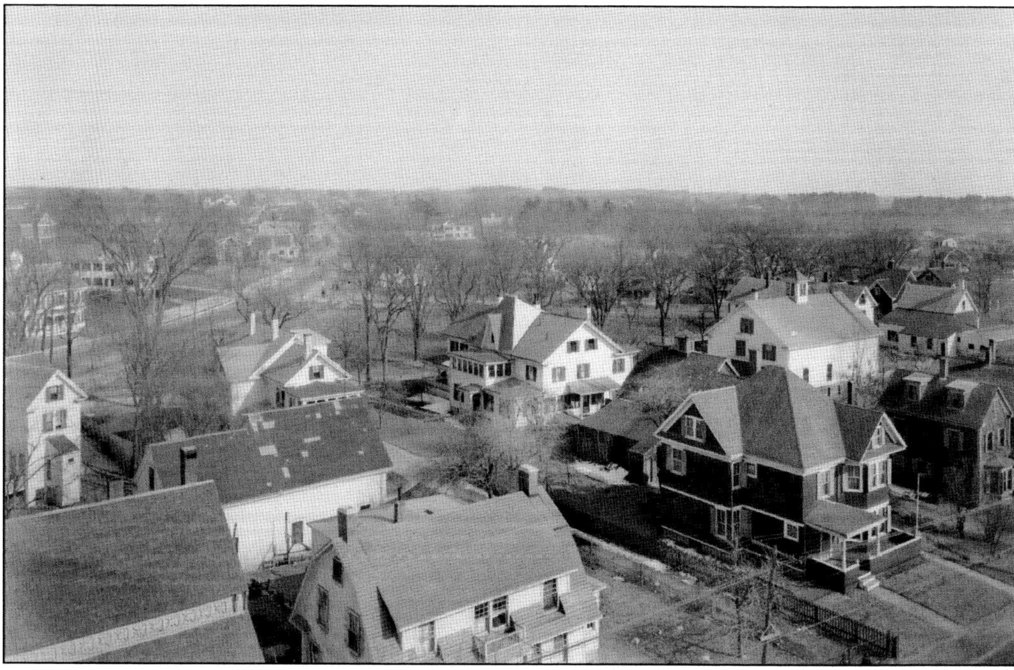

A NORTHEASTERLY VIEW FROM THE CONGREGATIONAL CHURCH, 1926. This view was taken facing northeast from the steeple of the Congregational church. Park Street can be seen in the upper left, near Faxon Park.

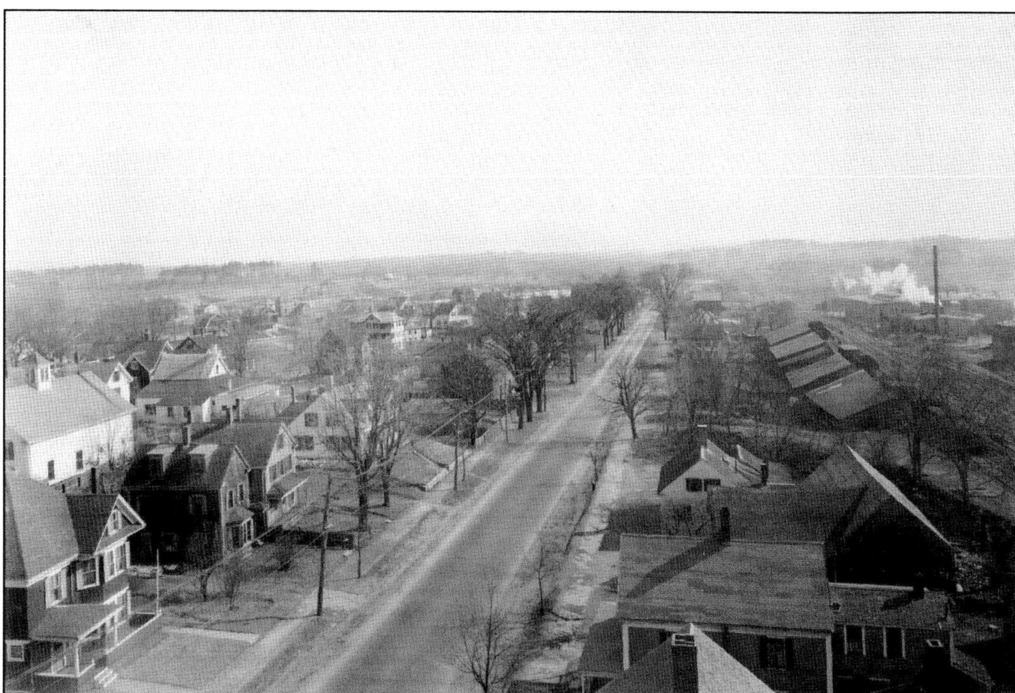

A SOUTHEASTERLY VIEW FROM THE CONGREGATIONAL CHURCH, 1926. Looking down Washington Street on Route 138, this view faces southeast.

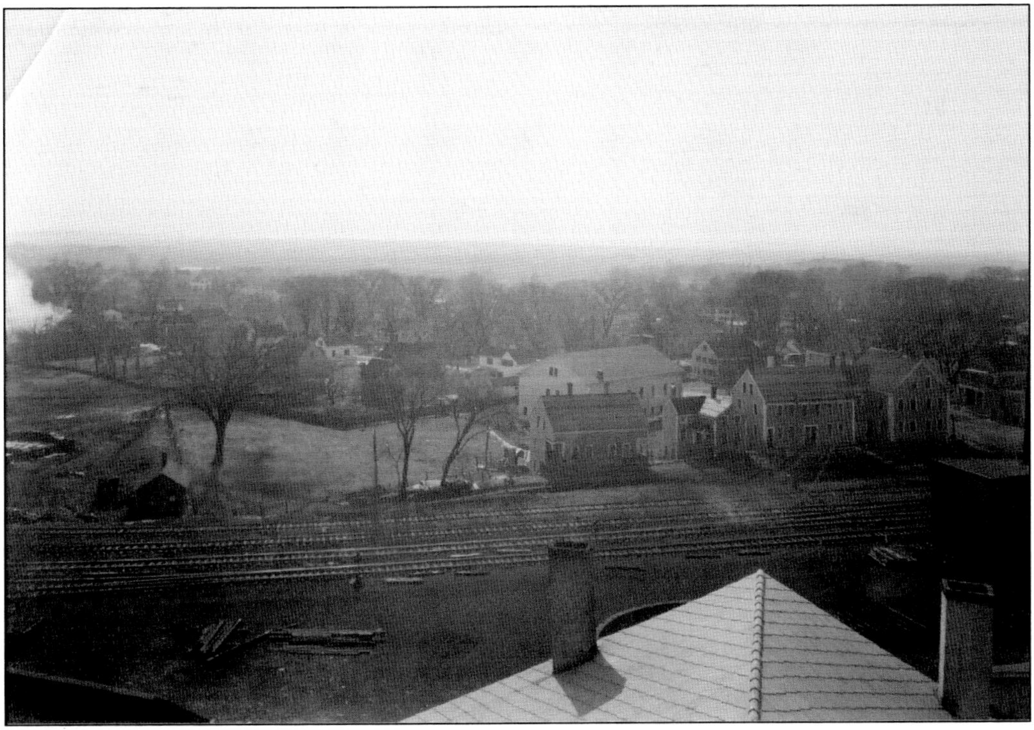

A Westerly View from the Congregational Church, 1926. This view faces west toward Morton Square.

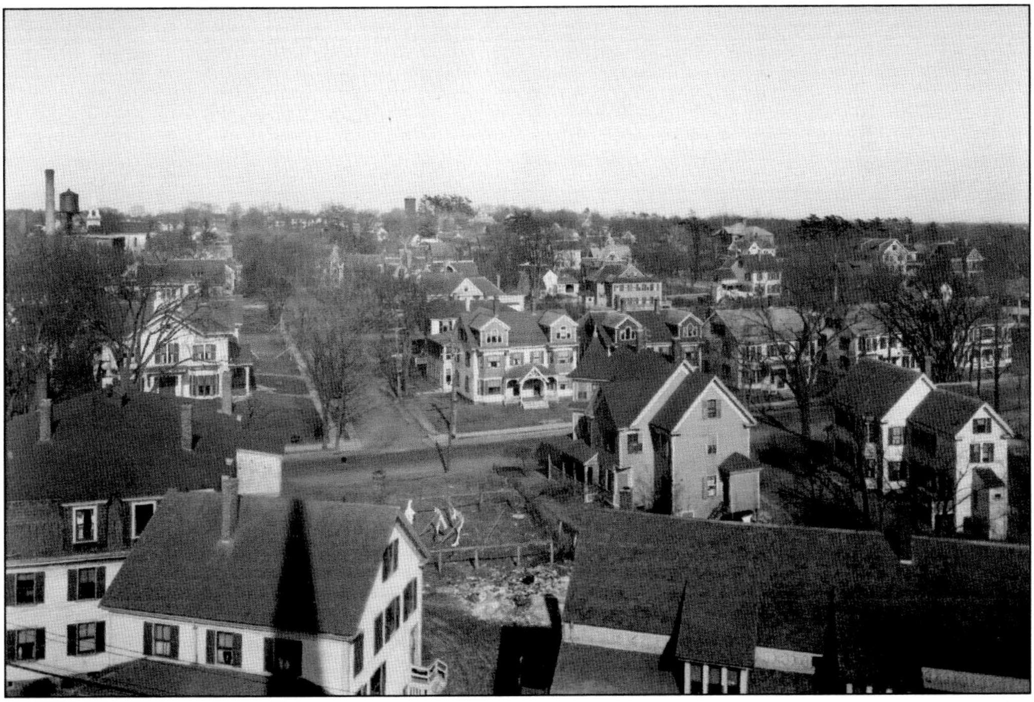

An Easterly View from the Congregational Church, 1926. This view from the steeple faces east, looking down Seaver Street.

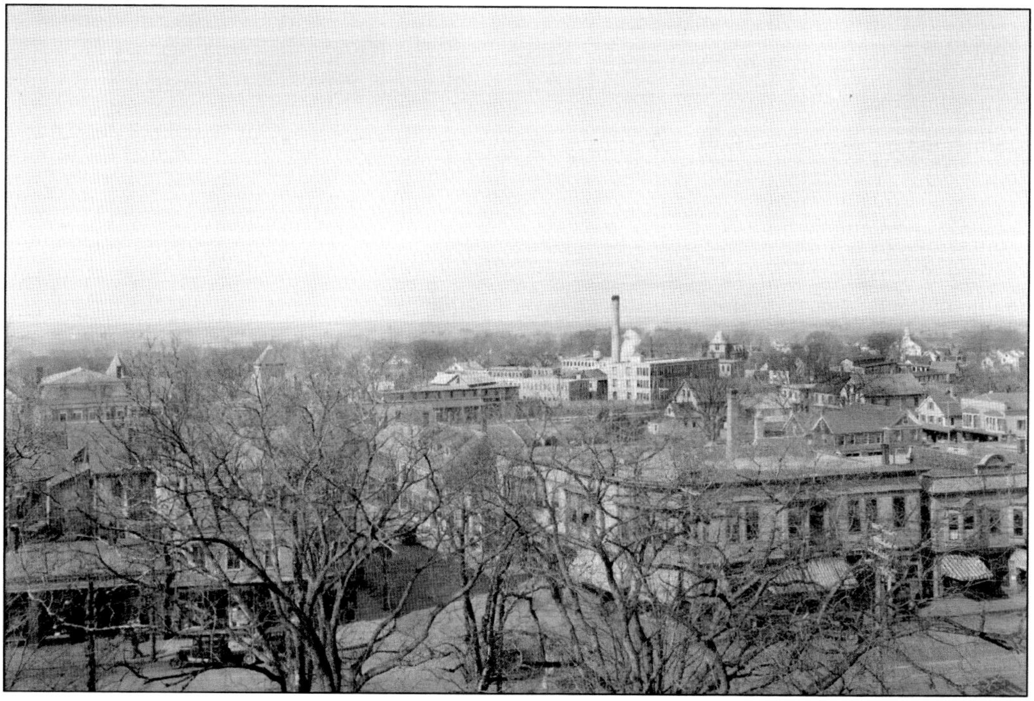

A Westerly View from the Universalist Church, c. 1930. This is a view from the steeple of the Universalist church, looking west down Wyman Street.

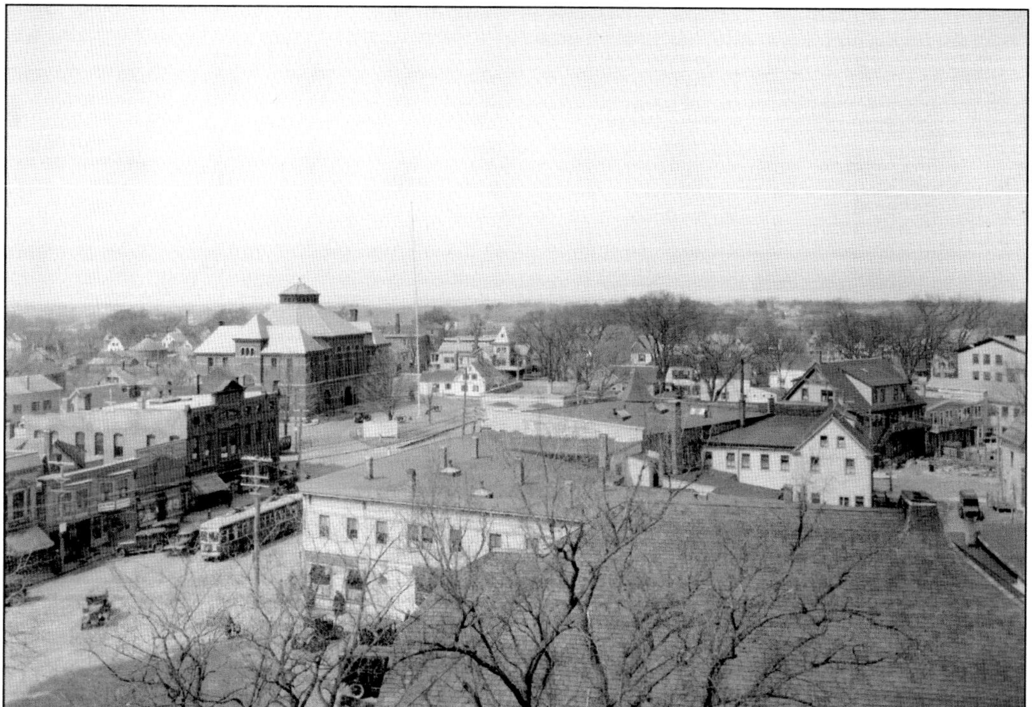

Another View from the Universalist Church, c. 1930. This view from the steeple looks northwest toward the Stoughton Town Hall on Pearl Street.

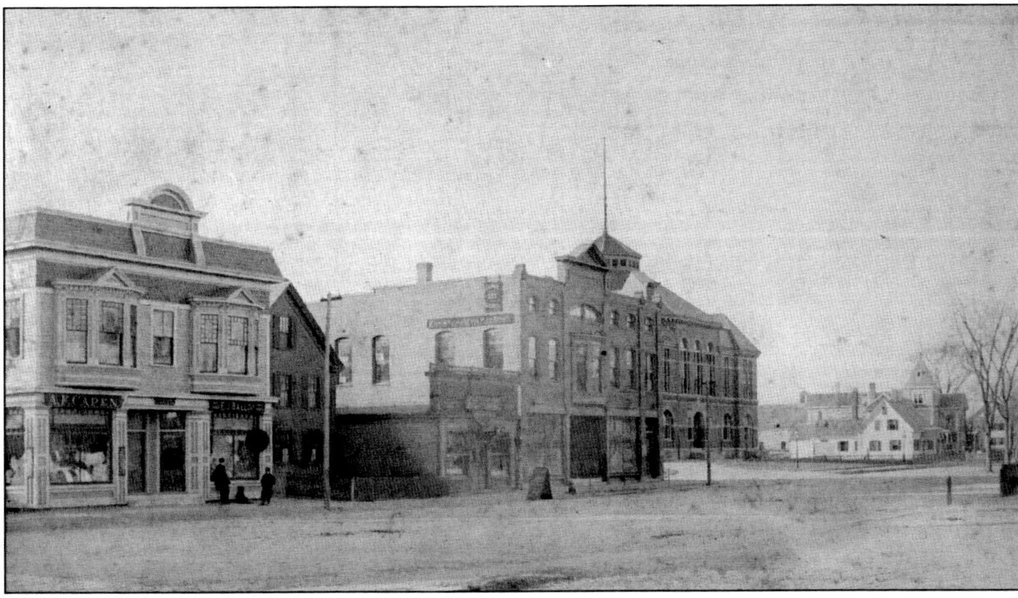

STOUGHTON SQUARE. This view of Stoughton Square shows, from left to right, the Ellis Block, which was built in 1888 and burned down in 1984, when Medical Pharmacy was a tenant; the Lucas House; Wilkins Drug Store; Monk's Cash Store; and the Stoughton Town Hall.

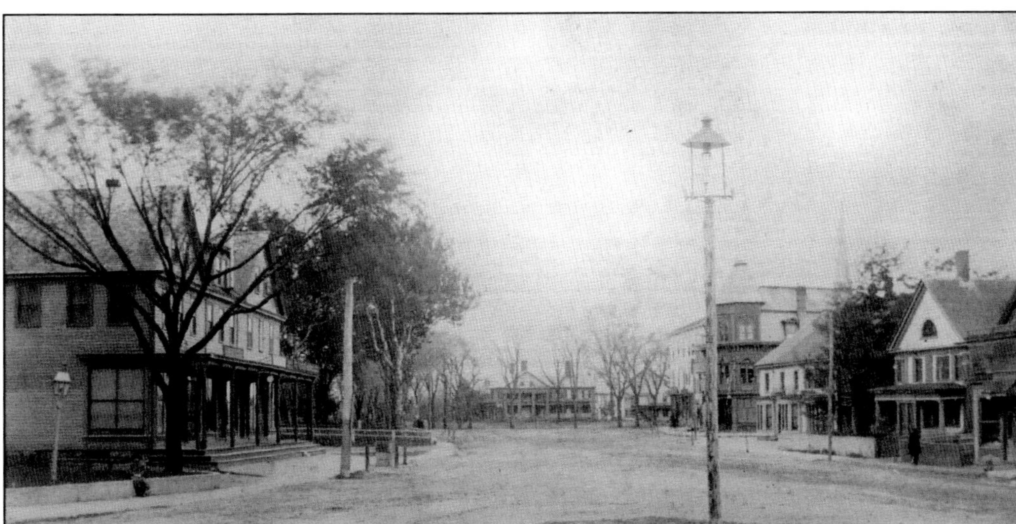

STOUGHTON SQUARE AT THE INTERSECTION OF WASHINGTON AND PEARL STREET IN A VIEW FACING SOUTH IN 1888. The double building to the left is Dr. Swan's Block, which burned down on April 28, 1892. In the center is the mansion home of manufacturer Martin Wales. To the right of that is Atwood's Market, and Darlings Block can also be seen. The old house and store of Joseph Swan is still standing on the corner of Wyman and Washington Streets. The home of Capt. J. Freeman Ellis was the structure with the half moon under the arch and was replaced with the Ellis Block later that year.

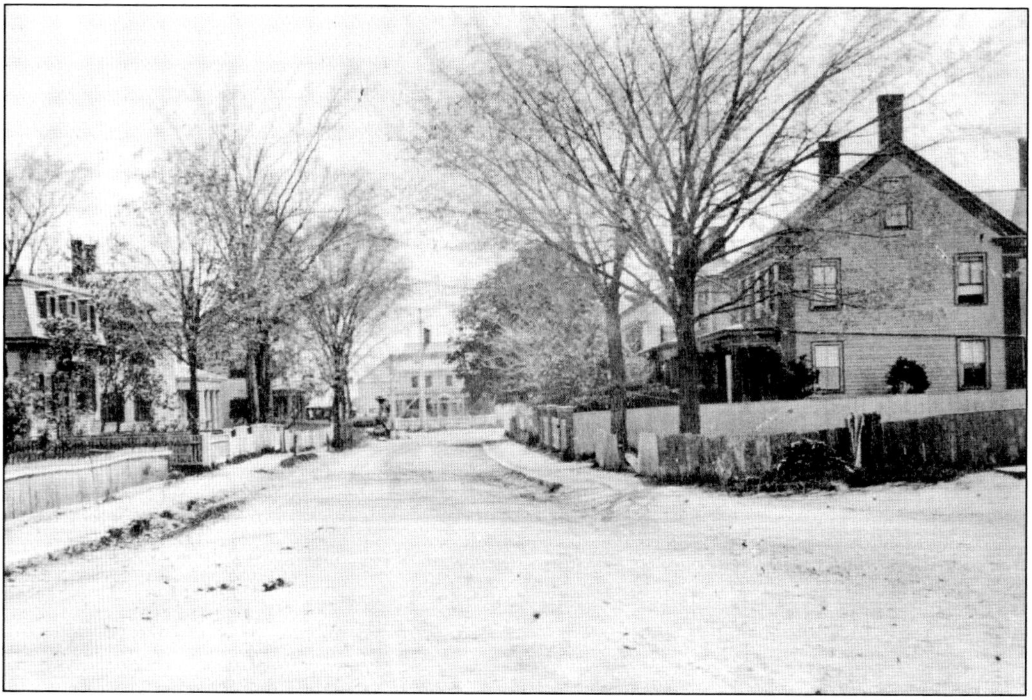

A VIEW DOWN WYMAN STREET. This is a view down Wyman Street before the Stoughton train station was built in 1888.

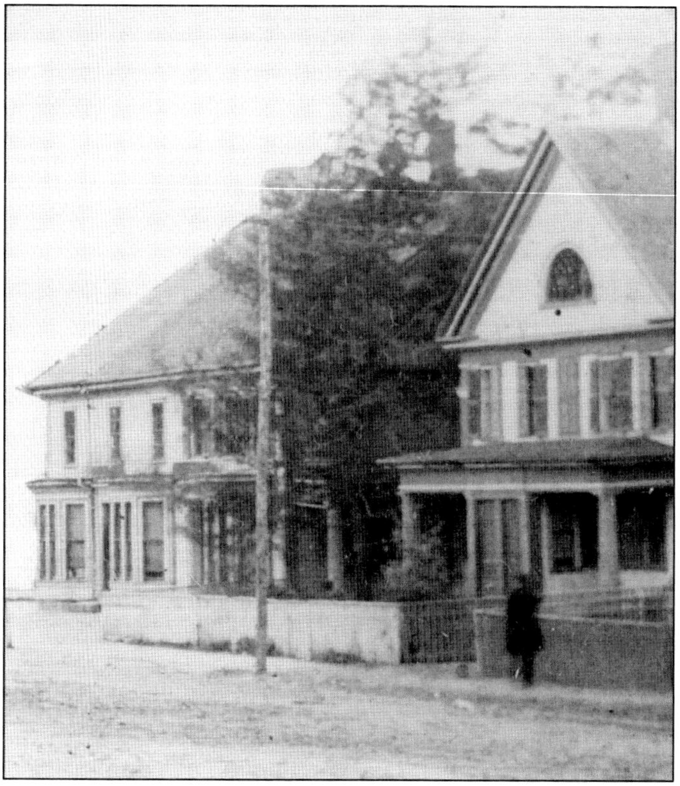

THE HOMES OF JOSEPH SWAN AND CAPTAIN ELLIS ON THE WEST SIDE OF WASHINGTON STREETS, C. 1888. The Swan house and store was replaced in 1892 with Swan's building at Wyman and Washington Streets. The home of Captain Ellis was replaced in 1888 with the Ellis Block.

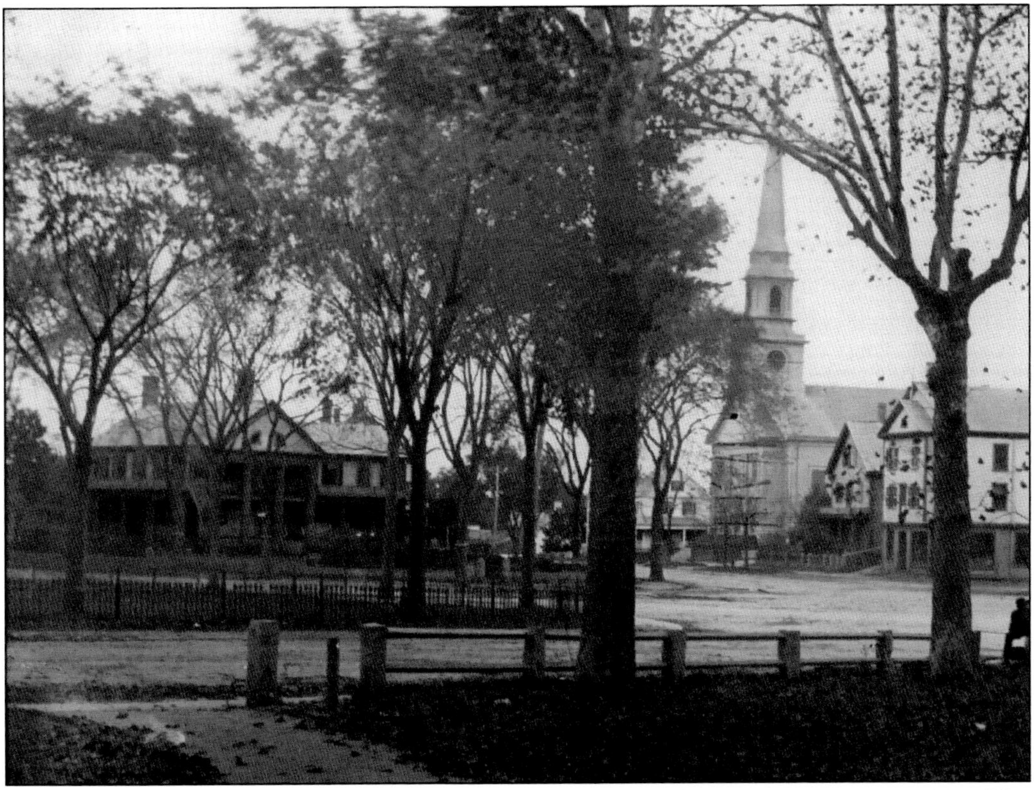

THE UNIVERSALIST CHURCH GREEN IN A VIEW LOOKING SOUTHWEST BEFORE 1897. The spire of the First Congregational Church can be seen on the right. Martin Wales's mansion home is to the left of the spire and the intersection of Washington and Park Streets.

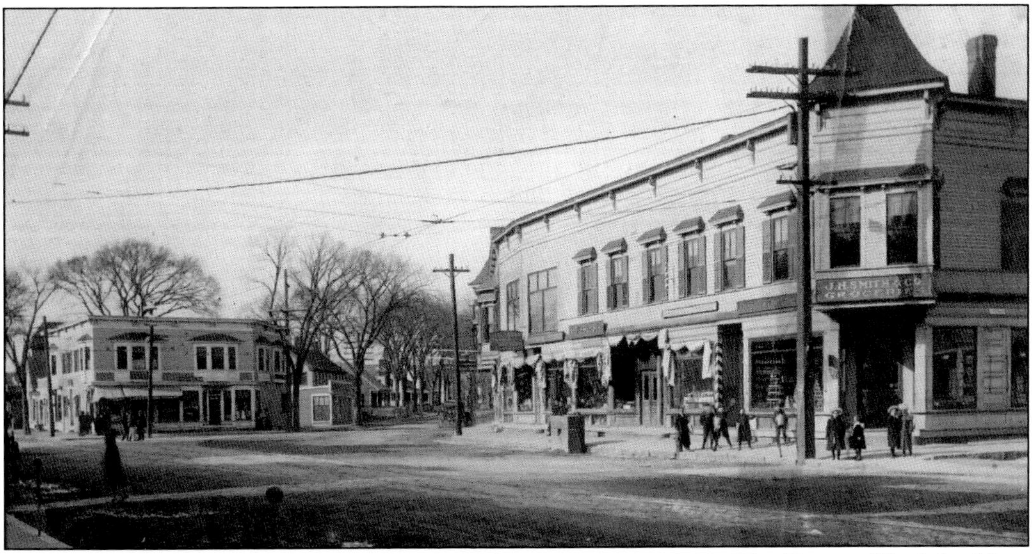

STOUGHTON SQUARE, IN A VIEW FACING NORTH BEFORE 1918. The Britton Block building can be seen on the left, and the new structure of Dr. Swan's Block that replaced the burnt structure of 1892 can be seen the length of Washington Street.

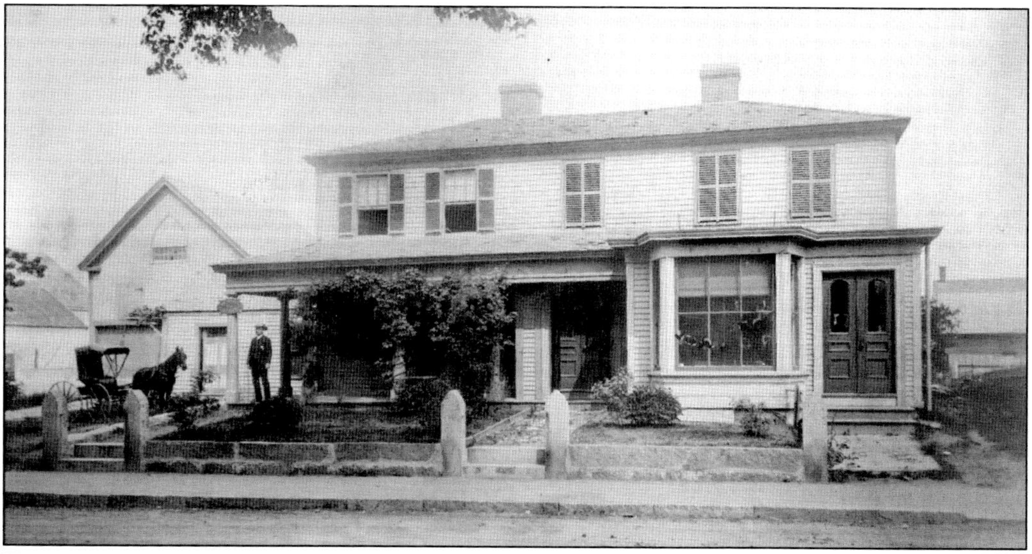

The House of Dr. Charles S. Young on Wyman Street. In this view, Dr. Young's sign is hung on the porch, and his horse and buggy stand ready. This house was formerly that of Abraham Capen, who ran the tavern at the corner of Pleasant and Park Streets in 1799.

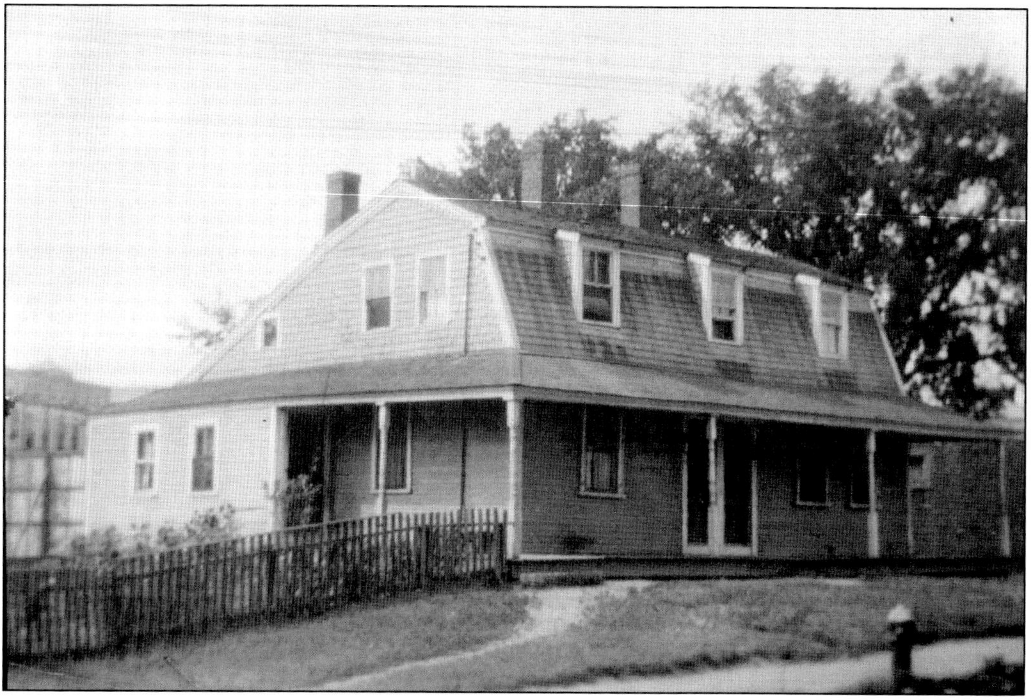

The Home of Benjamin Capen (1772–1858), on Morton Street. This unusual-shaped Cape was standing until recently, unchanged for many years. Benjamin Capen was the brother of Abraham Capen, the tavern keeper.

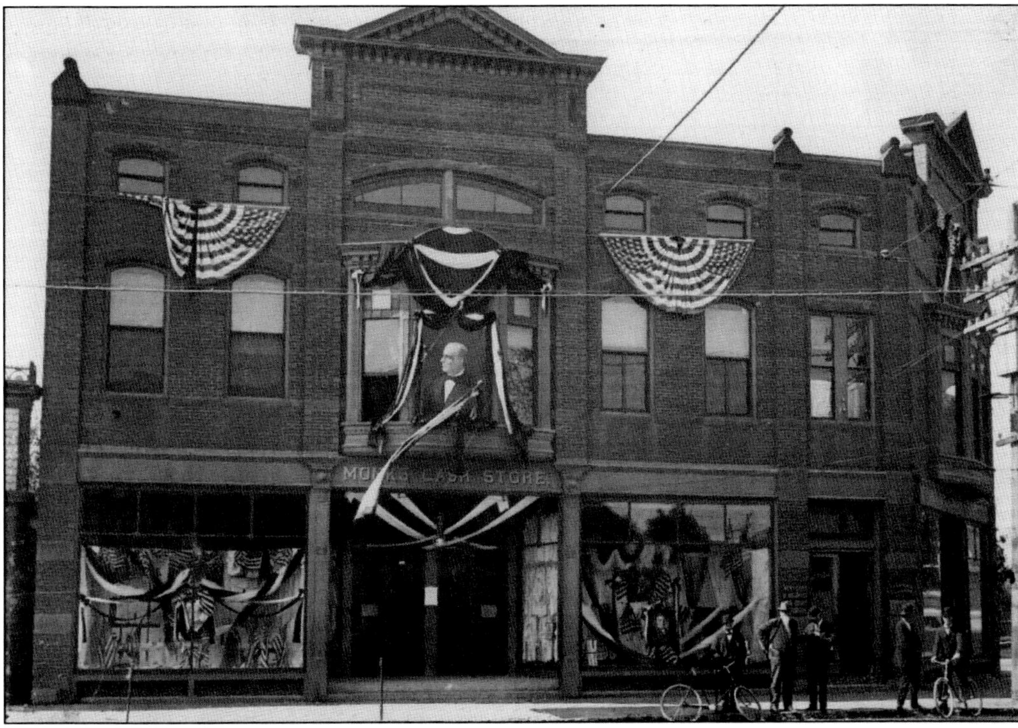

MONK'S CASH STORE, ON WASHINGTON AND PORTER STREETS. Monk's Cash Store is seen here draped in mourning for Pres. William Mckinley, who was assassinated in 1901.

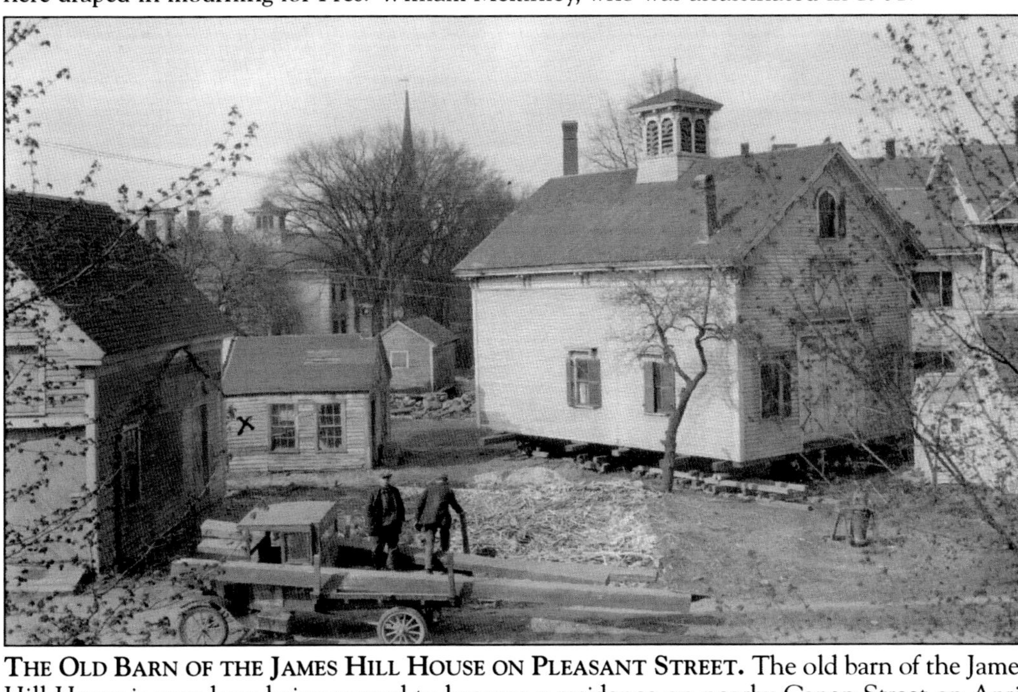

THE OLD BARN OF THE JAMES HILL HOUSE ON PLEASANT STREET. The old barn of the James Hill House is seen here being moved to become a residence on nearby Capen Street on April 26, 1922. The first residents would be Myron and Louise Pierce, and their daughter Dorothy operated a beauty salon on the upper floors.

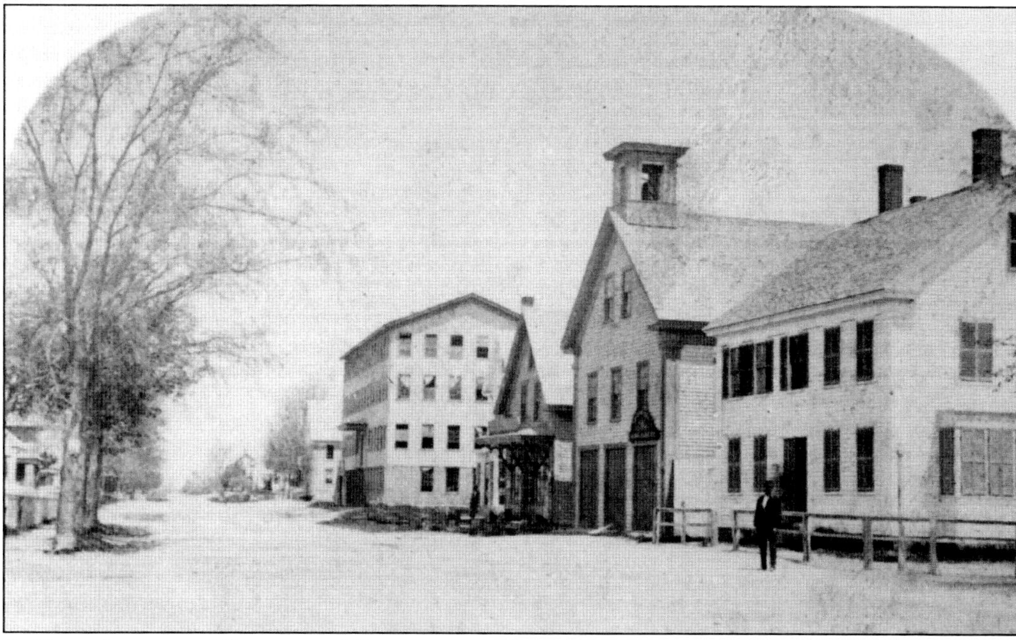

A VIEW LOOKING NORTH UP WASHINGTON STREET FROM STOUGHTON CENTER, C. 1885. Notice the large Fitzpatrick Shoe Factory off to the right. Also, the home of the Stoughton Fire Department can be seen, as well as another angle of the Washington Street Inn at the far right.

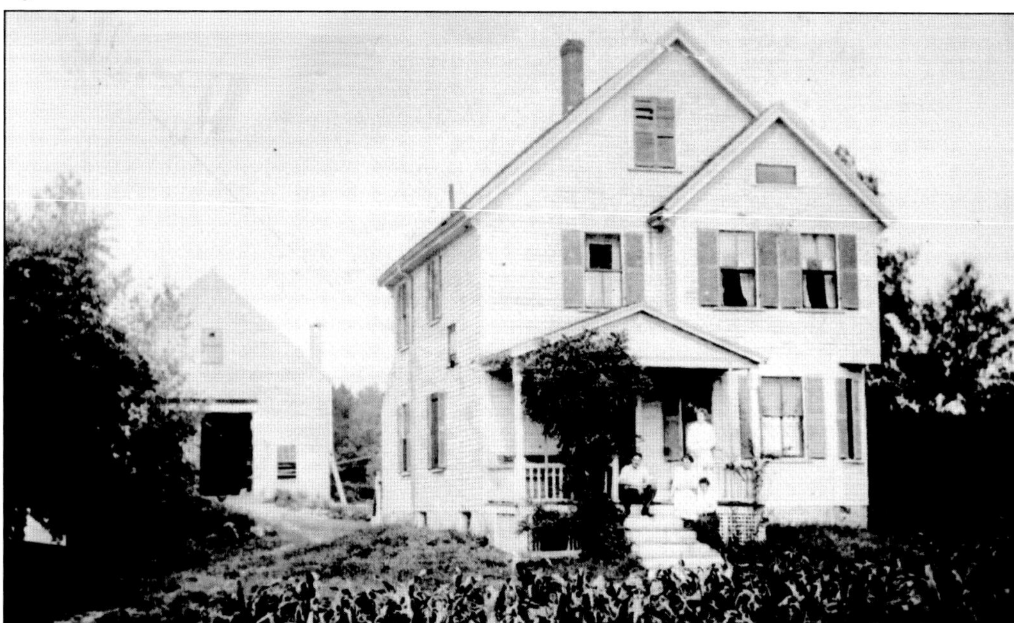

THE DEXTER-BARKER FAMILY FARMHOUSE, BUILT IN 1897. This property was located on the northern border between James Drake and Lucius Clapp's farm on West Street. The farm was owned by Edward Dexter. It was later owned by Frank Barker and, still later, by Dr. Charles Henry Gray. Dr. Gray was a graduate of Harvard Medical School in 1891. This late-19th-century farmhouse has continued to be the home of the author's family since 1965.

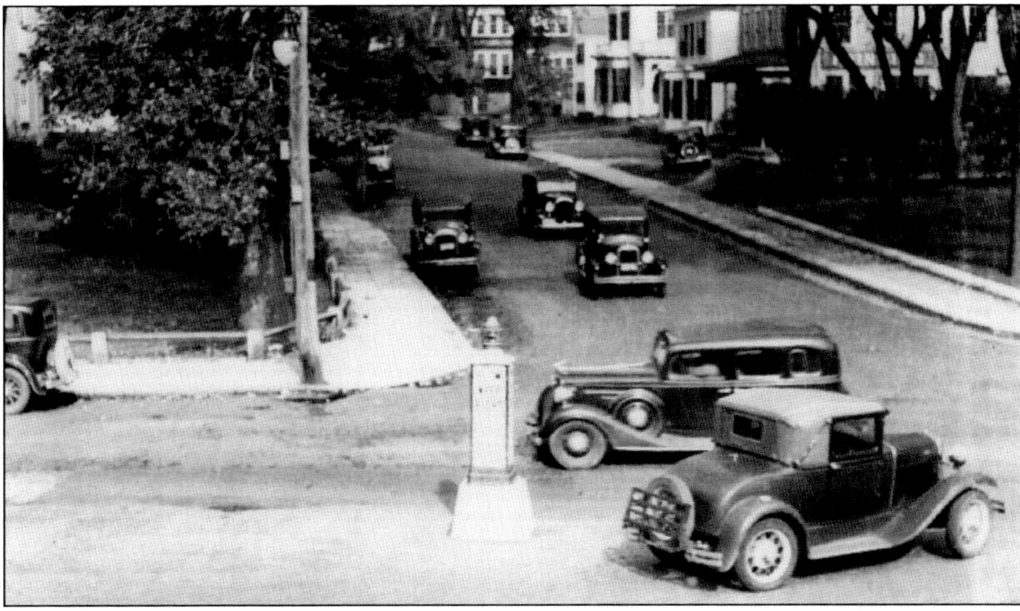

TRAFFIC IN STOUGHTON CENTER. This photograph, showing traffic in Stoughton Center at Pleasant and Washington Streets, was taken from the studio of John Cyrns Stiles.

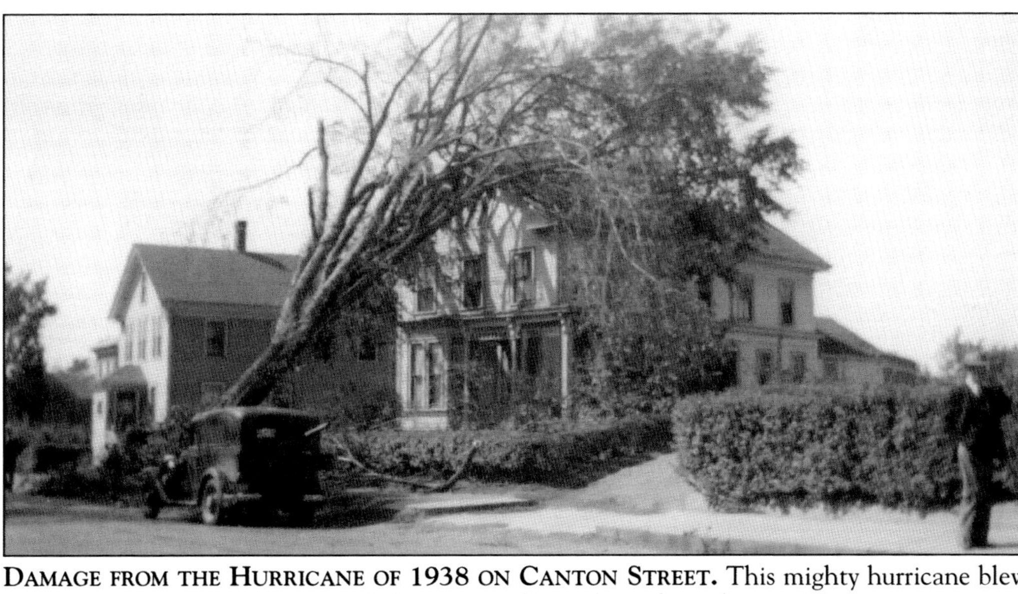

DAMAGE FROM THE HURRICANE OF 1938 ON CANTON STREET. This mighty hurricane blew down many trees that once graced the streets of Stoughton from the previous century.

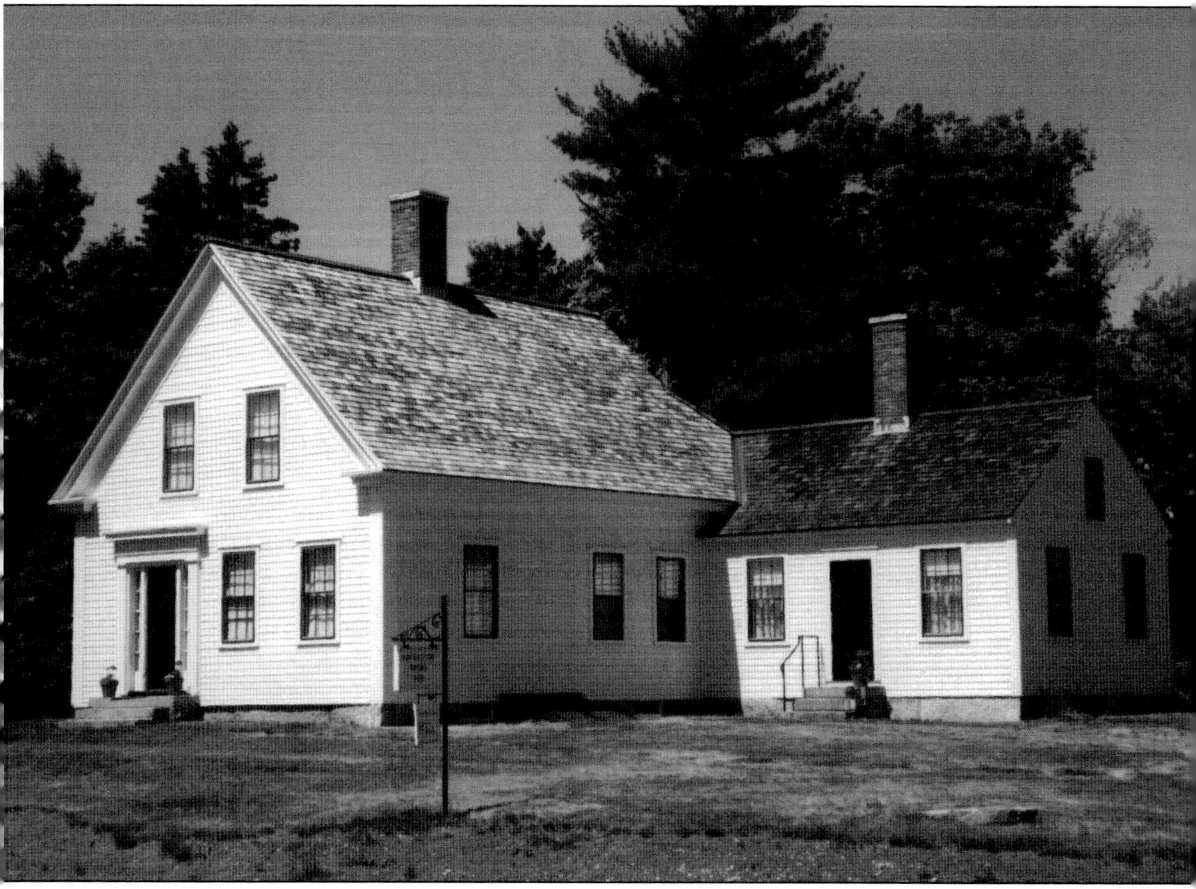

THE HOUSE MARY BARKER EDDY LIVED IN WHILE IN STOUGHTON. This is a photograph of the house that Mary Baker Eddy, the founder of Christian Science, lived in while at Stoughton from 1866 to 1870. This house at 133 Central Street was built on the foundation of an earlier structure. In 1742, Ezra Fisher built his home here. Alanson Wenthworth replaced the old structure in 1839. This property is open to the public by appointments only. It is a prime example of a small Stoughton farm that has not been altered by 20th-century influence.

Eleven

STOUGHTON RECREATION

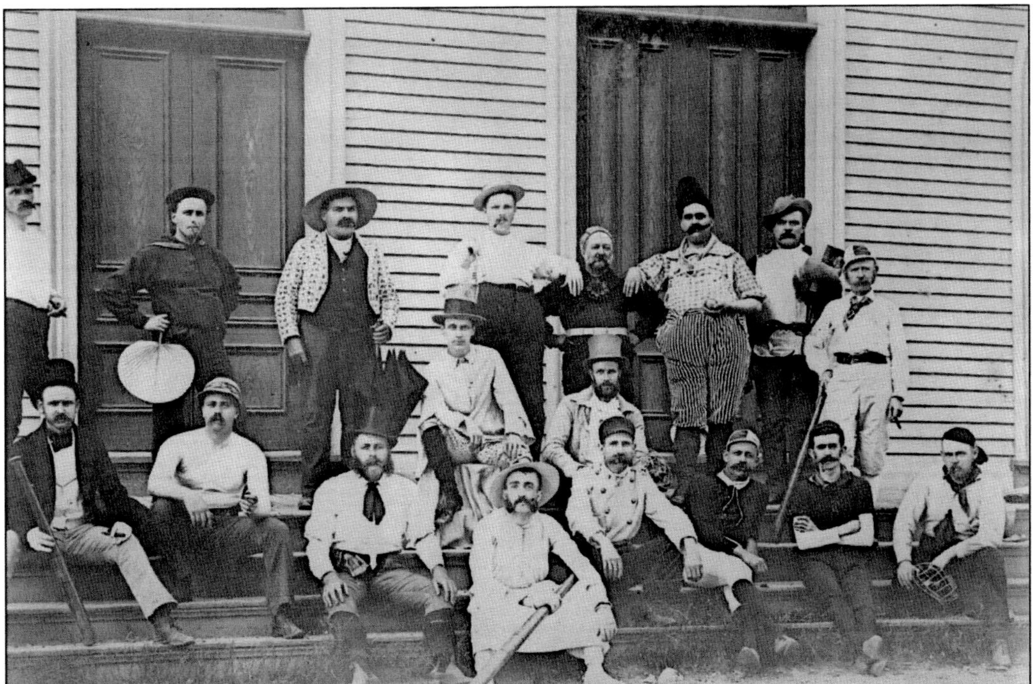

THE FAT AND LEAN MEN'S BASEBALL TEAM, C. 1880, IN FRONT OF THE UNIVERSALIST CHURCH. From left to right are the following: (front row) Lemuel W Standish, James May, Wilmot Fisher, Charlie Lunn, James Wellington, E.M. Elmes, Dr. W.O. Faxon, George Gardner, William Curtis, and Elliott Dodd; (back row, standing) Christopher Farrell, Judge Oscar A. Marden, William Taylor, Herbert I. Wood, Capt. J. Rogers, Ira F. Burnham, Dr. Charles S. Young, and Walter R. Swan.

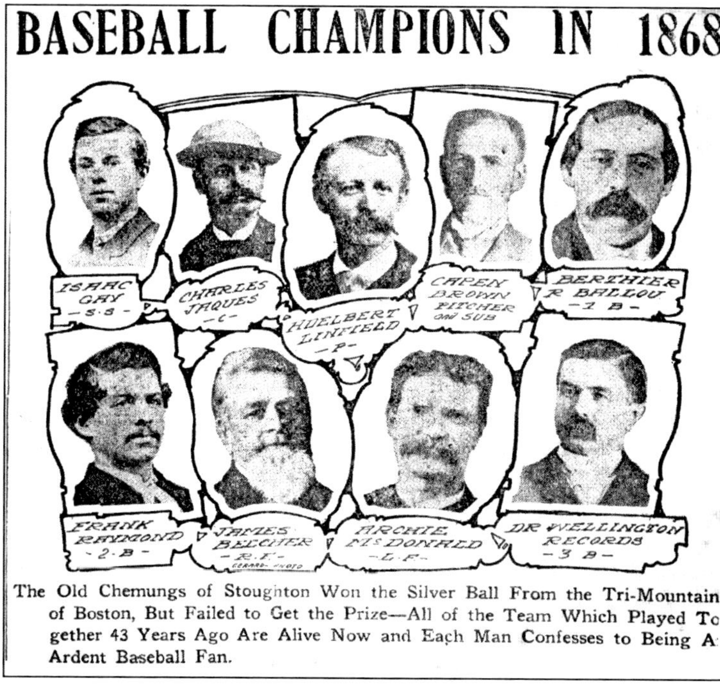

The Chemung Baseball Team Champions of 1868. This post–Civil War baseball team from Stoughton captured the Silver Ball from the Tri-Mountain team of Boston. From left to right are the following: (bottom row) Frank Raymond, James Belcher, Archie McDonald, and Dr. Wellington Records; (top row) Isaac Gay, Charles Jaques, Adelbert Linfield, Capen Brown, and Berthier R. Ballou.

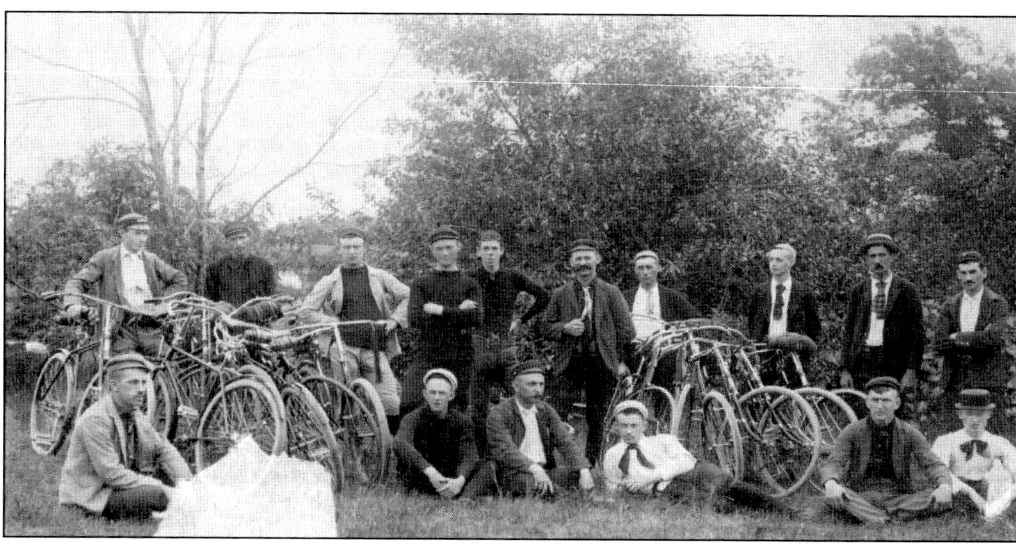

A Stoughton Bicycle Club Trip Photograph Taken at Rockland, June 26, 1892. From left to right are ? Ames, James Lehan, ? Douglas, George Fisher, Fred Reed, Larry Mead, Frank Burnham, John Kilbreth, ? Simpson, Louis Carr, Charles Putnam, ? Pond, Fred Hanlon, and Frank Johnson.

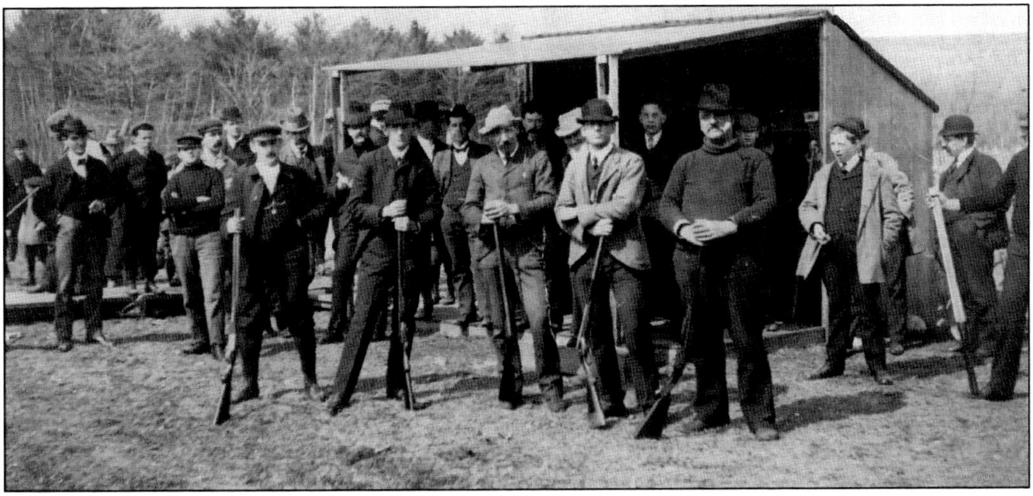

MEMBERS OF THE STOUGHTON GUN CLUB AT THE SHOOTING RANGE ON GLEN ECHO ROAD IN NORTH STOUGHTON, C. 1905. From left to right are Chester Morse, Hiram Belcher, Fred Curtis, Frank Linfield, Henry Francis, Charles Parker, Ernest Whiting, James Lehan, Joseph Porter, Arthur Wales, Billy Beales, Frank Gould, Stanley Leathers, unidentified, ? Harris, Ed Wales, Guy Cornish, Henry Botsch, Henry Dyer, Charles Gould, and Arthur Churchill.

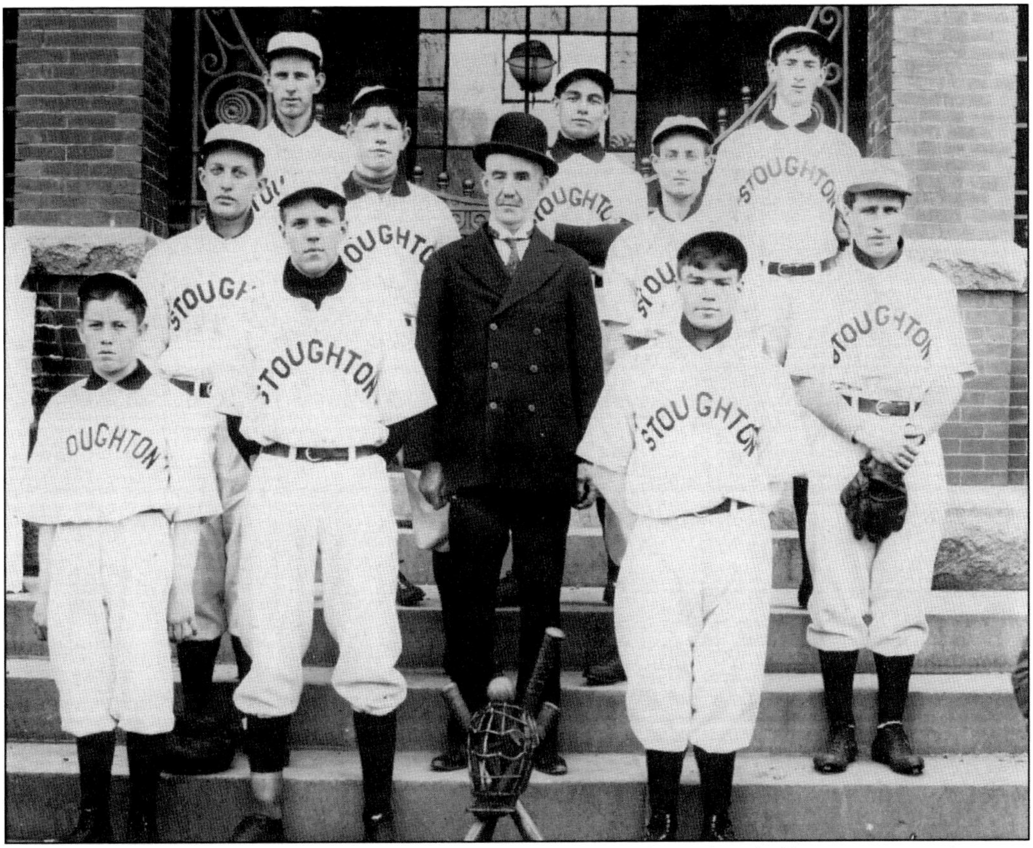

THE STOUGHTON BASEBALL CLUB, C. 1912. The Stoughton baseball team is seen here in front of the Stoughton Town Hall on Pearl Street.

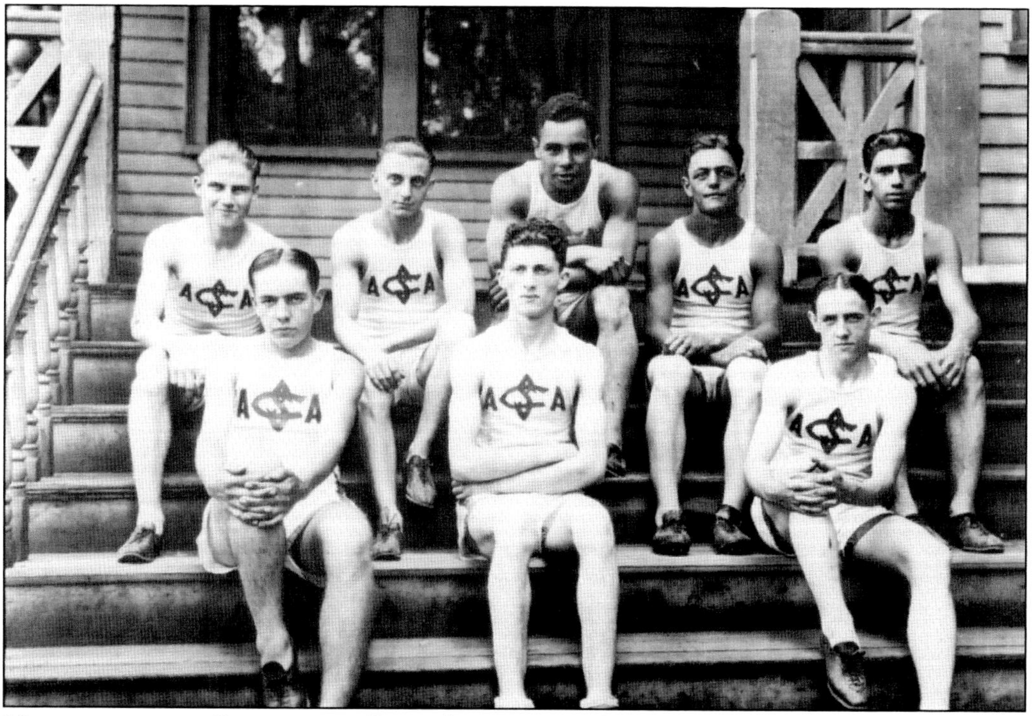

MEMBERS OF THE STOUGHTON CIVIC ASSOCIATION TRACK TEAM ON THE STEPS OF THE DRAKE SCHOOL IN 1923. From left to right are the following: (front row) Charles Klim, Gus Barbato, and Eddie Keogh; (back row) Eddie Keefe, Domenic DeMatteo, James Mitchell, Jack Hyde, and Guy Cimmarelle.

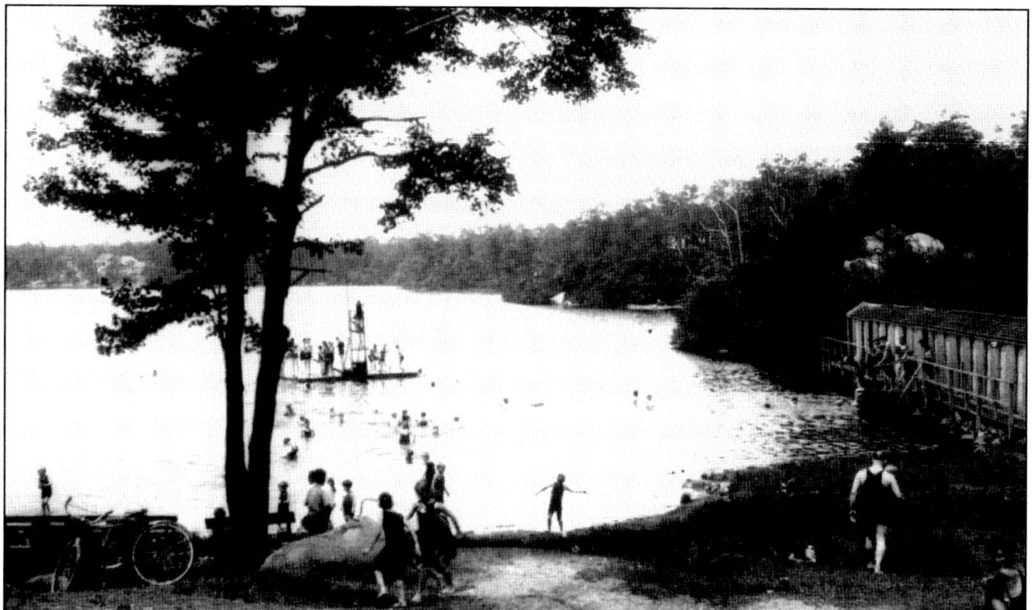

SWIMMING AND PICNICKING AT GLEN ECHO LAKE RESORT IN THE 1920S. George Monk opened this resort in Stoughton in 1895. A trolley would bring the crowds to the lake to fish, swim, and boat.